To Connor
on his 28th
Birthday 1994
January 19

With love,
your wifeves !
Susan

GOING FOR BROKE

GOING FOR BROKE

*Confessions of
a Merchant Banker*

RUSSELL TAYLOR

SIMON & SCHUSTER

LONDON·SYDNEY·NEW YORK·TOKYO·SINGAPORE·TORONTO

First published in Great Britain by
Simon & Schuster Ltd in 1993
A Paramount Communications Company
This paperback edition first published in 1994

Simon & Schuster Ltd
West Garden Place
Kendal Street
London W2 2AQ

Simon & Schuster of Australia Pty Ltd
Sydney

A CIP catalogue record for this book is
available from the British Library
ISBN 0-671-71291-8

Phototypeset by Intype, London

Printed and bound in Great Britain by
Butler & Tanner Ltd, Frome

Contents

Let no loans be made that are not secured beyond a reasonable contingency. Give facilities only to legitimate and prudent transactions. Make your discounts on as short time as the business of your customers will permit, and insist upon the payment of all paper at maturity, no matter whether you need the money or not . . . Every dollar that a bank loans above its capital and surplus it owes for, and its managers are therefore under the strongest obligation to its creditors, as well as to its stockholders, to keep its discounts firmly under control . . . The capital of a bank should be a reality, not a fiction; and it should be owned by those who have money to lend, and not by borrowers . . . 'Splendid financiering' is not legitimate banking, and 'splendid financiers' in banking are generally either humbugs or rascals.

> A letter to US national banks written in 1863 by Hugh McCullock, appointed by President Abraham Lincoln as the first Comptroller of the Currency

A copy hangs in the Banking Supervision Division (formerly Discount Office) of the Bank of England, and printed copies are available on request. My copy was given me by James Keogh, the last manager of the Discount Office, and the victim of his superiors' ill-judged introduction of Competition and Credit Control in 1981. It is to his memory that this book is respectfully dedicated, as well as to the management and staff of the Italian International Bank. All too frequently forgetting the strictures of Keynes, the IIB survived against the odds by never departing from those of Tawney.

It is necessarily part of the business of a banker to maintain appearances and to profess a conventional respectability which is more than human. Lifelong practices of this kind make them the most romantic and the least realistic of men. It is so much their stock-in-trade that their position should not be questioned, that they do not even question it themselves until it is much too late. Like the honest citizens they are, they feel a proper indignation at the perils of the wicked world in which they live – when the perils mature; but they do not foresee them. A Bankers' Conspiracy! The idea is absurd! I only wish there were one! So, if they are saved, it will be, I expect, in their own despite.

> John Maynard Keynes, *Essays in Persuasion*

An organised money-market has many advantages, but it is not a school of social ethics or political responsibility.

> R. H. Tawney, *Religion and the Rise of Capitalism*

Prologue
It Seemed a Good Idea
at the Time

'What experience and history teach us is this – that people and governments never have learned anything from history, or acted on principles deduced from it.'
Friedrich Hegel, *Philosophy of History*

BANKING IS AT THE centre of financial confidence and economic expectations, and those activities that create and destroy prosperity. So bankers are traditionally seen as authority figures, similar to fathers, schoolmasters and priests in their demand for respect and obedience. This they have long received; to which other business do we hand over our total wealth for safekeeping without question or security?

But do bankers still deserve our trust?

Three hundred years ago Blaise Pascal, the French religious philosopher, recommended that men should act as if God existed because if they did, and He didn't, nothing was lost, whereas if they didn't, and He did, then all was lost. This is the standard by which bankers need to operate, for they are supposed to be men of judgement and probity. Banks are the only businesses that we permit to borrow more than twenty times their net worth.

High Court writs may have silenced journalists, but Robert Maxwell's dishonesty was already known to bankers by the late 1950s, and was publicly proclaimed in 1971. Where was the judgement of Citibank, Swiss Bank Corporation and all four English clearing banks who, a few years later, were lending Maxwell some £2 billion of our money? What value the probity of Goldman Sachs and Salomon Brothers in New York, Nomura in Tokyo, Indosuez in Paris, or Samuel Montagu and Smith New Court in London?

These were all caught in the Maxwell coils in their hunt for fees. Even more disgracefully, so were Rothchilds, the house that publicly blew the whistle on Maxwell in 1969. Twenty years later, they were advising him in his New York battle for Macmillan.

The story of this book is less about the loans to Maxwell, the Reichmanns and all those other 1980s movers and shakers than about why many bankers, outwardly so normal, behave like lunatics. Politicians were appalled by the economic misery that followed the 1920s, the last time that bankers forgot that they were in a risk business. In the aftermath of the consequent worldwide banking failures of 1929–33, banking competition was regulated and banking activities separated, to protect voters from similar disasters. Legislation guaranteed the deposits of banking customers, either formally or informally, with the money of the taxpayer. This seemed safe enough, for bankers are meant to be 'facilitators', financial intermediaries specialising in a function which is very different from that of any other business activity or profession. The banker helps those he considers sound to achieve their aims. Except for government business and a few hundred multinational corporations, would-be customers solicit bankers, and not the other way around.

These legislative efforts have been fruitless. By 1988 Felix Rohatyn, for many years senior partner of Wall Street's Lazard Frères, was writing:

> We have created a gigantic financial house of cards . . . It is no coincidence that the explosion in speculation during the last few years has been accompanied by a significant increase in the level of illegal or unethical behaviour in the financial community . . . This speculative behaviour is not driven by individual manipulators, as was the case in the 1920s and 1930s but by institutions such as pension funds, insurance companies, banks and S&Ls backed, in may cases, by State and US government guarantees . . . the combination of highly volatile markets and reports of irresponsible behaviour by many of the financial community has undermined public confidence in the fairness of the system.

And just how competent are the guardians of the public interest? Financial centres, with their regulators, are more often than not competing for the favours of banks, as were New York and London over the last twenty years. The regulators of several countries, most noticeably those of Britain and Luxembourg, allowed the Bank of Credit and Commerce International, during the nineteen years of its existence, to defraud the public of some $20 billion, yet most bankers were aware of something wrong with BCCI by the early 1980s at the latest, which is why so few banks were caught in the debacle. During those same years, American regulators were silenced by politicians, as they allowed their friendly neighbourhood banker, with the active encouragement of America's largest and most reputable Wall Street banks, to steal at least $1,000 from every living American. And since 1990 banking regulators, from Japan to India, Scandinavia to Australasia, have watched helplessly as their constituents have admitted to scandals whose outrageousness would have been admired by the perpetrators of the worst frauds of the unregulated 1920s. None, however, admits to any inadequacies in their policing of financial markets.

Bankers often plan for the last war, just like generals, so it took them a while to forget the shock of the 1930s, and to realise that they had been made a protected species. However, by 1960 their new world had dawned, and bankers had come to think that the legislation which protected banking customers from their bankers also protected bankers from themselves. The banking crises of 1974 were the first great surprise; since then, banking mistakes have happened more frequently and on a grander scale.

The year 1974 was an intimation that regulating banking might not be as simple as politicians had hoped. The safety net of reform had freed banking egos from the traditional caution associated with those who must perform on the high wire. Local loyalties were despised in favour of multinational corporations and sovereign borrowers. Yet 'Put not your trust in princes' has always been a professional warning for bankers. By 1980, the valued corporate clients of yesteryear were using banking computers, and their profit-oriented treasury functions (once known as finance departments to the bankers who solicited them for business) were outdoing bankers at banking. Bankers also forgot the moral of Aesop's fable of the dog with two bones and, by coveting their neighbour's business rather than nurturing their own, lost their renown, the trust of their customers and a goodly portion of their shareholders' capital.

International lending requires greater skill than domestic banking, and the cost of mistakes is correspondingly heavier, as any Victorian banker knew. History, politics and competition with New York and Switzerland made London, as one American banker said, 'a warm place to do business' – the centre whose free and easy ways would allow the veriest tyros to try their hand at the risky game of international lending. Less than ten years after 1974 the risk could be discerned. The Third World debt crisis in 1982 exposed the world to a banking crisis graver even than that of the 1930s. Governments, banking regulators and auditing firms rallied around, for a key lesson had been learned from the experience of the 1930s – if we don't hang together, we certainly hang separately. The world's most important banks, just like Disney cartoon characters, had walked off the cliff edge – but all would be well provided they all stared resolutely ahead.

With the laws of financial nature apparently suspended, bankers ignored the aftereffects of their 1960s property and shipping binges, their 1970s energy and Third World lending blow-outs, and found even more interesting borrowers. The real risk of unrestrained banking will be discovered by us as the 1990s recycle, or resolve, the lending fashions of the 1980s. Upon this will depend the rate of economic growth and the length of the economic depression of the 1990s.

Among the better banking customers of the 1980s were the Reichmann brothers, Canadian property developers. Other people's money enabled the Reichmanns to bet against other people's perception of the best office areas for Toronto, New York and London. Canary Wharf in London's Docklands defeated the Reichmanns, just as it bankrupted its first builders some two hundred years earlier. This former wharf, which once specialised in bananas, may have cost the Reichmanns their fortune; it will certainly lose their bankers at least 75 per cent of the £2 billion that they advanced for this one dream castle alone. In total, the Reichmanns were the beneficiaries of some $12 billion from the commercial banks, and a further $8 billion from the securities markets – that is the commercial-paper, bonds and other securities-market debt raised for them by their investment bankers. At least a third of the commercial banks' total $12 billions of loan to Olympia & York is likely to be lost, though this is probably optimistic, since O&Y debt is trading in the busted loan market at only 40 per cent of its face value. Sod's law requires that whatever can go wrong, will go wrong, and always applies on this scale.

The Reichmanns trusted Mrs Thatcher. The bankers trusted the Reichmanns. No one remembered the admonishment that we were all taught as children 'Nothing to excess'. Originally carved above the door of the temple of the oracle at Delphi, one of the world's earliest management aphorisms may now be rewritten into banking procedures. Although O&Y is the world's biggest ever commercial failure, it is only a small part of a lending spree in the 1980s which must rank as the world's greatest commercial disaster. Worldwide, banks have lost not millions but trillions of 'other people's money', and the story of O&Y is just one of many. The value in 'impaired-value' loans – bankers' jargon for bust borrowers – is estimated to be at least $500 billion in total. A market has developed over the last three years, valued at some $12–14 billion in 1992. This is before any Japanese, or many European banks, have admitted their errors and faced up to their loan losses.

Good lending bankers are gamblers who have taken the pledge, but wish they hadn't, while the not so good, among whom I count myself, don't even know there is a pledge to take. The Reichmanns appealed to bankers. They were secretive, which was intriguing. They were certainly rich, having made the two largest corporate acquisitions in Canadian history. Their investments seemed inspired. By 1990, they owned a portfolio valued at $6 billion, which included the most blue-blooded of investments – oil and gas through Gulf Canada, energy and drink with Hiram Walker, and Abitibi for paper and newsprint. That portfolio is now worth a third less. This could be bad luck or it could be, as some critics have suggested, that the companies were raided for their cash, to keep the property empire afloat. Either way, it simply reinforces what bankers ought to remember, but don't, which is that what goes up must sooner or later come down again.

The Reichmanns were gamblers all right, with their lavishly fitted offices built in the cheap and unfashionable parts of Toronto and New York. They gambled that, by giving office users quality that they had never before contemplated, they could change the three rules of successful property development, which are location, location and location. Bankers could understand this; they, more than anyone, appreciate the value of marble and mahogany in presenting a flattering, or even false, image to the world. The Reichmanns were right about downtown Toronto. Canada's tallest building was built with jagged corners, to create double the number of corner offices, which command the highest rents with their panoramic views that gratify corporate egos. Two years later, in 1977, they used the profits of First Canadian Place to buy eight second-hand skyscrapers from a cash-strapped developer in the bankrupt city of New York. Another five years, and a tenfold gain on that investment, and the Reichmanns parlayed the banks into lending them the billions necessary to develop 92 acres of landfill close to Wall Street.

This home of junkies, a nightmare even for American developers, became an exceptional triumph for this Canadian firm. Buying out the leases of flagship Wall Street firms, techniques perfected with the

Reichmanns' Canadian developments, the World Finance Centre became the new 'in' address for the booming financial-services industry, as banking now likes to call itself. The initial cost to the Reichmanns of financing the move of their new customers was enormous, for the very success of the World Finance Centre destroyed much of the value of the leases that they were taking over in Wall Street's older buildings. As the location and name became fully accepted, sharply escalating rents on later lettings of the new offices justified these deals. There were two other factors working in the Reichmanns' favour, though these would become obvious only with hindsight: a final, late flowering of employment in Wall Street banks, with staff numbers doubling over the decade, and high inflation despite political rhetoric to the contrary.

Bank employment hit its apogee in 1988, according to a study by two analysts at McKinsey & Co., the world's best known firm of management consultants, and technology is now doing to bank employment what mechanisation has done to American farming all this century. In the summer of 1992, Olympia & York spelled out what this will mean to the bond investors who have lent $550 million against the security of 55 Water Street, New York City. Tenants are moving out of Wall Street's largest single office building and, by 1994, the net cash flow from rentals will be just about $5 million, more than a little short of the annual bond interest of $36 million. Modernising Water Street, for a couple of hundred million dollars or so, might attract new tenants but, since O&Y no longer has any money, bondholders must find this themselves. Even small investors might not need bankers to tell them that this is known as throwing good money after bad.

This is what the banks will do, though. The Third World debt crisis showed them that real money is not needed to increase banking assets and profits; since bankers first learned how to replace customers' deposits with money bought from the money markets, they have perfected new methods of calculating profit. The secret is to lend customers the money they need to pay the interest on the loans that they can neither repay nor service. This way everyone can pretend that bad debts are good loans, that losses are profits and that dividends are not being paid out of shareholders' own capital.

London's Docklands comprised, not Toronto's or New York's hundred acres or so of decay just a few minutes' walk from the booming commercial or financial centre, but eight square miles of dereliction, three to four miles away from the Bank of England. The government's original hopes for the regeneration of Docklands had been as a tax-motivated centre for light industry, media activities and craft enterprise. The initial failure of this much hyped scheme brought up the heavy artillery to support the government's initiative. The meeting between Margaret Thatcher, then prime minister, and the Reichmanns allied two 'can-do' believers in the market and its fashionable supply-side philosophies. This completed the hijacking of the original Docklands concept, with plans to build some 14 million square feet of office space, or some 20 per cent of the existing office capacity of the City of London. Docklands was to become a high-tech city of the future, supplementing or supplanting – the promoters were never very clear which it was to be – the traditional City.

But only as the stainless-steel-sheathed towers of Canary Wharf began to appear above their sleazy surroundings, did work begin on the transport links upon which their fate depended. What had worked in Toronto and New York might have worked in London, had adequate roads and railways existed, or construction funds been voted earlier, rather than being merely promised; had there been no other property developers; and had there been no recession. The loss of banking capital is now affecting London quite as much as New York. The back-office functions once envisaged for Canary Wharf are disappearing, as computers replace clerks and make middle management redundant. Where such functions still exist, the jobs can be exported. American banks and insurance companies, whose profitability was hit earlier and more savagely than their foreign counterparts', are already locating such clerical functions as they still need on the west coast of Ireland or within the Caribbean. These are cheaper alternatives to London's Docklands, and the staff are much more stable, since they have few alternatives for employment.

Dr Samuel Johnson remarked upon the fate of an earlier would-be London financier, commenting: 'Depend upon it, Sir, when a man knows he is to be hanged in a fortnight, it concentrates his mind wonderfully.' Similar prospects are now causing many a banker sleepless nights, for the plunging profitability of banking requires equal concentration, though the current round of mergers shows that the die-hards still hope that yesterday's solutions will work in tomorrow's world. It may be that the Reichmanns' great gamble of creating a third commercial centre to compete with the City and the West End will pay off and save the banks, but it seems unlikely. Nor has history much to promise those bankers prepared to defy

Hegel's dictum. Property values, and banking loans, were rescued by annual inflation of 15 per cent or so during the 1970s, which reduced the burden of debt at the expense of banking capital.

Then the bull markets of the 1980s enabled the banks to hide their many errors from themselves. The 1990s are not so kind. America's Federal Reserve Board (the central bank) is desperate to support the commercial viability of the banks it supervises, and to prevent the economy from suffering a 1930s debt deflation, and has been driving down the cost of money. In Europe, however, the costs of German unification are keeping interest rates at levels which, unlike those of the 1970s, are positive after inflation. Indeed, the real cost of money is now some 5–6 per cent a year, and the problem of property debt is twofold. Many of the 1980s dreams of the property developers can neither be sold nor rented, so these loans, which already account for at least 10 per cent of all banking assets, are increasing at a frightening rate; compounding unpaid interest at current lending rates means that bad debts are doubling every six to eight years, and destroying banking capital at the same rate.

However, if the banks become desperate sellers of their property collateral, their actions will destroy property values generally. This will put at risk business loans to individual and company customers, since the great bulk of these are secured on residential or commercial property. It will further undercut banking capital by devaluing the high-street-branch and other office property assets of the banks themselves. Positive real rates of interest ultimately destroy business enterprise, for no one risks money and effort when similar profits can be made from investing effortlessly in risk-free government debt. But the high interest rates, needed to satisfy the domestic concerns of the Bundesbank and the Bank of Japan, vitiate much of the Fed's recovery policy rather as, at another time of change, the Fed hindered the Bank of England's rescue efforts of 1931.

Rodney Leach, the banker who was with Rothschilds when he exposed Maxwell's fraudulent accounting practices in 1969, recently wrote:

> The slim returns and high risks of lending have given rise to the immutable laws of sound banking – moderation, knowledge of the customer's character, transparency of structure, the ability to repay principal, independent collateral, a proper business purpose, cash flow to cover interest. Abandoning these time honoured credit criteria, the banks substituted what? Proximity to fame? The assumption that other banks knew best, accompanied by a desire not to be left out?

The answer is partly that technology dragged banking from the nineteenth to the twenty-first century in less than three decades. Internal politics, and the assumptions of oligopoly, dictated that banks would invest to foil competitors, rather than to improve their service or reconsider the fundamentals of their business. Any group of managers, faced with such rapid change, would inevitably make mistakes. 'I don't know what effect these men will have upon the enemy, but, by God, they terrify me' was the reaction of Lord Wellington to the list of general officers sent him by the War Office, when he was fighting Napoleon's armies in Spain; it is fair to say such sentiments were shared by many practical bankers during the 1980s, as they considered the decisions of their superiors.

Most serious of these errors was the confusion over the banker's role in the postwar *Zeitgeist*, and the consequent misreading of banking history and function. The computer enabled bankers to make banks into large and centralised enterprises, modelled on most bankers' only experience of large-scale organisation – their formative years of military service during the Second World War or in Korea. Military organisation may, or may not, be appropriate for a business that requires judgement to be made on the basis of local conditions and face to face with the customer. What is certain is that centralisation of banking judgement led to its destruction, and senior bankers should have known of this danger. Warren Buffett, America's most successful investor and the rescuer of Salomon Brothers, calls it the 'institutional imperative' or the waning of rationality, when faced with institutional dynamics. This goes far to explain how bankers have failed themselves, their customers and their banks. If they are to restore their credibility and their businesses, bankers, like Mae West, now need to admit: 'I used to be Snow White . . . but I drifted.'

1

An Ill-Starred Voyage

'Bankers are just like the rest of us – only richer.'
Ogden Nash

NO ONE ACTUALLY SAID that the *Titanic* was unsinkable.
She was the apotheosis of the financial and engineering skills
of the English-speaking peoples. Her building was the high point of
Yankee money and Limey ingenuity. It was simply inconceivable
that she should sink. Nor was it ever claimed that the postwar
banking industry was safe for all time, though no one could imagine
that anything would go seriously wrong with a financial system that
was based on the dollar. Pax Americana, and the restructuring in
1933 of American banking laws, had made the world safe for bankers. America would maintain the world of WASPs, or white Anglo-
Saxon Protestants, and their money. It was equally unthinkable that
this system might collapse.

The *Titanic* was one of three sister ships intended by the White
Star Line to wrest leadership of the North Atlantic trade from its
great competitor Cunard, and to fight off the increasingly forceful
Hamburg-based steamship companies. She was designed and built by
Harland & Wolff, the most technically advanced and commercially
successful shipyard of the time. Ultimately, the *Titanic* was a casualty
of this bitter struggle between British, American and German industrial interests, and growing trade competition was exemplified by
the fierce pricing wars on the Atlantic shipping routes. As increased
capacity met slowing demand, American shipowners tried to profit
from the immigrant business, and to benefit from the regular pere-
grinations of rich American girls looking for titled European hus-
bands, while German competition with Britain included subsidies
for her merchant fleets. It was an axiom among all three that trade
should not only follow the flag, but be carried by it as well.

The White Star Line was controlled by the International Mercantile Marine shipping trust, the creation of Pierpoint Morgan, the

world's most powerful banker. The White Star Line had initially prospered under the joint ownership of Gustavus Schwabe and T. H. Ismay, who had recognised that the big profits in shipping were to be made on the North Atlantic routes. In the half-century to 1890, trade between Britain and America in cotton, tobacco and wheat expanded sevenfold. Immigration quadrupled the American population. As the century turned, shipowners realised that their real profit lay not in their mail contracts, not in the bulk commodities, nor even in the first-class passengers. It was in steerage, or third-class, passenger space for Europe's 'huddled masses, yearning to breathe free' and, as it made the profits, so size and passenger accommodation became more important than the coveted Blue Riband for the fastest crossing.

Ismay had died in 1899, and Morgan had then prevailed upon Ismay's weak and inexperienced son to sell him the White Star Line and take the chair of International Mercantile Marine trust instead. A Morgan partner exulted that this new company would 'practically result in our stretching our railroad terminals across the Atlantic.' Plans for the new fleet were devised in 1909, and the *Titanic*, with her two sister ships, was to have better-equipped and larger steerage accommodation than any of her competitors. She was also to have her millionaire suites with coal-burning grates and mock-Tudor half-timbered deck terraces, and the finest of these was reserved for Pierpoint Morgan himself.

The *Olympic, Titanic* and *Britannic*, these first fruits of American money and British technology, were intended to humble Cunard which stood in Morgan's way. Morgan first forced two of the leading Hamburg shipowners to merge and cooperate with him, and then initiated a vicious rate war with Cunard, offering third-class transatlantic passages for only £2, or £80 in today's money, intending to drive Cunard into his shipping trust, which would then determine Atlantic fares. Cunard were badly hurt, but they refused to sell to Morgan or join his scheme. These rate wars, and German acquiescence to the Morgan shipping trust, had forced Cunard to beg a sympathetic British government for help. The *Titanic* and her sisters were to compete with the pride of Cunard's fleet, the *Mauretania* and *Carpathia*. These, the very latest in speed, size and comfort, had been built with government subsidies which, though directed at Morgan, were justified on the grounds that the Cunard board had agreed to the conscription of its fleet in time of war.

Morgan was not yet ready to take on the British Empire. Most of his investors were British, and his London bank was an important source of revenue. So he offered the British government a deal; the White Star Line, though American-owned, would fly the Red Ensign with the ships crewed and officered under British Board of Trade regulations and available to the Royal Navy, should they ever be needed as troop transports. Though Morgan was at the Belfast launch of the *Titanic*, neither he nor the managing partner of Morgan Grenfell was able to use their reserved suites on her maiden voyage in April 1912. The loss of the *Titanic* was the death knell of International Mercantile Marine, which had always been a sickly company, with even the New York Stock Exchange refusing to quote its bonds. These were so heavily 'watered' by the front-end fees charged for merger negotiations* that even the most gullible of investors refused to buy them, and Morgans defaulted the bonds in 1916.

The Titanic is more than the memorial to the 1500 passengers, from the obscenely rich to the wretchedly poor, who died with her. The message from both the American Senatorial enquiry, and the British Board of Trade investigation, was clear. The loss of life reflected the complacent and self-confident arrogance of a people neither accustomed to defeat, nor realising that the world was changing around them faster than they knew. It was the beginning of the end of Britain's industrial leadership, and of London's financial might. The motives that made owner and captain of the *Titanic* drive the vessel at full speed through an ice field were similar to those that held back possible buyers of International Mercantile Marine bonds. It was the slowing of international trade, and the difficulty of making a reasonable return on investment. Competition was destabilising the markets in capital goods for the 'new lands' of America and Australasia had been opened, and the economies of western Europe industrialised.

From the 1870s onwards, Britain was generating savings at a rate unparalleled even by Japan today and, in those years, Argentina borrowed on better rates than the German government could borrow from its own citizens a century later. But the borrowing was private, and not State, and was to build British engineered railroads and docks, and financed by British imports of the wheat and meat of the Argentine. Capitalism's last great frontier was Russia, and eastern

---

* Morgan's fees for IMM were not unusual; when George Moore, the President of Citibank, joined the audit committee of the board of US Steel in the 1960s, the only matter in contention with the Internal Revenue Service was Morgan's fee from sixty years before. The IRS were arguing that this $57 million [over $1 billion today] was capital, and could not be offset against profits, while the company contended that it was most definitely a fee, and so deductible.

Europe, for the world was run by the nations bordering the Atlantic, and no one thought that either Asia or Africa had any role in this, except as consumers. Russian wealth was expanding, the opening of new companies accelerating, and between 1885–1914 the growth of the Russian economy outpaced even that of the United States. This was not sufficient to compensate for the slowing of other markets; moreover, the chaotic weakness of Russia's political structure, and German fears that Russian growth would affect its own industrial and military domination of the European continent, held back the investment needed.

As most Western countries began to be producers as well as consumers, protectionism grew. The encouragement of 'national industrial champions' slowed world growth as did, even more importantly, the very uneven distribution of the wealth created by the nineteenth century explosion of industrial techniques. The thesis of liberal capitalism developed its antithesis in Marxism, and the resulting synthesis has significantly improved the living standards of the average citizen of the world; Americans and Europeans probably enjoy a standard of living five times higher than that of their grandparents, and the Japanese some twenty five times greater. This political synthesis, today called social democracy, was not easily nor quickly achieved.

Europeans always preferred power to money for, like bankers later in the century, their neighbours' supposed good fortune seemed more attractive than the reality of their own and Germany, the Johnny-come-lately to the European high table, attempted to force the pace of history. European wars from 1914 onwards destroyed wealth accumulated over many centuries, and delayed Germany's emergence as the leading European power by nearly a century, as managerial ability allied itself to political incompetence. This ensured that Germany 'snatched defeat from the very jaws of victory' as President Abraham Lincoln had earlier remarked about the predecessor to General Ulysses S. Grant, the victorious commander of the US Federal armies, and the prophet of the bloodiness of twentieth century industrialised warfare. America was scarcely more politically adept for, though the era of British supremacy was dead by 1930, much of America's new financial strength was dissipated by its refusal to take on Britain's nineteenth century role as the world's lender of last resort. This dragged both America, and the world, into the Great Depression of the 1930s.

America and Germany, denied the geographical empires of the other European states, put their efforts instead into the development of business empires; many of today's multinational companies stem from those decades though it still took the political misfortunes of the twentieth century to persuade Europeans, and especially Germans, of the value of the American credo that 'The business of America is business'. Trade protectionism was the natural concomitant of economic nationalism; only after America's 1945 emergence as the world's financial and economic superpower did Washington adopt the British belief in the virtues of free trade. Even so, it was only in the late 1970s that international trade had recovered the same ratio to world manufacturing that it had enjoyed prior to 1914. The Uruguay round of GATT, calculated as a tonic to the flagging economies of the 1980s, is moribund after seven years of negotiations, though no politicians will admit to this, lest they be accused of causing it. That fear of public exposure is an improvement over 1930; the authors of America's Smoot-Hawley tariff laws were proud enough of their protection of American agriculture to put their name to an act which had, by 1933, reduced world trade to a third of its 1929 levels.

These twentieth century wars simply underlined that commercial vitality had passed from Britain to America and Germany. With it, went also the wealth creating ability that once underwrote London's financial preeminence, though this received an *erzatz* extension of life from the migration of American banks to London during the 1960s. Now, a century later, financial power is passing from America to Japan and Germany, business has exhausted the consumer society of its growth potential, and old habits are again resurfacing. Trade protectionism is still easier for politicians to sell than free trade, and neighbourly help to Russia and east Europe.

2

Holed and Sinking

'While the money is hoped for, and for a short time after it has
been received, he who lends it is a friend and benefactor; by the
time the money is spent and the evil hour of reckoning is come,
the benefactor is found to have changed his nature and to have
put on the tyrant and oppressor.'

George Rae, independent banker, author and later
director of the Midland Bank, in his 1886 edition of
The Country Banker

'THE STEREOTYPE OF BANKERS as conservative, careful, prudent individuals was shattered in 1929,' said Bernard Baruch, a
financier and politician who, despite the Great Crash, maintained the
fortune he had made during the 1920s as a Wall Street insider. But
Baruch was wrong. Over the next fifty years politicians and the public
were to prove more forbearing than he imagined. America's largest
bank, Citibank, almost destroyed by the losses it incurred in the
1930s, nevertheless became the cynosure of bankers the world over
during the postwar decades. Yet by 1992 Citibank had been required
to sign a letter of understanding with the Comptroller of the Currency,
which means that America's banking regulators consider Citibank's
managerial competence and financial health to be well below average.
Congressional critics claim that it is technically insolvent.

Indeed, had it not been for the 1930s banking reforms, bankers'
overcommitment to banking fashion during the 1980s would have
bankrupted many of the world's greatest banks and ruined their
managers, shareholders and depositors alike. In legislating so, the
politicians of the 1930s acted out of no particular love of bankers but
the realisation that economic prosperity – and their own continued
enjoyment of the perks of office – requires a properly functioning
economy. Those reforms meant that banking risks, though it took
time for bankers to appreciate this, were to be borne by taxpayers
and customers instead. Banks are necessary to world prosperity,

since they control the payments system; when businessmen no longer trust their banks to make payments to suppliers, business dies. Barter works in simple economies, but not in today's world.

This payments role developed from the banker's prime function of acting as a go-between for savers and investors – the lubricant for economic prosperity at regional, national and global levels. Since bankers always include among their number many who are over-enthusiastic, some who are incompetent and a few who are fraudulent, this underpinning of the world's commerce is always fragile. Once depositors fear for the safety of their savings, not only does this contagion quickly spread to other banks, but bankers themselves become equally fearful. A run on the bank reflects a loss of confidence in the bank as a safe home for savings, and affects company treasurers as much as individual savers. Just such rumours in 1984, which started among dealers in the Tokyo money markets, destroyed Continental Illinois, then America's eighth largest bank, and threatened the survival of two even larger US banks – Manufacturers Hanover and Chase Manhattan.

The world works on credit – not loans, as such, but the willingness to assume that goods will be paid for provided only that a bank confirms the creditworthiness of the other partner to the transaction. 'Credit' comes from the Latin word for 'trust' and it is credit, rather than loans, that fuels economic life. The credit generated by British banks, as banks, businesses and people transfer money among themselves through the payments system, and cheque and bill payments are met by banks before funds to cover them are received as cash, is 200 – 300 times greater than the amount lent by them. Similar ratios can be found in any industrialised society. The cancer that destroys economic vitality is the loss of this trust. It is then that bank customers worry that the money they put into their account, for transfer to business counterparts or family members, might never come out of the banking system. Once a run on the bank meant queues of desperate depositors forming opposite tellers' windows to withdraw their savings; now it is more likely to be telex messages from all over the world refusing to renew deposits, or demanding instant repayment.

The reforms of the 1930s assured depositors that, whether their bankers were crooked, incompetent or just unlucky, their money would be safe. Even though banks still fail, no major national bank has been allowed to lose its depositors' money since the 1930s. Even the customers of such rogue banks as the Bank of Credit and Commerce International had some protection. Unfortunately, ensuring that depositors are protected also protects bankers from the consequences of their own mistakes. Reform underwrote the survival of poorly managed banks, and so ensured that bankers would have nothing to control their ambitions, even though banking is no less competitive than other human activities. As bankers slowly appreciated what reform offered them, the second traditional control on bankers disappeared. Commercial banks became limited-liability companies a century ago, but unlimited liability curbed the natural ebullience of investment bankers, the riskier end of the trade, for the danger to the family's financial welfare reined in the wilder flights of banking fancy. By the 1970s, high rates of tax, the increased size and knowledge of their corporate customers, and growing competition from the commercial banks had persuaded most investment bankers to incorporate; the risk to personal fortune was no longer justified by the rewards of twentieth-century banking.

Once corporate and personal risk were eliminated, there was nothing to stop all bankers choosing the high-risk and high-return sectors of their industry. In addition to money, banking has always promised fame. Much of the excitement of investment banking is in its close and profitable involvement with the affairs of the world. Governments always need money, and bankers never refuse political honours – membership of the House of Lords for the British, senior rank within the Légion d'Honneur for the French, or a cabinet post for the Americans. But this is a limited market, and competing for it meant that, by the 1980s, banks had so destroyed, or spent, the natural advantages of a large, tied customer base that they had to lend, and lend on high-margin, risky business, just to survive.

Bankers have the measure of their legislators and regulators, and nothing keeps their ambitions in check, for the reason succinctly described by one of President Nixon's aides. Listing the benefits of the dirty-tricks campaign, designed to sew up the 1974 election, he remarked: 'With their balls in our hands, their hearts and minds are sure to follow.' While the commercial banks control the world's payment system, these have the same power of persuasion. So, although critics both in Congress and Wall Street question whether Citibank would still be solvent if the regulators were as tough on it as they are on smaller banks, no official in his right mind is going to insist on answers. The risks are just too great for, if there is such a thing as a global bank, Citibank is it.

Citibank has lived on the edge for much of its existence. Initially called City Bank, and founded in 1812, Citibank had first to be rescued in 1837, and was nearly destroyed again in 1920 by its Cuban and Russian loans. Only half of America's banks reopened after the politicians closed them in 1933, as a final attempt to halt the series of banking crises that started with the 1929 Wall Street Crash. Citibank survived, even though it had lost most of its shareholders' funds and many of its 1920s banking initiatives had been condemned as being against the public interest. Yet Citibank has never lacked a sense of its own worth or importance so, by 1945, it had restored its balance sheet and its morale from the public obloquy of the 1930s. Postwar demand for loans was exceptional, for companies and individuals were anxious to make up the time lost by fifteen years of depression and war. From 1960 onwards, Citibank used its London branch to escape American banking restrictions and renew its 1920s ambition to become the world's first universal bank, being everywhere and doing everything.

Citibank needed the world because George Moore and Walter Wriston, his successor as president and chairman, set the bank an annual growth target of 15 per cent a year. This was to get the blood running through Citibank's sluggish veins after nearly three decades of depression, war and postwar regulation. Together with the implementation of a five-year planning horizon, this was an effective tonic. However, the chosen growth rate was some four times the rate at which the American economy was growing, and twice that of the recovering continental European economies. But American goods were in demand everywhere, and Citibank's customers were expanding much faster than these averages. As the American multinational corporations increased market share, expanded overseas and developed new products for the emerging consumer society, Citibank had an exceptional opportunity to grow. However, if Citibank were to achieve its targets in the long term, it would have to take business from other banks or increase the size of the banking market. The former was unlikely. Citibank's international competitors were either nationalised banks or sacrosanct national businesses, and could look to their politicians for protection.

So, as the tide of American industry's imperial expansion ebbed, Wriston refined the Citibank mission; the bank would grow through the three 'I's, by banking for Institutions, Industry and Individuals. As even these grew to be insufficient, Insurance and Information were added to the pack. Wriston needed Citibank shares to be seen as a 'growth stock' by the new institutional investment managers, so expansion of Citibank's profits and earnings per share had to be regular and progressive, otherwise its share price would revert to ratings appropriate to that of other public utilities, such as the electricity, gas and water companies. This would make Citibank's physical expansion difficult, since raising new money from the stock markets would become more expensive. It would also ruin the value of the new share-option schemes for senior executives. So Wriston publically confirmed Citibank's ambitions of 15 per cent profits growth in the 1970s and John Reed, his chosen successor, did the same in the 1980s.

Neither achieved his aims for, at a compound rate of 15 per cent a year, or a doubling of size every five years, something had to give. Since it would not be Citibank's competitors, it had to be credit quality. Citibank culture is social Darwinism, internally and externally, and the bank works as close to the edge of capital adequacy and banking regulations as possible. Prudence is not an issue, Wriston was known as a 'ready, fire, aim' banker and Citibank believes in riskless banking; when a bank has a big enough market share, in enough places, then that diversification of lending means losses can easily be absorbed from profits elsewhere. This worked in the 1920s, and worked again in the 1980s. It did not work in the 1930s, nor will it work in the 1990s.

American regulators assess the health of their charges through a CAMEL rating, in which 1 is the highest and 5 the lowest. This acronym stands for capital adequacy, asset quality, managerial competence, earnings and liquidity. CAMEL ratings are never disclosed, but can sometimes be guessed from the action taken by the regulators. It is generally accepted that a bank has to be marked 3 – or occasionally 4 – before its board is asked to sign a letter of agreement, which is a memorandum setting out what the regulators expect of the bank's management. Such a letter is what the Citibank board had to sign in 1992. Banking is not an actuarial calculation, said George Moore, and he knew because he worked with Chairman James Perkins to save Citibank in the 1930s. Reed is now relearning that banking truth and, in referring to Citibank's property loans, which continued to be made well into 1990 despite clear evidence that property developers like Donald Trump were in trouble, professed that he was 'damned embarrassed because the critics were right, and we were wrong'. However, embarrassment in banking takes longer to work through than to apologise for; other banks have bad property loans, overoptimistic management buyout deals and too many overindebted personal customers, but Citibank's problem loans seem to be double the average of its competitors', while it still has outstanding debt from the Third World crisis of ten years ago.

In autumn 1991 Citibank recognised some of its mistakes when, for the first time in the bank's long history, Reed stated that the trend of future bad debts was such that it would be imprudent to continue to pay dividends to shareholders. Citibank is fighting loan losses expected to run at some $1.5 billion throughout much of the 1990s, with over $10.5 billion of its loan portfolio classified as no longer capable of paying interest. Citibank's capital is still leaking out of the bank faster than shareholders can pour it back in again, and is estimated to need at least $5 billion of equity to bring its balance sheet to the state of health required by the regulators. Moreover, Citibank no longer has its famous milch cow in consumer banking, accounting for 60 per cent of the bank's earnings in the 1980s; individuals are saving, rather than borrowing, now that they are no longer so certain that they will have a job next week. Corporate loan business is in the doldrums, too, as the recession deepens. Only Citibank's third core business, foreign exchange with its related dealing activities, is still doing well. In just four years to 1991, Citibank has written off $11.5 billion in bad loans, or more than the $10 billion of equity that it had in 1988. Since Citibank is no longer generating capital, its management has to cut costs by the amount of the estimated bad-debt write-offs, and raise extra capital to maintain the bank's independence.

Citibank has saved itself from the brink before, but this public mauling of its self-esteem will keep it, and world banking, quiescent just when the world desperately needs lively and supportive banks. For if losses destroy all of the bank's capital, it must close its doors and depositors will then lose some or all of their savings. Since world prosperity demands that major banks do not fail, those losses must be made good by others. 'Others' means us, for banking profitability rests on domestic customers, and we pay for losses either through taxes, with which governments rescue bankrupt banks, or through greater borrowing costs, lower deposit earnings and higher charges for banking services, or even through unemployment and business bankruptcy.

Mr Alexandre Lamfalussy, the general manager of the Bank for International Settlements, expressed fears as long ago as 1990 that a world economic slump might be caused by a shortage of banking credit. He remarked on the puzzling lack of commercial judgement in banks' borrowing and lending decisions and the 'propensity of the banking system to make repeated mistakes on a rather grand scale'. Lamfalussy's point was put more succinctly by Gordon Gecko, the chief banking character in the film *Wall Street*, when he proclaimed: 'Greed is good. Greed works.' Gecko was not simply mythologising the 1980s careers of Wall Street bankers such as John Gutfreund of Salomon Brothers and Michael Milken of Drexel Burnham, but the nature and history of banking itself.

The judgement of bankers concerns everyone, for their behaviour affects economic wellbeing. Bankers influence governments, for what cannot be raised through taxes must be borrowed, and the terms and conditions of loans are set by the preferences of investors and their bankers. Party politicians can temporarily get away with talk of a 'banker's ramp' – the evil gnomes of Zurich were long a favourite standby of economically illiterate British politicians – but if Britain regularly has to pay more for its borrowings than France or Spain, politicians will find that a hard reality to square with national pride. And bankers influence businesses even more directly. Commercial bankers the world over emulated Citibank, thinking it was a bank like themselves, whereas Citibank was in London proving that it could be just like Pierpont Morgan's bank, which was unique to its time and ownership. Only a tiny part of the banking industry is, or rather should be, concerned with either international or investment banking. Nineteenth-century bankers believed that money should be lent only to countries whose citizens wear overcoats; however good that is as a credit judgement, the brute fact of international banking is that there are certainly no more than a couple of dozen countries, and maybe 1,000 companies, to whom bankers can safely be 'international lenders'.

There are more investment-banking possibilities than that, of course, but these require a good understanding of the domestic environment. Yet adding 'international' and 'investment' together still keeps this as a tiny percentage of the banking market. The true reality of banking is not dealing with governments, nor lending to household names, but the humdrum financing of small business, the administration of the financial affairs of individual customers, and keeping the world at work by managing its payment system. Relationships between banks and business create the credit that buoys up prosperity, while bank loans fertilise the growth of businesses. These day-to-day activities, though important, are neither exciting nor fashionable, nor do they make a reputation for the bankers who do them.

Although there are 20 million business enterprises within the European Community, fewer than 12,000 of them employ more than 500 people. A similar ratio holds good in the United States. Excluding companies that have quotations on a recognised stock market, and so can theoretically borrow through the securities markets, over 70 per cent of business banking activity is generated by individuals and these small and medium-sized firms. These need commercial banks, not investment banks, for such companies have neither the size nor the credit rating to allow them access to the securities markets. Instead, they must rely on commercial banks as the intermediaries between other people's money and their talent, and to act as their anteroom for the parlours of the investment banks and the heady excitements of the securities markets. Few make it but, once commercial banks fail in this, their major function, national economies cease to thrive, because it is small companies that produce new ideas and, most important of all, new jobs. Business, like life, is a profligate process of natural selection, and commercial bankers are the financial midwives of the process.

Postwar bankers needed to be aggressive, for the dead years of depression and war had sapped the entrepreneurial vitality of many banks. However, governments, by preventing the destruction of banking-deposit, shareholder and management wealth, also ensured that banking capacity would grow faster than economic needs. Hidden from legislators and bankers by the capital-hungry nature of the postwar reconstruction boom, this overcapacity began to tighten banking margins from the 1970s onwards. Then the natural competitiveness of bankers was stimulated by the appearance of institutional investors, and their search for 'growth' stocks. The consequent requirement for banks to improve earnings per share meant that planning was increasingly based on a volume-driven, market-share approach to lending, which further weakened the responsibility of the individual banker.

Legislators were happy enough to go along with enthusiastic lending banks, whatever their reasons for being so. Henry Kaufman, a partner of Salomon Brothers until 1988 and long-time critic of lax banking practices, remarks:

Elected officials are often biased in favour of more credit creation, rather than less, because they see the economic activity that results, but they do not appreciate the associated risks, which come to the surface later on . . . excessive leveraging/borrowing, while ultimately debilitating for businesses, households and governments alike, is almost calamitous for governments . . . when fiscal policy is forced to be inactive, then the entire burden of economic stabilisation logically falls onto monetary policy. But this may compel the central bank to compromise its long-term goal of preserving a safe and sound financial system to the more immediate objective of reviving a flagging economy. Financial conservatism is the casualty. A more fragile financial system is the ultimate consequence.

It should surprise no one that bankers spend all their time and money on chasing the large corporate customer. The greed of bankers for money, first-class clients and personal honours needs to be understood as part of the nature of banking. Manufacturers can admire the machines in their warehouses or the efficient working of their production processes and, though sales may not be as high as hoped, can at least comfort themselves with technical comparisons that describe the superiority of their products to those of competitors. Banking as an esoteric service business offers no such concrete comforts, only the sense of satisfaction that comes from a reputation among neighbours. Centralisation and computers would destroy the community basis of banking during the 1970s, and with it the concern of bankers for their reputation.

Neither banking nor plumbing is necessary to life. The world for most of its history – like the majority of its population today – did without either. Yet bankers have much in common with sewage workers: as sewers link communities through the collection and disposal of their wastes, so banks link those same communities through their wealth. In so doing, they also immobilise surplus assets as savings which, sensibly invested, will create future wealth. When Birmingham was the workshop of the world, its manufacturers believed that 'where there's muck, there's brass', and organised crime in the United States today is said to do well out of the garbage business. No one needs to be told that controlling the flow of the world's gold, and regularly scooping out an insignificant handful on a percentage basis, is cleaner, more profitable and a lot more fun than shovelling shit, but that is part of the cause of bankers' greed; customers, on the whole, take their bankers and garbage collectors for granted and only notice them when the service fouls up.

Bankers are different from garbage collectors in one crucial respect, other than the money they earn. Rubbish is collected from individual households and businesses, transported to a centre, and destroyed in bulk. Banks must amalgamate, and then re-sort and re-deliver each individual financial item to separate recipients. These payments systems make banking the world's bookkeeper and financial postman. Bankers' functional monopoly died when computers became a cheap commodity product in the 1980s, but their managerial systems still assume a business oligopoly; neither owning the bank, nor able to assess their contribution to its results through profitability analysis, the only way for individual bankers to keep score is to pile up the money and the names.

Well into the 1960s, most banks were entirely dependent for their funding on the savings of individuals, and the cash surplusses of companies. These filled their coffers, and so enabled them to make the loans on which their profits depended. But from then on bankers began to borrow from each other, and through the money markets, on an unsecured basis. Released from the need to attract customers for their deposits, from the 1970s onwards bankers began to spurn prudence for growth, and banking judgement was institutionalised out of banking decisions as banking became an industry suffering from overcapacity, out-of-control spending, misunderstood technology and increased political involvement. President Reagan in the United States preached austerity in 1980, but practised the opposite, and the world economy took off on one of its occasional binges. That decade became the age of banking globalisation, since bankers had finally appreciated that the computer was something more than a replacement for the quill pen of an oppressed bank clerk. To allow prudence to affect lending and expansion plans would be to abandon the chance of joining the ranks of the dozen or so banking 'masters of the universe' that, it was confidently assumed, would dominate the financial world of the twenty-first century.

This was also the decade when Japan ceased borrowing for investment, and became a lender instead. Financed by the profit-fruiting of its hectic postwar capital investment, Japanese banks expanded pell-mell into the world at large while Japanese companies, raising and borrowing money at an effective negative cost – as the Tokyo stock market emulated Wall Street of sixty years earlier – became the world's most popular manufacturers. As this new financial power celebrated its wealth by throwing it around, everyone else tried to match it. The Japanese banks, which have been responsible for funding much of the world over the last decade, now have inadequate capital for their domestic business, let alone the rest of the world; they also have to face property and other non-performing loans conservatively estimated at $405 billion.

Scandinavia allowed its banks their freedom, and the bad debts that resulted from the consequent lending boom have destroyed many of the region's banks, while similar excesses appear to be having almost as bad an effect on those of the English-speaking countries as well. Of the Scandinavian banks, only the Danes have survived relatively unscathed; this might be because, as one Danish academic quoted in the *Financial Times* put it: 'Every year Denmark starts out with seventy-seven commercial banks, every year there are several mergers, but every year we still seem to finish with seventy-seven commercial banks. Much the same happens with the savings banks, except that there are twice as many of them.' Community banking may not be glamorous, but at least it seems to be safe.

Banking retrenchment burned out the loan collateral held by the Norwegian banks. As asset prices in Norway fell, interest rates net of the cost of inflation rose even higher in real terms and this further discouraged business activity. This slowing of enterprise affected the value of every form of real property, including the 32,000 tons of frozen salmon stockpiled as a result of overenthusiastic financing of fish farms. As the effect of compounding interest destroyed the value of collateral, the banks panicked, called in their loans, forced the sale of the security held to secure the loan, and these realised bad debts then wiped out much of their capital. Prices fell still further, for these banking policies set off a classical deflation of asset values, both of property and quoted securities, and the government had to step in, first with a guarantee fund to supplement banking capital, and then by taking over the banks. Deflation and business depression have now spread to Sweden and Finland.

There are only three ways of escaping such a debt trap, other than the substantial reduction of interest rates now being pursued by the Fed. All are unpleasant. Inflation, the choice of the 1970s, wipes out debts, but destroys the incentive to save, and weakens the capital base of the banks. Repayment, which has been chosen for the 1990s, requires much greater individual belt-tightening and worsens the economic recession; perversely, falling asset values and lower inflation often increase the cost of money and thus the likelihood of debt deflation. Financial and economic collapse is the third solution, and resulted from the actions of the politicians and bankers of the 1930s. These followed conventional wisdom, despite the protests of economists such as the American Irving Fisher or Britain's John Maynard Keynes, and their sound money policies drove the world into the same situation that engulfs Scandinavia now.

The UK, whose citizens are more highly borrowed than those of

America, has the worst of both worlds. Real interest rates are kept high by German domestic policies, because the legendary soundness of the Deutschmark and Bundesbank policy in general have been derailed by the unexpected economic shocks of reunification, while banking bad debts are on the American scale. Borrowers, whether individuals or businesses, are caught in a 1930s-style debt trap, where the compounding effect of high interest rates increases debt faster than it can be repaid. British and European policymakers, regarding the Exchange Rate Mechanism as today's equivalent of the pre–1914 gold standard, pursued as misguided a policy as that of the Fed in 1931; their efforts have brought about the very opposite of the stability for which they strive.

The Federal Reserve Board has been driving American interest rates down to keep its banks afloat. The Fed learned from its 1930s mistakes that high interest rates can compound bad debts, and so destroy the capital foundations of banks faster than shareholders can rebuild them. But the Fed is also conscious that central banks can only influence short-term interest rates, while the US economy and the world economy are both held back by the banks' general reluctance to lend. No sensible person risks lending to business if the same return, or better, can be achieved by lending risk-free to the government, which is why over 50 per cent of new American banking assets is government debt. But with 70 per cent of all private banking credit supported by property values of one sort or another, this reluctance to lend simply encourages debt deflation. It was this attitude that devastated business in the 1930s and destroyed Norwegian banking in 1990.

Since governments first prevented the natural commercial culling of banks, capacity has grown faster than demand, and bad banking practices are not penalised. The regulators, unveiled with so much enthusiasm in the 1930s, have proved incapable of keeping up with the technological changes in banking, and the entanglements of political and banking life. American banking traditions, with their subtle differences from English banking attitudes, fooled their enthusiasts at the Bank of England, and London's colonisation by Wall Street banks during the 1960s became a misfortune for banking shareholders and customers alike. Banking losses do not disappear, though banks can pretend that loans are 'good', as they did for most of the 1980s with their loans to Third World countries. If, in the end, bankers cannot recover the loans that they have made, banks must either offset these losses against profits or, if they are too great, write them off by reducing the value of their capital.

This makes for fearful bankers, fewer loans and slower economic growth, as we have today, or even no growth at all. The failure of the banking system in 1931 was so bad that it poisoned prosperity for a decade, and only rearmament for the Second World War provided an antidote. 1991 and 1992 are unforgettable vintages, though whether these will be equally poisonous for prosperity it is still too early to say. Without government guarantees, losses on 1980s business would have destroyed the world banking system by now. Bank reform will be on the 1990s agenda, for the excesses of the 1980s seem likely to bring about exactly the same debt deflation that followed those of the 1920s. The economic depression of the 1990s will probably not be as terrible as that of the 1930s, because now social-democratic governments spend 40–50 per cent of our money, including considerable sums on welfare payments, whereas in the 1930s it was only 10–15 per cent. Government spending will act as a stabiliser, but not a preventative, as Scandinavia has already proved.

Banking judgement might well have faltered when social unrest drove financiers to London from Amsterdam, and Dutch financial supremacy was destroyed by the political forces of the French Revolution. But no banker can be ignorant of what happened the next time round, when London gave place to New York. The celebrated American economist Irving Fisher helpfully spelled out the phases of a debt deflation for bankers, writing in *Econometrica* in 1933 that 'the public psychology of going into debt for gain passes through several . . . phases: (a) the lure of big prospective dividends or gains in income in the remote future; (b) the hope of selling at a profit, and realising a capital gain in the immediate future; (c) the vogue of restless promotions . . . ; (d) the development of down right fraud,' yet the shift of financial power from New York to Tokyo during the 1980s saw bubble-headed bankers repeating all the mistakes of the 1920s. Easy money quickly turns into spiralling asset values, and the roaring 1920s and depressing 1930s are part of folk memory but not, it seems, of banking memory.

Fisher's analysis is as true of the 1980s as it was of the 1920s, and regulators and legislators have discovered for themselves that the financial markets are difficult and dangerous places for the unwary or ignorant. Bankers know that finance is the 'quintessence of academic learning and a paradigm of fraudulence; it is a touchstone for the intelligent and a tombstone for the audacious, a treasury of usefulness and a source of disaster'. Even when bankers risked personal bankruptcy, a financial crisis every generation was needed to remind them of the continuing relevance of that warning, though it was first published in 1688 in *Confusion de Confusiones* by Joseph de la Vega, one of the first participants to write of the modern financial markets. The cost of government-subsidised banking mistakes, and the loss of bankers' personal liability, may well turn out to be considerably higher than imagined.

3

Slipping the Moorings

'Speaking from a perspective of sixty years in banking and
business, I have to say that banking is the surest, safest and
easiest business I have seen or known . . . if you're not actually
stupid or dishonest it's hard not to make money in banking.'
George Moore, writing in *A Banker's Life*
of his time with Citibank

BANKERS COMPETED DURING THE booming 1980s as if
money was going out of fashion, but that fashion was set well
before the 1950–70 postwar decades of expansion, or even the heady
1920s. Handling the payment transfers of shipowners, as well as
financing their shipbuilders, was good banking business and in 1905
the Midland Bank was accused by the Bank of England of 'unortho-
dox behaviour'. Midland had outraged the London merchant banks,
for whom the Bank was a cooperative club, by setting up both a
shipping department and a foreign-exchange-dealing function. Such
international business was considered to be quite outside the capacity
of a commercial bank.

Edward Holden, the managing director of the Midland, would
have none of this. He proclaimed it a necessary defensive tactic, to
protect British banking from the aggressive expansionism of continental European banks and to hold the growing foreign business of
American banks. Indeed, banking competition has always enabled
English-speaking bankers to enjoy the same character-forming pas-
times as their English and Virginian country gentlemen neighbours,
and their original clients. From its very inception Anglo-American
banking competition, just like fox-hunting, has offered 'all the
excitement of war, but only 25 per cent of the casualties'. Since the
triumph of American finance at the beginning of this century, though,
the odds have probably favoured fox-hunters more than bankers.

The defeat of Napoleon had given the world to London bankers,
and to the British government the key to world finance. London

merchant bankers preferred the frenetic excitements of international trade and the diplomatic round; the 'muck and brass' of industry was left to such banks as the Midland. These merchant, or investment, bankers had a small staff, and needed great flexibility in responding to changes in the financial world. They depended, as was said of the Morgan banks, 'on brains, blood and money'. These invented the modern financial world, now exploited to such good effect by nation states. Until 1940 banking history describes a world where bankers knew more, did more, and were more essential to the functioning of the world than any other group. Before national bureaucracies, treasury officials, economic statisticians and financial summits existed in their present forms, bankers did the job instead. Driven by its own needs, and the lack of any other source of economic analysis or financial information, banking developed intelligence services and administrative functions that either pre-empted or complemented those needed by governments.

There are real differences between banking skills, even if these are not the immediately obvious ones. Investment and commercial bankers both lend money, one of the riskier activities of banking. Investment bankers use an agency method of lending, an improvement on medieval banking techniques, brought to fruition during the ideological wars of the seventeenth century. These banks issue bonds or shares for sale to individual or institutional investors, and guarantee the success of the sale – and so the availability of the money – by underwriting them, a term acquired from insurers of the time. Commercial banks advance their own money as principals, a technique developed during the eighteenth century and perfected in the nineteenth.

However, the real difference is not technique, but style. Commercial lending is like the mass pheasant slaughter that so entranced Edwardian bankers. Just like a commercial banker, a competent shot runs little risk with these driven birds. A poor aim means wasting more ammunition than is desirable, but the only real risk in pheasant shooting is so rare as to be hardly a risk at all; this is that the gun in the next butt, having drunk too well at lunch, follows a low bird too far around and blows his companion's head off. Commercial bankers in the 1980s were already light-headed but, worse, they also went into investment banking. This is closer to hunting big game than pheasants; if a black rhino is not downed with the first two shots, and the hunter's companion has run, then at the ensuing wake the hunter's colleagues can happily divide his valuable possessions. Investment-banking deals are of great importance to their initiators.

Clients are rich and powerful, and must necessarily ask themselves 'Is he the sort of fellow I'd go tiger shooting with?'

Investment bankers prove their mettle only under fire. In the nineteenth century Junius Morgan, the father of Pierpoint, made his fortune, and the name of his bank, by raising £10 million for a French government beleaguered by catastrophic defeat and social unrest, and in the teeth of the Prussian leader Bismarck's threats that any such loan would be repudiated. To act for France was a banker's dream. The land reform of the French Revolution had resolved the nineteenth century problem of income distribution, though not political structure, so the immense natural wealth of 'France des villages' meant that this country, like Britain with its rapidly growing industrial base, was a net exporter of capital. But wars eat money, particularly lost ones, and no one else had the courage to step forward. Barings financed Prussia while Rothschilds thought France was doomed. French government bonds with a nominal value of 100 francs were issued by Morgan at 85 in 1870, so as to tempt investors with the exceptionally high yield of 6 per cent; this discount of the price to the face value of the bonds gave them a yield of more than twice that available on British government bonds. The government of the new Third Republic was appalled that France's credit should be assessed so low, though they had no choice but to accept.

Morgan was right to be cautious in his pricing; after the capitulation of Paris and the revolutionary explosion of the Commune, the bonds fell to 55. No doubt remembering the dictum of Nathan Rothschild, the founder of the London branch of the family bank, that 'when blood is running in the streets of Paris, I buy', Morgan gambled the whole worth of his bank on his earlier judgement. He supported the stock markets, and the syndicate he had put together to underwrite the bonds, by buying back all bonds offered him. His reward was a fortune of £1.5 million when the government of the Third Republic redeemed the bonds, buying them back in 1873 at their par value of 100 francs.

Bankers' central role in the creation and preservation of economic prosperity ought to make for prudence, for bankers have the inside edge in the money game. Before he threw the dice, Junius Morgan had done his homework; he knew that no French government since 1789, however revolutionary, had reneged on its predecessors' obligations. Bankers don't always win, any more than does the odds-fixing bookie or the house dealer at the roulette wheel, but none should ever lose spectacularly. That role is reserved for the punter.

Yet playing the punter is exactly what banks have been doing since the 1970s, for most have sought to achieve on an institutional level, and with other people's money, what Junius Morgan did alone and at the risk of his own fortune.

Modern banking was forged out of the furnace of European religious wars, and especially the Dutch struggle for independence from their rulers, the Hapsburg rulers of Spain and the Holy Roman Empire, known to contemporaries as being neither holy, Roman nor an empire. The profitability of banking depended on the activities of the merchants it served and, after their victory over the Spanish empire, the Dutch, English and French grew rich on the pickings from its carcass. Wars were fought to establish monopolies on the most lucrative of internationally traded goods – spices from Asia, slaves from Africa, and sugar and tobacco from the Caribbean and the Americas – and bankers financed both trade and war. As the British slowly prevailed in these wars, so London took over from Amsterdam as the world banking centre, and British governments used access to London, with its cheap international finance, as a potent weapon with which to support – or buy – allies. Governments favoured bankers who would do their bidding, and lend at the right price to favoured allies, just as American administrations would also do in the interwar and postwar years.

The cornerstone of London banking was the 'bill on London'. No different in principle from the trade bills used earlier by Italian and then by Dutch bankers, a trade bill is a postdated cheque used by a company to pay for goods. Since suppliers mostly need cash for their goods quite as urgently as customers need the credit of their suppliers, banks have traditionally done themselves – and others – a good turn by discounting these bills; that is, the financier buys the bill for cash from the supplier of the goods, but at a discounted price to give a profit, and then waits to collect the full amount of the bill from the buyer of the goods at the maturity of the bill.

Banks in England, though not in Scotland, were limited to six partners only, for English banking law until 1826 forbade joint-stock, or limited-liability, banking companies. Branch banking needed the capital strength given by incorporation and this legal prohibition, not fully repealed until the late 1830s, protected the business profits of the Bank of England. Successive governments acquiesced in these monopolistic practices; it suited them that the Bank, knowing the power of its legal master, would always agree to their financial requests. The small scale of English banks resulted in an active money market in London. This was where banks with a surplus of depositors' funds could buy the trade bills of banks that were operating in areas where the demand for credit was greater than the supply of deposits. English wealth and the London money market attracted continental merchants such as the Schroders, Rothschilds, Hambros, Kleinworts and Lazards. These quickly discovered that financing other merchants could be more profitable than trading, and was socially more acceptable.

Thus was the London 'merchant bank' born, for by 'accepting' trade bills, or effectively guaranteeing to make the payment whether or not the original buyer of the goods did so, merchant banks turned a questionable trade debt into the equivalent of a currency note. In England, though not in America, the issue of these had become a government monopoly before the middle of the century, operated by the Bank of England, so the acceptance credit was an attractive alternative source of banking credit and profit. The combination of an active domestic money market, fast-growing volumes of traded goods, and an expert and competitive group of predominantly immigrant international bankers turned London into the entrepôt of the world.

Trade and banking generate the ancillary, but equally profitable, activities that service international businessmen, such as shipping, insurance and commodity dealing. As early as 1836 a London Rothschild was boasting that the bulk of world trade, much of it never destined for Britain, was financed through London. There were dangers to financial stability in a fast-expanding, and faster-evolving, international banking network, and banking crises happened every twenty years or so in London, but they occurred with no less frequency elsewhere. London became a honeypot for traders from all over the world. The wheat of the American Midwest, the beef of Argentina and the lamb and butter of New Zealand became an ever expanding flood as the population and wealth of Britain grew. Timber from Russia and Scandinavia built the ships needed for this explosion of trade, cotton from the southern states of America fed the textile mills of Lancashire, while wool from Australia kept those of Yorkshire turning. At its base was British coal and iron ore, turned into steam engines, steel rails and, later, iron ships, and all exported to pay for food and raw materials.

As international merchants like the Morgans and Hambros turned into financial advisers and loan issuers for governments and large companies, their domestic equivalents developed into the high-street banks. Initially concentrating on the business of their local community, while Morgan was consolidating his hold on American industry, these tightened their grip on the domestic and international payments system. The railways, the steamship and the telegraph transformed communications from the 1850s onwards, opening up backward regions to industrial or commercial development. Some of the high-street banks began to specialise in the banking needs of larger companies, as well as lending them the money required for their expansion. The profitability of this commercial lending, when it was combined with efficient central control of credit decisions, enabled a few banks in each country to gain a dominant position.

These, through their 'correspondent' arrangements with similar banks in other countries, then created today's international payment network as well. This expansion of today's major commercial banks was most frequently achieved through the acquisition of less successful banks; bankers quickly realised that taking over another bank was a quicker way to profit than opening a new branch. Between 1875 and 1914, England's 120 high street banks were reduced to fewer than thirty. Then, over the next half-century, their number was reduced to four. The champion of this business cannibalism was the Midland Bank, which always preferred to buy weaker joint-stock banks rather than private partnerships. Midland believed that its shareholders were its natural customers, from whom it should solicit deposits and loan business.

Citibank was confined to New York City for most of its existence, but came to dominate the US commercial banking market in a similar fashion. Citibank's early growth, as a one-branch bank, was achieved through its ownership. Moses Taylor was one of America's outstanding businessmen, and Citibank served his widespread manufacturing and trading empire. Taylor's prudence also helped, and Citibank's conservatively managed and very liquid balance sheet always gained it more customers after banking crises destroyed its rivals. Only after the end of family management in 1920 did Citibank decide to challenge, rather than work with, the Morgans, Kuhn Loebs and similar Wall Street investment bankers. Though the commercial banker is the intermediary between money and imagination, and the function of this form of banking is to act as midwife to the creator of wealth, the pole position within the banking industry has generally been accorded to investment banking, the adviser to existing wealth and power.

Midland shareholders, like those of the other English banks, had grown used to an increase in profits financed by aggressive takeovers.

As the limit of domestic growth was reached, English banks, followed later by New York banks, looked beyond their borders. Midland's venture into merchant-banking territory, with the opening of a foreign-exchange department, was soon copied by its commercial-banking competitors, and all began to think of further expansion. The speed with which Russia was industrialising turned it into a gold mine for Western contractors such as Pearsons (now the owners of the London branch of Lazards as well as of the *Financial Times*) and manufacturers like International Harvester. So Midland's next challenge to the London banking establishment came in 1909, when it raised money for a Russian railway, through an issue of £3.4 million of 4.5 per cent bonds guaranteed by the Russian government. Further loans, and failed attempts to buy into a St Petersburg bank, led Midland into an agreement with Barings (the traditional London agent for Russia) and Hambros to syndicate Russian loans together.

Russian expansion by their domestic customers encouraged both Midland and Citibank to send out representatives to Russia, and these quickly persuaded their headquarters to upgrade them to offices, so as to recruit customers and lend money. Both retired hurt as the communist revolution turned bankers into ogres. This persuaded Midland to concentrate on domestic business and to develop internationally through correspondent banking, especially as it was able to recoup its Russian losses by working with Russian state banks during the 1920s. Citibank, though its Russian adventure faced it with a potential loss of 80 per cent of its capital, learned a different lesson. This was that for an international clearing bank, international loans could be less dangerous than they seemed: funds held on behalf of the defaulter for payments to third parties could be seized as security.

When the Morgans and the Hambros again took up the threads of international banking in London, their world had changed utterly. The 1930s legislation had split the house of Morgan into four separate banks. Morgan Grenfell in London remained as it was, commercially complacent but earning good money from its heritage, however deep its sleep. J. P. Morgan in New York chose to become a commercial bank, later merging with the much better-capitalised Guaranty Trust. The investment-banking business went its separate way as New York's Morgan Stanley and Philadelphia's Drexel & Company. The latter subsequently merged unsuccessfully with Harriman Ripley of New York, and then with Burnham in 1973 to become the 1980s envy of Wall Street as Drexel Burnham Lambert.

The Hambro family still controlled their bank, though it was now a quoted company and outsiders (such as the author) were joining the board. More importantly, Citibank, followed by other American commercial banks, had decided that international investment banking was where banking profit and interest were to be found, and London was the centre from which to do it. Yet the justification for bankers to look overseas for business, during the last years of laissez-faire economics, had died with the social revolution of this century. It was poor distribution of wealth that stultified the growth in demand for goods; classical liberalism was unable to cope with the trading and political strains that developed when Britain was joined by other industrialised countries, all looking to boost domestic demand through exports.

As power first began to leak away from Britain, in the 1890s, Pierpoint Morgan and Everard Hambro were close friends, each taking more than £100,000 a year (or $500,000 at the then prevailing rate of exchange) out of their businesses. A junior partner at Hambros earned some £8,000 a year – multiply by 40 for today's value – while a senior manager, the equivalent of a director today, earned £800. Edward Holden, the most powerful British banker of his day, earned only £6,000 a year as managing director of Midland, though he also received a special bonus of £15,000 a year and exceptional pension benefits; Midland's branch managers averaged £350 a year. For comparison, senior partners of Freshfields, the lawyers who have acted for the Bank of England almost since its foundation, earned about £5,000 a year at most, considerably less than the bankers, while their clerks, unlike those of the banks, could not expect a pension, and were unable to save out of their annual salaries of £60–70 or so.

Like most of the aspiring Victorian middle classes, legal clerks worked until they dropped, while the working classes hardly lived at all. The two radio operators on the *Titanic*, maintaining a twenty-four-hour daily watch with the latest in high-tech navigation devices, earned some £40 a year, in addition to which they lived free while on board; each individual telegram they radioed out for the *Titanic*'s passengers cost almost half their monthly wage. But though unappealing as customers to banks, these clerks and radio operators also needed banking services. From the start of the Industrial Revolution, local worthies took steps to ensure that the deserving poor had the means to save, provided only that they had the wherewithal. Parallel with the expansion of the commercial banks was that of the mutually owned saving banks. These offered simple banking services and, later in the nineteenth century, self-build cooperatives would develop into mortgage banks or building societies. Continental European governments developed post-office-based giro systems to enable their citizens to make small payments among themselves, and all countries saw a proliferation of specialised savings banks to support small-holders and artisans.

Anglo-American governments have always encouraged home own-ership as a means of quelling social unrest, by granting tax con-cessions or other benefits to mortgage lenders. Savings banks needed such support, because thirty-year mortgage loans funded out of savings accounts and the current-account balances of the working population would never receive the approval of banking academics. But the system worked. It was susceptible to inflation, since that would discourage bank saving and encourage speculation in prop-erty, and was more vulnerable in America than in Britain. Americans expected their housing costs to be fixed, so mortgage loans were at a fixed rate; in Britain, they could be varied as the cost of money changed. Without realising what was happening to them, inflation began to destroy the principles on which savings bankers had oper-ated since the nineteenth century.

This was the rule of three for American savings bankers: borrow at 3 per cent, lend with a margin of 3 per cent (i.e. 6 per cent for a mortgage) and be on the golf course by 3 p.m. But savers were not satisfied with 3 per cent on their deposits when prices were rising at 5 per cent and banks were charging nearly 30 per cent on their credit-card loans. The mutual-fund companies took advantage of this gap, and created money-market funds that offered small savers the level of interest rates that banks paid to each other, rather than the rates they offered to their customers on their savings accounts. Inundated by complaints from these important local constituents, legislators accepted that nothing could be done about the loss of Regulation Q, or the specific banking privilege that enabled the savings banks to offer slightly higher deposit rates than their com-mercial-banking competitors.

All banks were suffering from the money-market funds, for the 1933 law had not envisaged the computer, nor imagined that it would be possible to offer banking services by post, over the tele-phone, or from newspaper and TV advertisements. Instead, local US politicians gave the savings bankers wider banking powers. This was equivalent to rearranging the deck chairs on the *Titanic*, for nothing can alter the basics of banking; if banks lend at less than the cost at which they borrow, sooner or later they go bust. This was what was happening to the savings banks. Legislators, regulators and bankers tried to hide this unpleasant reality by some Mickey Mouse accountancy procedures that turned actual losses into apparent assets. When this failed, the politicians widened the savings banks' authority, to tempt more entrepreneurial managers into the industry. No one quite got what they wanted, though the new managers were certainly imaginative when it came to using other people's money.

In 1946 the actor James Stewart had celebrated the mortgage bankers who were rehousing America's victorious GIs in Frank Capra's film *It's a Wonderful Life*. Few went to see it, despite the popularity of star and director, for mortgage bankers are the epitome of the sound, boring, pinstripe-suited banker; the public, just like the industry, prefers its bankers to be ogrelike Pierpoint Morgans. This story of a banker driven to suicide when he discovers that a friend and employee has been embezzling the savings of his neighbours and customers, became a smash video hit during the 1980s though within a somewhat restricted circle; James Stewart became regular party entertainment, together with booze, girls and property deals, among the crooks, chancers and incompetents who then took over many of America's savings banks, or savings-and-loan companies. By the time their embezzlement is cleared up, and depending on how long it will take to sell such property as survived the various scams of the managers, compound interest will have doubled the $200 billion of American savings that went missing.

Savings banking is not expected to be risky, though investment banking is, and it was once accepted that this was a much more dangerous activity than commercial banking. The ratio of 265:1 between the earnings of Everard Hambro and a Midland branch manager, or even that of nearly 5:1 between Hambro and Holden, reflected this. There were many years when partners had to put money into their business, rather than take it out, for investment bankers have no automatic prescription to profit, as is given by the payment function of commercial banking. Moreover, investment-banking partners had their personal fortunes on the line, and all knew that this was no legal fiction, for regular banking crises thinned out colleagues at an alarming rate. Only the clever and prudent survived. This risk was not only that of ownership structure, but of the business itself. The surest banking profits come from the administration of money, or from fees earned from advising the owners on how to invest it. The former business is controlled by the commercial banks, who also have a major part of the latter through their branch network. The riskiest banking business is dealing in money – once the preserve of the investment banks – or lending it.

All banks did the latter but, again, the commercial banks concentrated on the local or national business, a surer source of income, though less glamorous, than the household-name multinational corporate or governmental borrower. But bankers have always been judged, not by the profitability of their business, but by the number of scalps that they have taken, and the ethos of investment banking is collecting the freshest, bloodiest scalps of all. George Moore, as the clever and ambitious Yale graduate assistant to the chairman during the 1930s, helped rescue Citibank from bankruptcy and the odium heaped on it by a congressional inquiry. But it was also Moore, president and later chairman, who ensured that Citibank would escape US banking restrictions by transferring many of its activities to the more complaisant arms of London's 'Old Lady of Threadneedle Street'.

Following Citibank's example, commercial banks increasingly searched for investment-banking deals. This was done partly to achieve institutional growth, but also for banker's personal gain. Bankers believe in the commandment: 'Do unto others as you would be done by, but do it first.' Salaries and share-option schemes leapfrogged almost as fast as the business, for commercial banks inevitably followed the Citibank pattern. These changed from a federation of small local businesses in the 1960s – the bank in miniature, as Citibank branches were described in the 1920s – to computer-controlled, worldwide distributors of money in the 1980s, while the incorporated investment bankers attempted to outdo them as money and securities dealers on a global scale.

Salomon Brothers ceased to be a private partnership in 1981; Warren Buffett became chairman of Salomon in 1991, after the senior management were disgraced by their attempts to corner the market in US government bonds. Buffett issued a statement to shareholders promising to reform a salary structure based on cronyism, and in which one employee had been encouraged to negotiate a deal that netted him $23 million a year, a wider differential than that enjoyed by Pierpoint Morgan but with no business risk. Others earn similar sums and, though much of this is bonus, the only risk to employees is that they earn no more than their basic salaries, or lose their jobs. But these minimums are many hundreds of thousands, if not a guaranteed few million of dollars; neither Salomon employees nor modern bankers bear the risk of personal bankruptcy which their predecessors assumed was the inevitable corollary of such income ratios as these.

Moore, tough and talented salesman though he was, always kept his 1930s experiences at the front of his mind. They were reflected in his business decisions, the strategy of the bank that he influenced or led for two decades, and his insistence that senior Citibankers not only knew of the bank's past mistakes, but why the decisions looked right at the time they were taken. Moore had no family money, though he was always paid well enough to be able to save from his salary and, like Holden a generation earlier, when he retired from Citibank it was with only his pension and his savings of some $500,000.

Moore made his real money after he left Citibank, but his successors would be different, wanting both to level the differentials between investment and commercial bankers, and to make capital from their banking employment. These new arrangements allowed bankers to plan the bank's growth on the comforting assumption that 'heads I win, and tails the taxpayers lose'. Memories of past disasters faded with present glories and, by Moore's retirement in 1970, the revolution in banking practices which he had set in train made Citibank, and banks generally, appear invulnerable. His successors would not display a similar prudence in their hunt for fame and fortune.

4

Dropping the Pilot

'The calling is hereditary: the credit of the bank descends from father to son; this inherited wealth soon brings inherited refinement. Banking is a watchful but not laborious trade. A banker . . . can feel pretty sure that all his transactions are sound, and yet have much spare time.'

The English economist Walter Bagehot, describing bankers in *Lombard Street*

ONLY THOSE WHO BELIEVE in the tooth fairy will ever understand banking, for bankers are the most credulous and optimistic of people. Who else but bankers would venture their reputations and their money, as well as that of others, on projects which are but dreams, often requiring financial support over many years, and sometimes having no certainty of immediate, let alone continuing, success. The only protection that bankers have against such optimism is a lively sense of their own financial risk, and their memories. Banking memories become the precedents by which banks are managed, for these are the records of similar business ventures, the characteristics of certain types of promoters, and the profitable, or costly, result of earlier banking decisions. Unfortunately, the exaggeration of the business cycle, which happens once or twice in every generation, allows bankers to bask in public esteem as share and property prices float into the empyrean, and forget their own business experience as they smile serenely at their customers, asking them: 'Do you really have enough, or would another million or so help?'

Economists still do not understand the workings of the business cycle but it is certainly true that banking generosity helps develop a bubble mentality and bankers, just as much as ordinary folk, succumb to the charms of booming profits and rising property values. Elderly gentlemen bore on that no good will come of such glad-handedness, for they have seen it all before, while prosaic statisticians mutter that nothing goes up for ever, and super-bull markets always end sadly. But no one listens. Caution is fine in theory but hard in practice, since there is nothing quite so entrancing as the prospect of instant wealth without much effort. So each time the business cycle accelerates into boom, everyone persuades themselves that economic laws have been suspended. Stockbrokers' 'buy' circulars transmute sows' ears into silk purses, and bankers forget all the lessons, so painfully learned, about the evanescent nature of loan collateral.

Disbelief and cynicism, even among those who can remember similar episodes, are banished by the healing touch of banking generosity, a surprisingly efficient analgesic to the financial pain of management mistakes. But then, with a sudden clap of thunder, the tooth fairy turns into a wicked witch, those bubble fortunes dissipate and all that is left are bankers, who smile no longer as they ask for their money back. For the sanity of bankers returns with economic reality, and they again appreciate that easy come, easy go applies as much to themselves as to their customers. Robert Maxwell is merely the latest and best-known example of how bankers and entrepreneurs fall out of love. This is how it has always been since modern banking emerged from its medieval chrysalis nearly five hundred years ago. There have been three exaggerations of the business cycle this century, first during the 1920s, then the 1970s and finally the 1980s. During those booms wealth, at least as measured by the indices of share and property prices, doubled every three to four years. Those with sensitive hearing, and not too greedy a disposition, benefited from them, but for others the clap of thunder announced their coming bankruptcy in 1929, 1973 and again in 1987.

Robert Maxwell was able to loot more than £700 million from the pension funds of his British companies, in his desperate attempts to shore up an overborrowed empire, so destroying the retirement expectations of some 32,000 people. Such funds did not exist fifty years ago and, twenty years ago, were too new to attract even Maxwell. These looted millions went to banks, as collateral for their loans to Maxwell's private companies, or as cash with which to buy the shares of his two quoted companies, and so buoy up their price. Although many of Maxwell's victims have spent their lifetimes working for companies that only briefly came into the Maxwell web, neither this, nor the busy but expensive burrowing of accountants and lawyers, will save them.

The professionals now belatedly worrying over the financial

interests of the ostensible owners of these missing funds have recovered about half, but their chances of acquiring the remaining millions are slim; the banks have them and prising them away will be no easy task. This should surprise only the naive, for setting up and managing pension funds has been the most stable of all the banking bonanzas of the last four decades and was, indeed, the cause of my becoming a banker. But pension-fund management is not a business that has ever much concerned itself with the ordinary pensioner. The legal owner of pension funds, for all that these represent deferred wages, is the company.

Bankers make their money out of the rich and powerful. The world for most of its history has been poor, with such capital as existed very unequally distributed. Though the laissez-faire political economy of the nineteenth century made the world rich, its replacement this century with popular democracy has brought both greater prosperity to industry, and a better spread of savings among individuals. European wealth was rebuilt under American tutelage and in fear of communism; as reconstruction and international trade put money into the pockets of workers, these then recycled it into those of house builders, mortgage banks and the manufacturers of cars, washing machines, TV sets and similar goods. America adopted the British policy of free trade, and the consequential explosion of trade among America's allies encouraged businessmen to invest even more.

Wealth not only increased but spread, from the shores of the Atlantic to those of the Pacific. This revolution in business, and its governance, transformed the way that bankers got their money. 'Engine Charlie' Wilson was the postwar president of General Motors, and is credited with the claim that 'what's good for General Motors is good for America'. In fact, this was a calumny by his political enemies, after he took a cabinet post under President Eisenhower, for his actual remark was that 'what's good for America is good for General Motors' and reflected his 1951 decision to form a pension fund for GM workers. Engine Charlie's action forced businessmen and politicians throughout the world to emulate him, and stock markets, while remaining gambling clubs for the would-be rich, became, in addition, professionally managed markets for the capital created by these new forced savings.

Seven years after GM had begun to democratise capital, I graduated from the University of Oxford to become, in 1958, Mobil Oil Company's first ever economist. This says little enough about their needs or my skills, but it did improve my report writing, for the academic style of the two-handed economist – 'on the one hand this,

but on the other that' – was not appreciated by busy bosses who
wanted simple answers to complicated questions, such as the effects
on their business of Britain's failure to strangle the newly emerging
European Economic Community at birth. Though the oil industry
offered intellectual stimulus, contrary to my hopes on graduating,
no fortune appeared to go with it. It took another Wilson, Harold
of the Labour Party, to make me jump from industry to the City
with his remark to the House of Commons that 'Britain is no longer
a welfare state, but a windfall state'.

I was aware of these windfalls since a banker friend had told me,
a couple of years earlier, of how he had been called unexpectedly
into the office of his general manager. To his surprise, he was
informed that he had been allocated shares in the flotation of one
of the new commercial television companies, that these had already
been sold for him, and that he could expect the profits to be added
to his bonus for that year. These tax-free capital gains were more
than twice his annual salary, and he protested that he disapproved
of the government's decision to allow commercial television to compete with the BBC, and would not accept this money. He was told,
with no little abruptness: 'This is a bank, not the Salvation Army,
and you're working here and, if you're told you've made these
profits, you've made them and you'll take the money whether you
like it or not.' Banking paid much the same as industry, but bonuses
like that put the comparison of taxed salaries into a different light.

Most of us would have been hard put to explain what 'the City'
actually did, but we all scented freedom and the ability to turn
our brains and imagination into something immediately useful; the
banking mentality generally prefers money now to bureaucratic
power later. It was unusual in the 1950s for a London bank to
advertise for staff, but then Robert Benson, Lonsdale, which, after
some reluctance, had agreed to pay me some 20 per cent more than
the £800 a year I was earning at Mobil, was unusual. RBL was not
a partnership, the traditional ownership and management structure
for London and Wall Street banks, but a company quoted on the
stock exchange; nor was it a front-rank 'acceptance house' but a
member of the lesser 'issuing houses' club. RBL had started life
financing North American railroads and cattle ranches by selling
bonds to British savers, like many of the acceptance houses, but it
had long since switched to domestic business.

The New York banks had shown that domestic companies created
a customer base that was more profitable, and less chancy, than
working for foreign governments and their offshoots, but raising

money for domestic companies was regarded by many blue-blooded London acceptance houses as beneath contempt, and this snobbery ensured that most were slowly dying. These had always made their real money from financing foreign trade, for slow communications meant that nineteenth-century firms needed at least £4 of working capital for every £1 of fixed capital. But 'trade' was socially unacceptable, however profitable it might be. To maintain their social standing, the London merchants promoted their business as lending to foreign governments or, slumming it a bit, financing those countries' infrastructure – such as the bridges and railroads, docks and harbour works. Of course, these were all essential to the foreign trade that actually made the money.

Draconian controls on borrowing and lending overseas meant that the traditional business of the London merchant banks was virtually dead, but RBL and its shareholders had benefited from the return of a Conservative government in 1951, since this had immediately dismantled government controls on business, sold back the steel industry to private investors, denationalised the road-transport industry, allowed private money into television and encouraged existing companies to raise money for expansion through rights issues. Inspired by their Scots chairman, for Edinburgh had a better reputation as an investment management centre than London, RBL had become one of the most innovative and successful of these New York-style investment banks. I was to become half of a two-man 'research department', RBL being one of the first investment banks to develop an investment-management department; advising the new pension funds was to be a key business of the future, and RBL was setting out its stall.

The London banking tradition slowly acknowledged the inherent conflicts of interest within finance, and by the latter part of the nineteenth century the industry was organised to protect the interests not only of bankers but also of users, provided, that is, that these were wise enough to heed the overriding market imperative of 'buyer beware' and go to the appropriate type of bank for their needs. To reconcile the different needs of issuers and buyers, investors and marketmakers, banks had different management skills, ownership structures and attitudes. The investment banks, or issuing houses, looked after the interests of the company, in their design and pricing of the negotiable securities that they would issue on its behalf, and that would then be quoted on the stock market. Stock jobbers 'traded' or 'made a market' as principals in these issues, ensuring 'liquidity', or the ability of investors to buy and sell at will, at their own risk.

Stockbrokers, often called private banks in Germany and other parts of continental Europe, acted as agents in the management of wealth, and so protected the interests of the investor. Commercial banks gradually lost their right to deal directly on the stock exchange; instead, they shared commission with the stockbrokers. A similar, though less defined, pattern existed in New York, where the trust banks, which had originally started as estate managers in the early part of the nineteenth century, specialised as money managers, together with the stockbrokers. However, American investment banks, unlike their London counterparts, were permitted to be stock-exchange members, and so acted both as principals for the company and as agents for the rich. These investment banks specialised among themselves; the best, like the Morgan bank, only acted for companies, while others acted as the sponsors of their issues, 'distributing' bonds or shares among investors on behalf of the issuing bank. Some New York investment banks specialised as securities dealers, or marketmakers, a function which was further eased by the use of 'specialists' on the New York Stock Exchange. These were similar to London's stock jobbers except that, in return for certain monopolistic privileges, they guaranteed to buy and sell the shares of the companies in which they specialised.

Investment bankers mostly prefer the higher profits, lower staff costs, and greater prestige that come from advising governments or companies on how to raise money, or the excitements of dealing in the markets. Investment banking needs placing power, or people to pay cash money for the promised income and hope of capital gains represented by the bond and share certificates that bankers create and sell. All banks have some committed customers whose money they manage, and the fees for such advice covers overheads when the issuing business is quiet, but they need many more than these in-house clients if they are to succeed as an issuing house. If the reputation of a bank with its buyers depends on the quality of the governments and companies it advises, then its reputation with its issuers depends on the amount and price of the money it raises for them, and the ease with which it does it. Customers must receive the cash they expect for the bonds or shares they issue, so this is guaranteed by the issuing bank for an 'underwriting' fee of 2.25 per cent which, though small as a percentage, is large as an absolute. Underwriting is insurance for the issuing house, which passes the bulk of this risk to its friends for a sub-underwriting fee of 1.75 per cent.

Underwriting is important to the banking club because the risks, though great, are infrequent, whereas the rewards are both good and regular. Not all underwriting fees are passed on to the fund for which the bank accepts the underwriting, and the salaries of some of us at RBL were occasionally fattened with an underwriting cheque, but the rule of the game is that rough is taken with smooth, and that greed needs to be restrained. Not all issues go well, and then the underwriters must stand behind their guarantee and pay for the shares at the underwritten price, regardless of the price in the market. Buying shares needs money, and banks expected to lend staff the money to do this. This was not altruism, but practicality, for bankers must eat their own cooking. The best way to learn banking lessons is to lose money, for those memories hurt and linger.

Commercial banking structures were designed to give young managers the chance to make small loans, while investment managers can understand the emotional vagaries of investment markets only by putting their judgement to the test. It is better for banks that their staff learn by losing small sums, which both bank and employee can afford, than assume that the world works on pure logic. This is not something that the average personnel manager can understand, and the consequences are seen in today's lending and investment errors. No one can ever be persuaded that certain actions will not work, for any one with talent will always be convinced that it can be done right. The old style of bank training accepted that arrogance; the new style does not even admit that there is a problem. The result is modern bankers who experiment with risk-taking only when they are entrusted with sums of money that their banks cannot afford to lose, and within an institutional environment in which no one is held accountable.

The secret of a successful issuing house is distribution, either directly to substantial investors such as insurance companies or indirectly, through other banks, to their controlled customers. These underwriting fees are, and always have been, more than an extra source of banking profit. Though the foundation of banking relationships is reputation, the mortar that holds them together is underwriting income and, occasionally, the exceptional profits that come from the direct sale – today called private placement – of scarce and attractive shares. Pension funds promised to become as important an investment sector as the insurance companies and Phil MacPherson, RBL's chairman, recognised that these could transform the placing power of a bank. Managing large sums of other people's money gives banks strength within the underwriting club, for these add to 'underwriting firepower'.

The New York message for London bankers had been reinforced by Siegmund Warburg, who was to say later to Anthony Sampson in *Anatomy of Britain*: 'In the sense that bankers provide money for industry, they're becoming less important but in the sense of being consultants – what I call financial engineers – they're becoming much more important.'

The Great Aluminium War was to transform banking practice, first in London and then on Wall Street. Aluminium was one of the industries of the future, but British Aluminium was an undercapitalised and outdated producer of this metal. It was heavy with British establishment figures: its chairman was Lord Portal, who had been the wartime Chief of the Air Staff, and Geoffrey Cunliffe, the son of a First World War governor of the Bank of England, was managing director. The company was advised by Hambros Bank and in 1957 Cunliffe, arrogant and tactless, had shocked Olaf Hambro, its seventy-three-year-old chairman, by telling him that he was taking his business to Lazards, where one of the partners was a personal friend.

Cunliffe had also snubbed Siegmund Warburg, who had settled in London at the end of the war, and he was rather less forgiving than Olaf Hambro. His London banking company (now S. G. Warburg) had only been formed in 1946, but this was no banking tyro. The Warburgs have been bankers in Germany for even longer than the Rothschilds, though rather more discreetly, and have been an influential business and banking dynasty in America since the 1850s. The bank had done well in its first decade in the City and, in 1957, Warburg joined the top table of the 'banking club' when his takeover of Seligman Brothers gave him a seat on the Acceptance Houses Committee. So it was unfortunate for Cunliffe that a poorly judged investment in Quebec had left British Aluminium in a hopeless financial mess, with the shares halving in value to well under £3 when the board of directors cut the dividend.

This gave Warburg his opportunity. Early in 1958, he was approached by American Metal Climax, also an aluminium smelter and formerly the US subsidiary of the German Metallgesellschaft group. These knew Warburg through his American and German banking cousins, and believed that Warburg might be prepared to consider something revolutionary – a friendly cross-border takeover which would give the American company control of British Aluminium. Warburg approached the BA board, only to be rebuffed, for the company was not for sale to foreigners and certainly not through the agency of a *soi-disant* English banker. American Metal Climax were gentlemen in the English style, disliking public embarrassment, and withdrew. Warburg was not, and did not, for he had done his homework: London, after half a century of financing America and another half-century living off its accumulated fat, now had no future unless it could spend the next half-century selling its ailing companies to better-managed and richer American firms. This analysis particularly appealed to Warburg because it required brains rather than capital, and therefore suited his new bank.

But to achieve his objectives, and become a real power in the City, Warburg would have to ruffle some feathers. If he could not acquire BA through cosy chats over lunch with its directors and bankers, he would either have to withdraw and accept defeat, or fight. This would be revolutionary, for it meant acting, not merely as a behind-the-scenes adviser to a company, but as a committed proponent in the acquisition of a company against the wishes of its board of directors, and would involve buying shares in the stock markets on behalf of the hostile bidders. Warburg determined that BA should be his first such venture and, by the spring of that year, he had interested another US company in BA's potential. Over the summer Warburg quietly built up a 10 per cent shareholding in BA, on behalf of the US Reynolds Metal company, and then persuaded the Birmingham-based Tube Investments to become the British end of a buying partnership. This brought Schroders and Helbert Wagg, TI's City bankers, as allies into the Warburg camp.

These manoeuvres, and particularly the buying of BA shares through the stock market, had not gone unnoticed by Portal and Cunliffe. Bad managers though they might be, British Aluminium's board could not bear the thought that the company's future – or, rather more importantly, their own – might be decided over their heads. BA had powerful allies, for Olaf had persuaded Cunliffe to continue using Hambros in partnership with Lazards. As a first line of defence, in May the two banks recommended that the BA board obtain shareholders' approval to an increase in the company's authorised share capital from £9 million to £13.5 million. These new £1 shares were not to be issued but kept in reserve for the pending battle. With this ammunition in hand, Portal asked his bankers to consider another American company as what would later come to be called a 'white knight'; this was the Aluminum Company of America, or Alcoa.

Warburg's second approach to BA was in the autumn, when Sir Ivan Stedeford, the chairman of Tube Investments, suggested to

Cunliffe that some form of partnership would be beneficial to all three companies. This proposal was even worse in BA's eyes, since the Americans had not gone but were now joined by a self-made Birmingham businessman, and both were still dancing to Warburg's tune. Once again, Cunliffe refused to talk. So in November Stedeford, on behalf of the two companies, formally bid £3.90 a share for the 9 million shares of BA in issue, subject only to the 4.5 million shares remaining unissued. The bid was private and followed club rules: it was a board-to-board approach, and without reference to the shareholders, the legal owners of the company. Cunliffe was able to refuse outright. Using the unissued share capital, Portal and Cunliffe had bounced Alcoa into buying a third of the company, so the TI-RM offer was unacceptable.

The Alcoa agreement, under which they had bought 4.5 million shares for £3 each, had already been signed, and was only subject to Treasury consent for the overseas sale of a British asset. Cunliffe was delighted to snub Stedeford and Warburg with this coup, which he had arranged without informing his shareholders of the higher TI-RM alternative. Stedeford was outraged by this treatment. Happily for Warburg, this behaviour reinforced the prejudices of the practical Midlands businessman against the fat cats of the London establishment, and he was delighted to call a press conference with Warburg and bring the Aluminium War out into the open. Then, in the first week of December, the Treasury, whose agreement to either deal was necessary, told the BA board that it was up to the company's shareholders to decide between the Alcoa and TI-RM offers.

An approach to shareholders would have been suicidal for Cunliffe, since any half-competent investor was bound to accept an immediate £3.90 for shares, rather than see Alcoa buy a third of BA for £3 a share, and so dilute the value of existing shares. This was too high a cost to pay for the value of Alcoa's management expertise, whatever that might be, so BA had to switch its defence from business logic to emotion. If Britain could not hold on to her empire, at least her bankers could protect BA from this Yankee threat, and an appeal to the flag might obscure the hypocritical self-interest. Olaf Hambro's eminent reputation, combined with his business and family connections, lined up the whole of the City establishment on BA's behalf except the three banks committed to the TI-RM bid.

Olaf was flanked by his cousin Sir Charles Hambro, who, in his early thirties, had become the first ever executive director of the Bank of England with responsibility for protecting sterling during the confusion of the 1930s, once Britain's currency had ceased to be convertible into gold. Refusing the governorship of the Bank of England in preference to the family bank, he later commanded the Special Operations Executive, promoters of armed resistance and spying throughout the occupied world. But Sir Charles was not only tough, he also had great charm and diplomatic ability, proved by his close working relationship as Britain's nominee on the Combined Development Trust with General Groves, the strongly anglophobic US Army head of the atomic-bomb project and chairman of this Anglo-American body designed to establish a uranium monopoly. Jack, Olaf's other cousin, was much more of a buccaneer. The war had enabled him to relive the family merchanting origins, as managing director of the United Kingdom Commercial Company. This secretly government-owned trading company had the sole objective of denying the enemy the raw materials that their economy needed, whether by cornering resources, subverting suppliers or even capturing cargoes already purchased and dispatched. Once the war was ended, Jack was delighted to return not only the company's capital to the Treasury, but a handsome profit as well.

Despite this impressive leadership, the peasants were definitely restless. The growing band of institutional investment managers shared Stedeford's distaste for BA's secret dealings, done on behalf of owners by directors but without their knowledge. As these mutterings were heard, they were made known to a wider audience by the financial press. For the first time ever, bankers were forced to take newspaper advertisements to explain and justify their actions, and from the last weekend of November the actions of Hambros, Lazards and Warburgs became front-page news. To counter this opposition, fourteen of London's best-known banks pledged a war chest of £7 million. Rowe & Pitman, the Queen's stockbroker and with partners intermarried with the Hambros, were strong-armed into deserting Tube Investments, for whom they were the official company brokers, to join forces with Cazenove, the City's other major blue-blooded stockbroker. Together, these would fight Warburg in the stock market, for the City consortium replied to the TI-RM bid with a higher bid of £4.20, though for only some of the BA shares.

No one doubted that the merchant princes of the City would see off this interloper and keep the 'Great' in 'Britain'. By New Year's Eve, BA's allies had either bought, or had pledged to them, some 2 million shares. They felt confident that the victory was theirs since, even though their funds were now running dry, the government had come out openly for them. Cameron Cobbold, the governor of the Bank of England, joined with the chancellor of the exchequer in asking Warburg to stop buying in the market, saying that this was also the wish of the prime minister. Warburg refused, for he knew that with the deep pockets of TI and RM behind him, he could win any bidding war and that this was now the decisive moment. As the New Year dawned, the TI-RM offer was increased to £4.25 a share, and Warburg sent his stockbrokers into the market to sweep up any potential sellers, buying hundreds of thousands of shares a day. By 9 January 1959, the TI-RM group controlled BA, owning more than 51 per cent of its shares.

London's banking elite were stunned not only by their defeat, but by the lionisation of Warburg and TI by press and investors alike, while they were characterised as stuffy and out-of-touch dinosaurs. Olaf Hambro wrote a bitter letter to *The Times*, blaming the financial press for allowing Warburgs to frustrate the wishes of the City. But once the club rules were breached, most members adapted; all the major London banking dynasties can remember, when forced to do so, that those who are not born into the banking club can enter it by kicking down the door. Rothschilds, Morgans and Hambros had all in their time done to others what Warburgs had just done to them. Warburg was proved right when, over the next decade, seventy of the one hundred largest British companies would buy or sell themselves, sometimes in a friendly way but more often than not in an orgy of merging, diversifying or expanding.

These changes propelled Warburgs into the premier position among the merchant banks and forced new blood to the top of the old-established banking dynasties. A year after the battle, Olaf Hambro went to Siegmund Warburg in his office and, embracing him, cried: 'Siegmund, haven't we been awful fools?' The irony of these events lay less in Cunliffe's earlier behaviour to his staunchest defender than in Warburg's closeness to Olaf. Olaf's son Jocelyn remarked to me years later:

> It was amazing, quite amazing, because Siegmund had been a protégé of my father and Tony Rothschild, and the first half of his bank's name, the New Trading Company, came from Rothschild's New Court building. They thought that all they had to do was to say 'boo' to this chap, and he would go away, for my father had never dreamed of buying shares in a company without its agreement . . . He was appalled at the way the banking club disintegrated around them. It showed the power of cash, of course, and the growing strength of institutional fund managers.

Morgan Grenfell had put £500,000 on the table for British

Aluminium, and refused to deal with Warburgs for another fifteen years. This was despite Warburg's rise to pre-eminence in British corporate finance, their growing success in the international Euro-markets, and Morgan Grenfell's own imitation of the Warburg style. London bankers were anti-Semitic in the normal fashion of British society at that time, but not too much so, for virtually every blue-blooded London banking dynasty was originally Jewish, and more often than not German Jewish. Morgan Grenfell reflected New York banking where, for more than a century and until at least the 1970s, there was a sharp division. Wall Street was split between the business, culture and habits of 'dusty money', or the WASP banks (of which J. P. Morgan was the leader) with client industries such as steel, mining, railroads and engineering, and 'our crowd', or the German-Jewish banks led by Kuhn Loeb.

The latter group, ironically, drew the ire of the former for supporting the Germans in the First World War although it was the former, secure in their strength after the Allied victory, who then arranged the inter-war German reparation loans. But 'our crowd', with their concentration on textiles and retailing, would be best placed to exploit the consumer society that blossomed after the Second World War, while their tradition of securities trading would benefit them in the new world of institutionalised savings. Banking mergers in the 1960s paralleled those of industrial companies and, over the next two decades, what had been personally directed banking businesses of 200–300 people, turned into complex corporate bureaucracies employing several thousands.

The greater resilience of American capitalism saved Wall Street for a little longer than London but, in 1970, Morgan Stanley itself partially incorporated. This was to conserve the capital of the firm, for even this most blue-blooded and well-endowed investment bank was forced by the competition of relative parvenus such as Salomon Brothers and Goldman Sachs to protect its issuing business. This meant more dealing in securities, once anathema to the Morgans because it was a both riskier and heavier user of banking capital. But incorporation was also to protect the partners from the perils of unlimited liability, for Wall Street had become a tougher place in which to make money. All remnants of unlimited liability were swept away in 1975, as were regulated stock-market commissions. This was necessary insurance for the partnership for, a year earlier, Morgan Stanley had junked its long-standing policy against hostile takeovers. It set out to do to Wall Street what Warburg had done to London fifteen years earlier. Thereafter, Wall Street emulated London, but at twice the pace and with ten times the aggression.

The London opposition to Warburg was neither that he was Jewish, nor that he represented American money, nor even that his deal was bad for shareholders since both Hambros and Lazards acknowledged, to themselves at least, that the TI-RM offer was better than theirs. It was much more that he was a newcomer, and his behaviour threatened what Ron Chernow, in his magisterial history of the 'House of Morgan', calls the London Gentleman Bankers' Code. Proper banking behaviour required that:

> '... banks did not try to scout out new business or seek new clients but waited for clients to arrive with proper introductions ... they refused to take on new companies unless the move was first cleared with their former banker ... This meant no advertising, no price cutting and no raiding of other firms' clients.'

As Chernow says of this code

> 'The object was not to compete, at least not too openly. Such an arrangement worked to the advantage of established banks and kept clients in an abject, dependent position. But it was a stylised competition – a world of sheathed rapiers – not a cartel, as it often seemed. The elegance of the surface often blinded critics to the vicious underlying relations amongst the banks.'

Quite how vicious these could be would become apparent during the 1980s. By then the incorporation of the investment banks had reduced the personal risk of bankers, so the dropping of the code meant also the end of gentlemanly self-restraint. As bankers vied for success, fame and money, based on an ability to win at all costs, so competition ushered in a self-feeding frenzy that would embarrass even sharks.

Competition does not necessarily lead to stability within an industry and, in certain instances, can create inherent instability. This seems especially true of banking, where personal relationships are paramount, and banking judgement can only be assessed long after the event. The banking club effectively acted as a damper on greed, though helped by social attitudes; the initial energies of the 1840 wave of German and American bankers, such as Hambro and Morgan, were seduced by English life, and a later generation of German invaders, such as the Speyers and the Kleinworts, then came to show London what banking work really entailed; finally Midland

and Lloyds came from the provinces in the 1900s to stir up these sleepy aristocrats of commerce. Since banking reform the risks of revolution have been less, and the rewards greater. As Warburg himself wrote towards the end of his life,

'I remember some people in very good houses who talked very nastily behind my back: "Do you know this fellow Warburg? He starts in the office at eight o'clock in the morning!" That was considered contemptible. Most of them came to the office at ten o'clock. I was awful.'

S. C. Warburg in its early days was truly Prussian, with staff appointed only after an assessment of their handwriting, expected to be in early, work late, detail every conversation and telephone call, suppress their personalities for the sake of the firm and even, when necessary, to have two lunches. This was certainly not the style of the assimilated London banks, to which all in the end succumbed. Though the Rothschilds have never converted, they became as anglicised as all their competitors, with an ethos based on Eton, Oxbridge and the Guards. Warburgs themselves have now been transformed, and their Prussian discipline has been ameliorated by English guile, and establishment approval bought with the acquisition of Rowe & Pitman.

The later practice of the Gentleman Banker's Club in London, taken to New York by the Morgans, attempted to split the functional interests of issuing, distributing, dealing and advising between narrow specialists, all called investment banks or stockbrokers, but each of which was recognised for its particular skill. Banking profits and standards were maintained by club rules, for those who transgressed were blackballed, or otherwise summarily expelled. In many ways unfair to individuals, who might have been imaginative rather than crooked, it was a cheap and effective method of enforcing investor protection. It did not work for fools, of course, but nor does its much more expensive replacement of government regulation, and the famous 'chinese walls' which are supposed to stop colleagues from talking to each other. 'Buyer beware', as this system was known in law, prevailed in both centres until, in the 1930s, banking reforms imposed the regulatory structure of the SEC on New York banking.

The 1986 'Big Bang' in London was a replay of Wall Street's 1975 'Mayday' and brought the practice of both centres into line, and the UK 1988 Financial Services Act is a would-be self-regulatory copy of America's Securities and Exchange Commission. Legislation to resolve the many different conflicts of interest within the financial markets was first passed by the Dutch in 1611; that was unsuccessful, as was similar English legislation a century later.

Nothing yet suggests that either America's SEC or Britain's FSA will be any more effective in reconciling the inherent conflicts of interest within the financial market than was the original Dutch law of 1611. That attempted to outlaw the 'short selling' of Dutch East India stock, but such speculation is the oxygen of securities markets. The sale of shares not owned, in the hope of buying them cheaper when the price has fallen, or the alternative purchase of shares by those who don't have the money to pay for them, is what creates market liquidity. Securities markets don't work if owners of shares can't sell when they need to, anymore than deposit banks can survive once they fail to repay their depositors on demand. Denied the protection of the law Dutch bankers, like their English counterparts a century later, simply created their own club morality.

5

Setting the Course

'A bank lives on credit. Till it is trusted it is nothing; and when
it ceases to be trusted it returns to nothing.'
                                    Walter Bagehot *Lombard Street*

INSTITUTIONAL FUND MANAGERS HELPED Siegmund Warburg put the Gentleman Bankers' Code to the knife, and they
changed banking even more fundamentally. The growth of irrespon-
sible investment funds – for when many are accountable, no one is
truly responsible – would enable banks to borrow without credit.
The spread and growth of prosperity, and of institutionalised savings
such as pension funds and mutual funds, has taken place only since
the 1950s, as has the substantial growth in the financial resources
of large manufacturing companies. The arrival of these wholesale
funds freed banks, whether long-known investment houses or newly
formed commercial banks, from the tyranny of a deposit-collecting
branch network, and allowed banks to change their approach to
funding their loans. Walter Wriston's predecessors at Citibank
would have considered his instructions to his subordinates of 'You
get the business, and let me worry about the money' as mad, bad
and dangerous to the bank.

This change would take time to mature, for bankers live well and
long, and their memories of past mistakes are vivid. But, by the
1980s, the very best Wall Street names were vying to find the most
dishonestly managed savings banks. These were paying the highest
rates for $1-million-plus deposit packages, and the investment bank-
ers had no cares. Both their finder's fees, and their clients' money,
were guaranteed by the US government. What was slowly forgotten,
as new developments made banking prosperity seem a fact of life,
is that banking is risky, and never more so than when business
conditions are difficult and bankers ambitious. When the hard
money policies of the 1980s ushered in a new boom, banking had

ceased to be profitable, but bankers could not alter the course upon which they were set.

Banks and fleas are similar in that

> Great fleas have little fleas
> upon their backs to bite 'em,
> And little fleas have lesser fleas,
> and so *ad infinitum*

and the commercial banks are the great fleas of the financial world. Branch networks, and correspondent arrangements with foreign banks, allow commercial banks to siphon wealth directly from the economic activities of society. Investment bankers are the little fleas, for it is off other people's money and business connections that they feed. Until well into the 1960s, the world's wealth was not only owned by individuals, but directly owned by them. The majority of people had few savings and could afford only the simpler services of savings banks, building societies or mortgage banks, and post-office giro systems.

Banks were for the successful and the rich, and only the commercial banks and the insurance companies had the skills necessary to administer the private and business affairs of a widely spread group of wealthy customers. These, together with the private banks and stockbrokers, administered the wealth of the nation, while investment banks needed wits if they were to live off the money that these others managed. Though the relationship between society and bankers is better than between fleas and host, for the former is symbiotic while the latter is parasitic, both require that the host be healthy, if they themselves are to thrive. A century ago London banking was beginning to sicken, and the weakness of the British economy was thrown into vivid relief by the First World War. This cruelly exposed the relative backwardness of British industry. Strengthening traditional Scandinavian business links with a strong commercial-bank shareholding connection would therefore be a good diversification for Hambros.

C. J. Hambro & Company, the London merchant bank founded in 1838 at the same time as the predecessor of the Morgan banks, ceased to exist in 1920, when it merged with British Bank of Northern Commerce Limited to become Hambros Bank Limited; the 'Northern Commerce' disappeared shortly after the merger in consideration of the feelings of the bank's American and

Mediterranean clients. That merger, also, brought to an end the partnership's unlimited liability to its creditors, and replaced it with the protection given to personal wealth by incorporation. The partners of C. J. Hambro became directors of Hambros Bank Limited and, though they might lose jobs, salaries and shareholdings if the bank failed, the family fortunes would remain intact. Nevertheless, though the legal structure had changed, partnership attitudes continued to run Hambros until well into the 1970s, by which time C. Hoare & Company was the only London bank still to retain unlimited liability.

BBNC had been founded in 1912 by a group of Scandinavian banks and businesses. These connections, and the very latest accounting systems acquired from the Midland Bank, meant that by 1920 BBNC was nearly as large as C. J. Hambro. The merger reflected luck, as well as the Hambro family's ability to see what was happening to London rather earlier than their colleagues. The founders of BBNC saw advantages in becoming both more 'British' and allying with a first-class London name, and the Hambros knew the bank and its management well, for they had cooperated on a large Norwegian kroner war loan to the British government. This loan had arisen from the diplomatic work of Eric Hambro, Olaf's eldest brother, on behalf of the British government during the First World War.

The Hambros had other, more personal, reasons for looking favourably on the merger. Thirty years previously Everard Hambro, Olaf's father, had seen close banking friends ruined. Everard, who was to remain chairman until 1925, had made C. J. Hambro one of the most aggressive and innovative of London merchant banks. Between 1881 and 1883, Hambros had led an enormous loan for Italy, intended to establish for it a stable gold-backed national currency. Despite falling stock markets and Rothschilds' spoiling tactics, Everard succeeded, and obliged his old rivals to close their Naples branch. The value of this Italian loan was greater in prestige than in profit, but competition for business was tough and the two houses had been contending over Italy since the bank was formed.

Hambros had been loyally supported in their battle with the Rothschilds by Barings but, in 1890, this bank was itself in trouble, facing a crisis of confidence as word spread that it had overdosed on Argentinian loans. C. J. Hambro had a considerable holding of the same loan, so self-interest as well as good fellowship motivated Everard's actions. Barings was the oldest merchant bank in London, and one of the largest, and its name was on some £15 million of acceptance credits, held by firms throughout the City. Failure would not only destroy old friends and allies, but create a worldwide financial collapse in which no London bank would be safe. Once aware of the danger, Everard worked all one night to produce a rescue plan with Lord Revelstoke, Baring's chairman and the man whose aggressive impetuosity had caused the problem. At 8 a.m. the following Saturday, Everard and Revelstoke presented this to Lord Rothschild, chairman of his family bank, who initially refused to help believing, and hoping, that this major competitor was doomed.

The Bank of England, when approached later that morning, took a more generous view, despite their shock at this being their first inkling of the coming crisis. The 1866 failure of Overend, Gurney & Company had taught the Bank that it had a more general duty to London banks than merely looking after its own business interests, together with those of the government and its friends. Then the failure of the Bank to come to the help of a leading London house – and, indeed, the last of the 'native English' banks – had precipitated a financial crisis and economic depression. In the years since then, London's dominance as the centre of the world financial system had become even greater, and no one could tell what might happen if Barings failed, though it was possible to guess. As the Committee of the Stock Exchange asked rhetorically after the event, if Barings had gone, 'what securities would have been saleable, what bills could have been discounted?'

The Bank's total reserves were only £11 million, so government support would be essential for any rescue operation, supposing that one could be mounted. That same Saturday, having arranged that the three of them should meet the following Monday with the chancellor of the Exchequer, William Lidderdale, the governor of the Bank of England, joined Revelstoke and his cousin and colleague, Francis Baring, in Everard's office at C. J. Hambro. The partners' lavatory, as myth has it, was as confidential a meeting place as any to be found, for it was essential that City confidence be maintained as long as possible; there was smoke but, as yet, no sign of the fire. Any action that Lidderdale could take would depend upon the nature of the problem, but the Baring accounts, which he first saw that afternoon, were a hopeless mess, and it was impossible to tell if Barings was insolvent or just illiquid.

If Barings was insolvent, and had lost all its assets through bad debts, little could be done except organise the bank's liquidation. This would have to be done in as controlled a fashion as possible, otherwise the ensuing panic would destroy many other houses which, though solvent, would be killed by their inability to realise their assets quickly. If, however, the bank still had a value, despite the Argentinian losses, and was merely facing a liquidity crunch, because the loss of depositers' confidence meant that the bank was incapable of holding its deposits or meeting payment on trade bills due, then the authorities could help. By Wednesday, revised accounts showed that Barings had good assets of some £25 million against liabilities of £21 million, and, by Thursday, these had been verified by two directors of the Bank of England. The following day Lidderdale put an ultimatum to the chancellor; either the government supported the Bank, or it would be the first to dishonour Barings' bills. Faced with this, the cabinet reluctantly agreed to underwrite half of any losses the Bank might sustain from its purchases of Barings' paper, made in the twenty-four hours commencing at 2 p.m. that Friday, 14 November.

Confident of government support, Lidderdale immediately set up a guarantee fund, with a seed-corn contribution of £1 million from the Bank. This was doubled when Glyn Mills, Baring's bankers, promised £500,000 and shamed Rothschilds into a similar contribution. Another £3.25 million came from a consortium of acceptance houses, including Hambros. During Saturday, the British commercial and overseas banks were approached and by the 2 p.m. Saturday deadline, with the regional banks making their promises, news of the impending crisis finally reached New York. By this time, however, the fund stood at £17 million, and it was all the fashion to be seen as a guarantor. Panic was averted, since no one had cause to fear any loss from holding Barings bills, once the guarantee was in place.

A new limited-liability company was established to take over the business of the old Baring partnership, but the cost of rescue was ruin for Revelstoke and his senior partners. Lidderdale had copied a similar rescue plan mounted by the Bank of France the previous year, but the importance of the Bank's action was the speed and secrecy with which it was implemented, and the concern it showed for the health of not only London depositors, but the world financial system in general. Lidderdale was a hero, though not given a title, for 'he is not rich enough for a baronetcy' the chancellor reported to the prime minister. But Lidderdale's action marked the Bank's coming of age; it had matured from using the regular financial crises to improve its own market position, as in 1866, to recognising under Lidderdale that its duty as the central bank was to maintain the solvency of the London banking system – and therefore that of the world at large – as 'the lender of last resort'.

The need for such a lender is that all banks are middlemen, or intermediaries, and banks use other people's money in the ratio of ten to twenty times their own equity. Confidence underpins banking; without it, the money flows out faster than central banks can pump it back in again. The revolutionary change that Lidderdale had introduced, and that had made the government gag, was to support a named house. The principle of central banking support was enshrined in the writings of Walter Bagehot, based on earlier Bank experience, which was that the central bank should lend to the market and allow this to sort the sheep from the goats. Jeremiah Harman, a director of the Bank of England quoted by Bagehot, had given the classic description of this function during the 1825 panic:

> We lent [gold] by every possible means and in modes we had never adopted before; we took in stock on security, we purchased Exchequer Bills, we not only discounted outright but we made advances on the deposit of bills of exchange to an immense amount, in short, by every means consistent with the safety of the Bank, and we were not on some occasions over nice. Seeing the dreadful state in which the public were, we rendered every assistance in our power.

Lidderdale recognised that rescuing an individual house could avoid market panic, and be less disruptive to the financial system as a whole than the Bagehot proposals. These new principles were severely tested by the outbreak of war in 1914, for this not only brought to an end the freedom of capital and personal movement, which had allowed the London merchant banks to flourish, but left all of them with a crisis of liquidity. Many of their customers and creditors had become the 'enemy', while much the same was true of the merchants themselves. This cosmopolitan society, which had run a worldwide entrepôt business based on the telegraph and the 'bill on London', now found themselves under suspicion as enemy agents. Neither the lost trust, nor that merchant society itself, would ever be regained.

The business of the London merchant banks had ended with the bang of August 1914, though it would be nearly fifty years before Warburg finally rammed home this message. Long-term borrowers migrated to the richer and cheaper money fount of New York, while economic autarchy made the bill on London irrelevant. Fortunately for the Hambros, the merger of C. J. Hambro and BBNC had created a London hybrid, an acceptance and issuing house with a strong commercial banking business. In this, it was similar to Morgan, prior to 1933, and to German banks. This was the universal banking pattern which American banks would aspire to during the 1980s, and which any British bank could have followed, provided only that it had the necessary skills and a willingness to argue with the Bank of England.

The Lidderdale system collapsed during the crisis of 1931, when the Bank of England's inability to help the Austrians in any worthwhile way alerted the world to Britain's loss of financial supremacy. By 1945, the system was back in place under American leadership, and only now in the 1990s is it again being tested to destruction by the narrow domestic policy focus of Germany's Bundesbank and the Bank of Japan. Success, whether among central or private banks, assumes that bankers should do unto others as they would be done by, for banking is an uncertain trade, and bankers never know when they might need friends. Seven years after its rescue, Lidderdale asked Barings for a loan of £35,000 on inadequate security of £10,000, stating: 'My request is for an advance on my bare word that I will repay it if I can.' The money was lent immediately. The Bank of England had many occasions to look for similar friends during the sterling crises of the 1960s and 1970s.

In the early 1950s, when Sir Charles Hambro set out to rebuild the bank's Scandinavian connections, which had become inbred and cautious during the years of depression and war, he naturally turned to Marcus Wallenberg, with whom he had worked when Swedish ball bearings and special steels had been vital to the British wartime production of aircraft engines and anti-tank guns. The Wallenbergs controlled both Stockholms Enskilda Bank and many of Sweden's most important companies; their role as industrial 'godfather' would be strengthened by the postwar development of the Swedish welfare state, which ensured that those who were rich could stay rich, but those who wished to become rich would need to go elsewhere.

Scandinavia was Britain's second largest trading partner, at the time when the postwar need for timber, board and paper could create a virtuous business circle for the bank. Imports into Britain could be financed on three-or six-month acceptance credits which, unless the bank was flush with cash and wished to hold the paper, would involve the bank simply guaranteeing the importer's credit, while the bank could finance the exporter's development of new paper mills through the bond market. The problem was the Bank of England, and the weakness of the currency. The use of sterling to finance the trade of other than British customers was disallowed, and the desire of the merchant banks to raise bond finance for their overseas customers was frustrated by the Bank's need to protect its reserves of gold and dollars. Salvation was to come from an unlikely quarter.

The US government had a reputation for impounding the assets of those nations that it did not like. As the popularity of the anti-communist US Senator Joe McCarthy waxed, the enthusiasm of the Russians for keeping their dollars reserves in American banks waned. But the Soviet-bloc countries needed to hold dollars, for this was the only currency in the world that was untrammelled by restrictions. Since American industry was rebuilding the world, the dollar was also the best store of value; everyone else wanted American goods, and their currencies were all valued in comparison to the dollar. It was almost certainly a Soviet-owned bank in Paris which gave the eurodollar market its name, for this bank's telex sign-off was 'euro-bank' and, as the Russians searched the markets for banks that wanted dollars but were not American banks, that signature became very familiar. But it was a central-bank policy decision that gave the market life: in 1957 the Bank of England, more than mindful of the commercial interests of its charges, allowed British merchant banks unrestricted freedom to borrow and lend in dollars. Jocelyn Hambro remembers:

> It was about then that Anglo-American came to us with a request for a large loan, and we were keen to do it, but it was going to be tricky getting the Bank's permission and Anglo were in a hurry. Then Kern, who ran our Swiss office and, like all good Swiss, was razor-sharp on currency trading, said: 'Why bother with sterling? Let's offer it to them in dollars, and book it here.' That's how we got into the euro-dollar lending and, of course, after the Bank's approval, we could book similar business in London. It was very profitable, since the deposits were cheap, for no one had much idea of what to do with them, but both my father and Charles were worried about this busi-ness. We had no lender of last resort, since the Bank would only rediscount sterling paper and, at the time, we all reckoned that the market might disappear one night. That's why, for the first three or four years, we used to show this eurodollar business as a separate item in the accounts.

The market structure was in place for the rapid exploitation of the new euromarkets, once the Bank gave its blessing since, two years earlier in 1955, the UK Treasury had encouraged the British local-government authorities to borrow directly in the money markets. These were attractive borrowers, for they came with the implicit guarantee of the British government and, in no time at all, these 'parallel' markets were challenging the old-established discount markets, while local-authority bills were a higher-paying alternative to Treasury bills. But the main impetus for the euromarkets came from Citibank when, in 1961, Walter Wriston invented the negotiable certificate of deposit (CD).

US banking regulations prevented banks from paying interest on deposits in current accounts, and set maximum rates of interest for time and notice deposits. The Fed could also determine the maximum rate of interest of CDs, and so controlled the pace of bank expansion, American banks had been issuing CDs for years, but these were simply a documentary confirmation of a deposit for thirty, sixty or ninety days or whatever. They were not competitive with their equivalent securities, the commercial paper (CP) issued by the major industrial companies through their investment banks. The investment banks made a market in these CP issues, to help investors who suddenly needed their money back. Banks could not do that, or even hint at it, because of Fed regulations, so, more importantly, Wriston arranged for the Discount Corporation, a Wall Street investment house in which Citibank had a large shareholding, to make a market in Citibank's CDs. This was in parallel with the market Discount Corporation made in three-month Treasury bills and CP issues, and so promised investors a similar degree of liquidity on their bank CDs.

With the promise that investors could realise their money legitimately and whenever they wished, negotiable bank CDs became more popular than CPs, and helped banks regain their share of the US deposit market, which they had been losing. Since the Fed had no authority over the eurodollar markets, there was a regular and substantial use for eurodollars, too. On eurodollar CDs, there was no Fed interest-rate maximum, nor were there any reserve requirements. European banks could buy American banks' CDs, and gain a turn on the interest margin by funding them with eurodollars. American banks were soon the largest users of these new markets and, as the brokers began to work the markets, these began to swell with the dollars earned by US companies working overseas, and with tax-flight money tempted out of Swiss accounts.

Hardly had this interbank money market in eurodollars got going, before it was given an unexpected boost by American legislation.

Reconstruction and free trade had succeeded beyond all expectations, and so had American spending on the Cold War. Political action was taken to protect the value of the dollar by making foreign companies pay 1 per cent more to borrow in America. The consequence of President John Kennedy's 1963 interest-equalisation tax (IET) was a perfect example of the law of unintended consequences, which would continue to surprise legislators and bankers during these years. These actions of the US Treasury, paler versions of British action to protect sterling from 1914 onwards, had no effect on the value of the dollar but, instead, loosened the control of the Fed over American banks.

IET, when taken together with other regulatory taxes, meant that American banks could lend to the overseas subsidiaries of their corporate customers more cheaply from the euromarkets than from New York. The banks could offer more on dollar deposits in London than in New York, so surplus pension-fund money, like that of General Motors, could get better deposit rates from US banks in London than were available to them from stateside branches. IET transferred the financial capital of the world from New York back to London, but made the dollar the currency of London banking. Literally within weeks of the announcement of IET, London was back in business as an international issuing centre. Warburgs, and then Hambros one day later, announced the first ever eurobond issues. These had all the style of the old days. They were on behalf of overseas governments, with the issuing banks acting as paying agents for the interest coupons attached to the bonds. They were bearer bonds, giving legal ownership to their physical possessor, though their modernity was attested by the country of issue.

Luxembourg was starting on its career as a world financial centre, appealing to all those doctors and dentists who believe that the less their tax authorities know of their financial affairs, the better. A eurobond market of $90 million in 1963 had grown to £3,000 million five years later, while euromarket deposits went up sevenfold to $15.5 billion. Citibank, the most aggressive and imaginative of the New York banks, turned increasingly to its London branch, using it to take advantage of the euromarkets but also recreating its investment-banking business, under the more congenial attitude of the Bank of England to matters of banking supervision, at least as far as foreign banks were concerned.

If the euromarkets had made a breach in the regulations, an even larger one had been made in bank defences. For all their many centuries of existence, bankers had regarded their competitors with the gravest of suspicion, and no bank would ever lend to another without collateral, preferably good trade bills. Neither the Bank of England nor the New York Clearing House (the forerunner of the Federal Reserve Bank of New York) would ever help its charges unless they had security to offer in exchange for help, and this did not include finance bills, even from the most respectable of houses. 'Pig on pork', as London bankers described finance or accommodation bills, were treated with the utmost discretion, because if such bills were the only security a bank could offer, what then was its equity, or where its prudent governance?

Now banks would lend to others, not even directly but through brokers, and not with collateral but simply on their request for money. Where banks led, others would follow.

6

Make All Speed

'I have known a man to come into my office, and I have given him a check for a million dollars when I knew that they had not a cent in the world.'

Pierpoint Morgan

ONE MORNING ON HIS way to work, some sixty years ago, Charles Mitchell called in on J. P. Morgan to borrow $12 million in his own name. The chairman of Citibank needed to pay for 50,000 Citibank shares bought the previous day by Citibank's investment-banking affiliate. Unfortunately Hugh Baker, the president of City National Company, in taking the shares from the market had not thought how he was to finance their purchase, and Mitchell was his only hope.

The explosion of American middle-class wealth during the early years of the century, and especially during the Jazz Age boom of the 1920s, had enabled Citibank to stake its claim to be a universal bank, a financial business that would act for governments, companies and individuals alike. In 1929 the *New York Times* welcomed Mitchell's merger between Citibank and the Corn Exchange bank

as giving America, for the first time, the largest bank in the world. In a way, it had been a matter of mortification that, with the post-war United States outstripping Great Britain not only in the field of industry but of home and international finance, London should still possess the premier institution [Midland], measured by total banking resources.

This merger was planned to give Citibank the largest branch network in New York City, but the board of the Corn Exchange had required Citibank to underwrite its share-exchange offer at a cash price of $450; that meant buying shares to keep the share price high. This was not that easy during the boom, when the shares peaked at just under $500 each, for Citibank shares were overpriced compared with their asset value of $50 a share or their minuscule yield; the shares paid a dividend of only $4. But Baker's was a forgivable oversight, for after the October 1929 Wall Street crash had sent all prices tumbling, he and his dealers at City National were hard put to it to support the market price of Citibank's shares. By November it was impossible, and attempting to staunch the selling flood had already exhausted City National's borrowing facilities with Citibank itself.

With Wall Street in panic, there were no other lenders to be found and, if City National was to be saved from bankruptcy, Mitchell had to buy the shares himself. City National was Charles Mitchell's own creation, the successful merger of one of America's largest retail stockbroking firms, which Citibank had bought in 1915, with Citibank's own investment-banking activities. When in 1920 Citibank's controlling families had recognised that they no longer had the desire or the ability to run the bank, they also wanted fresh blood, for Citibank's balance sheet was in tatters; uncontrolled expansion of lending to Cuba and Russia, under the last, incompetent family manager, had almost immediately turned into enormous losses. The tough and plain-speaking Mitchell seemed the ideal candidate to rescue the bank and, over the next ten years, Mitchell transformed Citibank, using the foundations laid by predecessors.

Citibank had grown rich and powerful on its ethos of 'ready money', and Mitchell was not going to forget its traditions. If he allowed the Corn Exchange merger to go through with Citibank shares well below the $450 level, the cost of redeeming this pledge would drain the bank of cash during the worst financial crisis in its history. Mitchell voted the shares bought with Morgan money, together with all his other Citibank stock, to kill his own dream and to concentrate, instead, on building up Citibank's cash reserves. By December 1930, even without the Corn Exchange merger, Citibank had overtaken Midland to become the largest bank in the world.

This business pattern was the one that most banks, led by Citibank, would attempt to replicate in the 1980s. The only difference between then and now is that Mitchell's bank had a clearer and more comprehensible identity. There were three quite separate businesses. National City Bank (today called Citibank) was the domestic and international commercial bank. City Bank Farmers' Trust (another of Moses Taylor's former businesses) administered and managed the affairs of the wealthy. City National Company was the investment bank, dedicated (at a price, of course) to turning the successful into the rich. Each of these activities was separately managed, though all had Mitchell as chairman, and were separately owned. This avoided the tiresome legislative difficulties that aimed to prevent American bankers from doing what Citibank had done, for, in fact, the other two banks were controlled by trustees on behalf of National City Bank, and fed all their profits into it; the three together composed the bank.

British weakness gave Citibank its first opportunity to compete with the Morgans and London banks, for Baring's failure opened Argentina to American banking competition. The real boost to business came with growing American commercial success in Central and South America. These initial efforts were turned into solid success with Citibank's purchase of the Connecticut-based International Banking Corporation in 1915. This American-owned bank operated very profitably in Asia, for it set a thief to catch a thief, employing Scots and English managers to compete with the London-based British overseas banks, all fighting for a share of business in any market governed by, or within the reach of, British imperial power, such as China. Although the interwar State Department was unable to sanction government loans because of the power of isolationism within Congress, it nevertheless flexed its muscles by using the British pattern of approving would-be borrowers for political correctness, and then directing them to its favourite Wall Street bankers. These rarely refused the honour and Citibank, with many others, would come to rue the German reparation loans, as well as investment loans to Latin America, made under such auspices.

City National was the means to compete with Morgan and, fertilised by introductions from Citibank's lending divisions, it sought out the smaller emerging companies, as yet unknown to Wall Street. But while Morgans only sponsored issues, Citibank distributed them as well, and Baker, under the overall guidance of Mitchell, turned America into a shareholding democracy. City National's 2,000 salesmen introduced Americans to the delights of international bonds and domestic shares, all coming with Citibank's 'seal of approval'; not least of their wares were the shares of Citibank itself, for if his branch manager was buying, what harm could come to the customer? By the middle of the decade City National was underwriting nearly twice as many issues as Morgans and Kuhn Loeb combined.

Citibank was equally innovative within banking, for the success of small savers' accounts had persuaded Mitchell not to use these simply to fund business loans, the traditional function of individual deposits within a commercial bank. Instead, some were recycled back to the same market as small unsecured loans. Banking for the blue-collar worker and small businesses had made the California-based Bank of America one of the fastest growing in America, a surprise to most bankers, for commercial banks normally had no time for this market sector. Citibank's willingness to follow suit meant it was able to kill off some New York loan-sharking, garner favourable publicity for itself, and still earn interest margins of two to three times its normal level.

Commercial bankers' great need is for deposits, the basic raw material of their business, and the more widespread their branch network, the greater their chance of collecting the peoples' savings. The search for deposits would have driven commercial bankers to expand anyway, but eighteenth-century experience proved that branching out promised greater security; even if panic affected banking depositors in one part of the country, the odds were that other parts would not hear of it. Opening new branches was expensive in capital, and the caution of customers meant that it took years for a branch to break even on revenue account, let alone make a return on the capital invested. Bankers believed that expansion was in the interests of their shareholders, depositers and managers; size enabled banks to diversify their business loans as well as their deposit sources. This reduced banking risk; a setback to a particular industry, once generally known, or a local misfortune, such as crop failure, could and did destroy local banks, by bringing about a loss of confidence and so a run on its deposits.

When bankers discovered that taking over existing banking offices made expansion more quickly profitable and could be financed not by real money but by issuing shares, the case for cannibalism needed no further arguing. Of course, this argument swung both ways, for those that did not eat would get eaten, so banking size and bankers' paranoia grew hand in hand. As early as the first decade of the century, British politicians were disgustedly claiming that bankers' only justification for mergers was that their rivals had either completed one themselves, or were about to do so, and their actions were legitimate self-defence. The expansion of the commercial banks from the 1870s onwards was a reflection, also, of improved control: the invention of the telegraph, the laying of a transatlantic cable, and finally the introduction of the telephone enabled large numbers of geographically scattered offices to be monitored. Better communications encouraged the expansion of bankers' customers, too; as these grew, so did their banks, desperate lest their absence from the field allow a competitor to make a breach in their relationships.

Although there has never been any other empirical evidence that banks benefit from economies of size – above balance-sheet totals of £100 million or so – initially this expansion and centralisation had a beneficial effect. Midland could afford the very latest bookkeeping technology, imposed its credit-control systems on the banks it took over, but still left the local manager with considerable autonomy. But the 1920s, and then the postwar decades, also showed that expansion and centralisation could have more unfortunate effects, because contrary to general opinion and even that of many bankers, banking is less about lending than managing money. But the development of unsecured interbank lending made it easy for bankers to forget this, as well as the fact that customers deposit funds, not only borrow.

A service business thrives only by responding to customer needs, so it should be no surprise that banks, in forgetting their function, also lost their two major franchises, which were the very pillars of commercial-banking profitability. Lending to undoubted commercial names was one; the other was managing their money, and that of the rich and successful, many of whom were shareholders or managers of those selfsame corporate customers. Bankers live and die with their customers; only close contact with customers ensures that banks get off the industrial hearse before it gets to the crematorium. This is the importance of relationships in banking, as opposed to the trendy 1980s transaction-based dealmaking. Though among the earliest to appreciate the profitability of shipping, Midland failed to understand this changing market, and stayed with British owners and yards as they sank.

Until the 1970s all bankers needed to be conscious of both sides of their balance sheet. Those banks that have survived the centuries, such as C. Hoare & Company, are those that ensure that they align their interests with those of their customers, and organize their business so that loans, though desirable for their higher profits, are not essential to their survival. Indeed, after their 1930s fright, most bankers became excessively cautious, concentrating on making profits through the liability side of their balance sheet; liabilities are a bank's deposits while its loans are its assets. Bankers, in very general terms, tend to specialise; some like to lend, others prefer to get their hands on other people's money. Liability bankers are the ones who build up the liability, or deposit, side of the balance sheet, or attract the customers who want to have their money managed in the securities markets.

Bankers earn their money by ensuring that savers and borrowers alike can each obtain the characteristics they want in their deposits or loans, and the key to the working of the financial markets, and of banking itself, is bridging the 'maturity gap' between my needs as a depositer (I need my money now) and yours as a borrower (my business needs the money, and I can't repay you yet). Bankers risk both their reputations and their bank in satisfying these contradictory needs of savers and borrowers, as they also do with the chance that borrowers may not repay them. These 'liquidity' and 'credit' risks, to use the jargon, are what destroys banks, since any bank that cannot repay its depositers on demand ceases to be a bank. The reward for shouldering these risks is the 'spread' between the rate banks pay for their deposits and what they charge for their loans, or earn on their investments. The chance that banks may lend, or invest, money at less than they have to pay for it is another of their calculated gambles, that of 'interest' risk.

The willingness of bankers to transform 'maturities' by lending for longer periods than any particular group of their depositers are prepared to commit their money is their 'value-added' service. Savings banks are the most extreme version of this, for the repayment of a house mortgage can take thirty years. Though Anglo-American experience indicates seven years as the likely maturity of a mortgage, savers are unwilling to commit their money to any bank for anywhere as long as this. In theory, all banks run enormous liquidity risks, for most deposits are repayable on demand, and must be repaid whatever the contract might say, while loans can be reimbursed over many months or years. In practice, the necessity of banks and the modest volume of their loans, compared to the amount of credit created through the relationships of customers and banks with each other in the payment system, mean that the law of big numbers works to obviate that risk. What banks lose on the swings is made up on the roundabouts, for one bank's borrower is another's depositor.

Until the 1960s banks were funded by the current-account balances of their customers, or the savings and deposit accounts designed to appeal to longer-term savers. The bulk of these came, and come, from private individuals and small businesses, for neither have the time, resources or standing to use the money or securities markets directly, and so must use a bank as an intermediary. Banking skill is managing the balance sheet in such a way that a bank can safely earn the higher margin on longer-maturity loans while funding them with cheaper and shorter-maturity deposits. Until the appearance of the money markets, bankers needed to nurture customers; partly in the expectation of referrals of other business, it is also because banking profitability and security depends upon customers using as many of the facilities of the bank as possible.

The most important banking task until the 1970s was the morning meeting, when the financial position was examined. This was the responsibility of the chairman of the bank; when Moore was running Citibank, he used the very latest information and communication devices to bring together his most senior colleagues, the latest information on the Citibank's position, and securities-market experts to decide the bank's money policy. To establish a bank's treasury position required intimate knowledge of its depositers, for otherwise bankers could not answer questions such as: 'Which of our large deposits are due to be repaid today, and how many might be renewed?' Equal insight was needed into the financial affairs of its borrowers, for a bank's funding needs could be established only when it knew which of its loan commitments would be drawn down; how many loans were due for repayment, and whether they would be repaid or, more likely, rolled over and renewed; how many trade bills were due; and what assets could be sold.

With these questions answered, bank directors could estimate the size of the bank's funding gap, the cheapest and surest way of funding this, or the most profitable way of using any surplus. Banks expected to have a surplus until the arrival of unsecured interbank lending; this was the bank's reserve, available to meet unexpected withdrawals of deposits. Always before 1914, and for the banks of major countries up to 1930, these reserves were kept in what American bankers called 'high-powered money'. This was specie – gold or sometimes silver coins – and the currency notes of the central bank. This was the money that customers wanted during financial panics, and Moses Taylor's Citibank grew strong as it became known for its ready money, regardless of conditions. Very prudent banks, like the nineteenth-century Citibank, would keep as much as 40 per cent of their total assets in reserves.

This was costly, for neither gold nor currency notes have ever earned interest, while deposits have to be paid for, though the payment is not always interest. Services, such as running a current account or making payments, are costly in bankers' time, and these traditionally remunerated themselves by not paying interest on current-account balances. Even though paper money is everywhere triumphant today, and short-term deposits with other banks have replaced these real reserves, balance-sheet structure, and reserves against the unexpected, still go to the heart of banking security and profitability. Economists describe this as the matching of the maturity structure of the bank's assets with its liabilities. Bankers traditionally faced two main constraints on their lending growth; one was getting the money, and the other was pricing it. Businessmen need certainty in their investment decisions, and the cost of money is one of their most important considerations. Investors take the risk of fluctuating interest rates from bankers and businessmen both, because the price of the bonds they buy carries it instead.

Commercial bankers once carried this risk through their loan pricing and, when bankers wrongly forecast interest-rate trends, as frequently happened – and still happens, though it is now hidden by their use of swaps and the derivative markets – the interest spread on their loans turned from positive to negative. As these banking losses mounted, the banks were forced to cut back on lending, to reduce the cost of this interest mismatch. The risk of earning less on their money than they were paying to depositors also meant that banks had to be cautious about their gearing. Merchant banks who lent more than five times their capital were considered less than prudent during the late nineteenth century and, as late as the 1960s, commercial-bank gearing of more than ten times was considered daring.

CDs removed the liquidity threat to banking, but did not change the risk of negative interest rates. In 1966 the Fed, which still controlled the rates at which American banks could borrow, forced money so high that CDs became unsaleable, and the banks had to borrow from the Fed at penal rates – or use the euromarkets. As was intended by the Fed, this destroyed banking profit margins, and so slowed the expansion of banking credit; what was unexpected was the bankers' response. To avoid this happening again, and at a time when all Wall Street banks were increasing the ratio of loans to capital, American bankers passed on the risk of interest-rate movements to their customers. Customers could borrow as much as they liked in future, but would no longer know the cost. Loans were priced at the cost of money, normally the London interbank offered rate (LIBOR), together with a margin for the bank, and would be repriced every three or six months.

Large businesses saw no reason why they should pay a margin over the cost of money to their commercial bankers, once these ceased to perform the function which justified that profit. The invest-ment banks were keen to encourage them in this attitude, for the businesses came to them instead, since they could raise cheaper, though equally variable, money for the companies by issuing commercial paper on their behalf. Then the 1970 bankruptcy of Penn Central, the blue-chip railroad company, gave temporary respite to the commercial banks. This crisis in the New York commercial-paper market caused another credit crunch, which frightened the Fed, and from then on, American banks were allowed to pay whatever rates they chose on 'wholesale money' of CDs of $100,000 or more. The CDs of the banks became even more popular than commercial paper, however big the issuing company.

But company treasurers remembered that, if necessary, do-it-yourself financing could be cheaper, and was often more flexible, than using the commercial banks. So the large corporations began to recruit bankers during the 1970s, to ensure that their finance departments would understand the tricks of bankers. By the time the lunatic behaviour of some US money-centre banks in the early 1980s reversed the favourable pricing of bank CDs, the banker-influenced finance departments of the large industrial corporations had become profit-centre treasury functions. These appreciated that the credit ratings of their own companies were at least as high – and often higher – than those of the banks, and that any financial analysis the banks could do, they could do as well. Confronted by an industry that was not prepared to talk sensibly about differential pricing, the larger corporations realised that they had no need of an intermediary in their dealings with each other; smaller companies paid instead for this error in banking strategy.

Banking needs good salesmen, and the best salesmen traditionally ended up as bank chairmen, but selling energy has always needed to be monitored by a lively sense of self-preservation. This could come from the family, keen to make more but not at the price of losing what they had, or from the financial constraints imposed by the balance sheet. All these constraints had gone by 1970. The postwar Citibank board would be uneasy with Moore's Mitchell-like drive, but the New York bank would continue to be a predator; with Moore out of the way, the memories of the 1930s would also fade, for Mitchell had rescued Citibank from its postwar errors only to push it into deeper trouble. Citibank's official history admits that between 1929 and 1933, the bank lost two thirds of its capital. Moore, who was there, reckoned that the bank's losses were $433 million, rather than the $167 million of the history, and that the bank and trust company were left with only $137 million of capital; the investment bank found no buyers, and had to be liquidated.

There was a double irony to Midland's support for Citibank during the 1933 American banking closure. Citibank would rebuild itself on the back of the postwar recovery of American industry, and follow its worldwide expansion. Central to Citibank's strategy would be its exploitation of London, which it would develop as America's offshore banking centre, enabling it to sidestep US banking regulations. And what Moore and Wriston's Citibank of the 1960s and 1970s would do today, others would do tomorrow; in doing just that in 1980, Midland emasculated itself. Though Citibank's earlier excesses had stimulated American politicians into placing shackles on the freedom of the banks, neither Moore later, nor Mitchell earlier, was exceptional in this drive for size. Indeed, Mitchell was merely copying, albeit with even greater aggressiveness, what Holden had done for Midland earlier in the century.

The 1929 Wall Street collapse was certain to bring blame on to bankers, for the ending of the bull market ended the middle-class dream of instant wealth, but the Fed acted promptly and by the time 1930 dawned, it seemed that the new supervisory system had justified itself. The Federal Reserve Board system of regional reserve (or central) banks had been established in 1913 to prevent banking panics. Congress had finally accepted the need for a supervisory bank after the 1907 crash, which had resulted from the reckless behaviour of the US trust banks. These, instead of concentrating on managing the affairs of the wealthy, fancied themselves as lenders, and exploited legislative loopholes to achieve their ambitions. The crisis, the worst in American banking history until 1929, had taken a year to develop, helped by rising speculation in mining and railroad shares.

Only the calming presence of Pierpoint Morgan in his Wall Street office sufficed to bail out the finances of New York City in 1907, rescue several trust banks, and save the stock exchange together with a large investment bank. The fact that this narrow escape from financial disaster had to be engineered by America's most hated banker had galvanised Congress into action. Not everyone was persuaded that America needed an equivalent of the Bank of England, and the inability of the US Treasury, in 1991, to use the looming bankruptcy of the Federal Deposit Insurance Corporation to shoehorn banking 'reform' through Congress shows that American public policy, even today, is still divided over the same issue that split the founders of the republic – the Jeffersonian belief that the industry

needs plenty of bankers, and banking should not be made a monopoly through government regulation; and Alexander Hamilton's fear
of indisciplined lenders. So, though the Fed existed in 1929, it was
politically weak, financially inexperienced, and Jack Morgan had
nothing like the authority of his father.

The Fed initially responded well to the 1929 crisis, for the finance
of the 1920s stock-market bubble had come from US companies.
These earned higher rates by lending to investment bankers, who
needed the money to finance their share-buying clients. Interest rates
on these 'call-money accounts' were consistently higher than those
offered by the deposit accounts of the commercial banks and these,
fearful of losing their relationships, acted as agents in the placing of
call-money accounts. As soon as the crash occurred, the companies
wanted the greater safety of a commercial-bank deposit, so the Wall
Street commercial banks took over the bulk of these share-supported
loans. The Fed ensured that the market was flooded with money;
neither it nor their commercial bankers wanted distress-selling by
the investment bankers.

These were kept afloat, to sell their shares at a better time. The
securities markets stabilised, politicians announced that business
recovery was around the corner, but neither business recovery nor
confidence reappeared. And public confidence received a further
shock when, in the following year, the Bank of the United States
was allowed to die. This grandiloquently named bank aimed for the
immigrant market and, despite its unpopularity with both 'dusty
money' and 'our crowd' banks, had become New York's fourth
largest bank by the time 1930 showed up its inadequacies. One in
every ten New Yorkers banked with it, even though the bank was
certainly badly managed and the ownership probably dishonest.
Citibank and other leading members of the New York Clearing
House could not agree among themselves how to share the rescue
of this retail bank; none was foolhardy enough to take it on alone.
Their failure turned the 1929 financial crash into a worldwide economic disaster, because the Bank of the United States not only had a
name that fooled depositors, but was also a member of the Fed
system; collapse despite this membership combined with its name
to cast doubt on the soundness of the US government itself.

This national credit crisis was then worsened by the Fed's shilly-
shallying; in principle, the Fed was prepared to support its members
with cash, but in practice waited for the banks to come to it, which
was against all nineteenth-century experience. The Fed should have
been aggressively forcing liquidity on to the market, like Jeremiah

Harman a century earlier, but its policy discouraged the banks instead, for its lending rates were two points higher than the market, and confidence was fragile. Banks were fearful that, if they were seen to be borrowing from the Fed at penal rates, their depositers would jump ship even faster. The result was a deflationary spiral as Citibank and its Wall Street competitors liquidated loans, built up their cash reserves and waited anxiously for the coming crisis. Business activity collapsed as deflationary pressure within the world's richest economy sent all other economies spinning into turmoil. As factories closed, and banks failed, America's consequential Smoot-Hawley protective tariffs act set the world on to a beggar-my-neighbour path of tit-for-tat trade protectionism.

The 1931 failure of Vienna's Credit-Anstalt dominoed through Austrian banking into Germany, and collapsed all East European banks. A run on sterling forced the British government to go cap in hand to American bankers even after they had cut civil-service and armed-forces salaries by 10 per cent, and reduced pensions and unemployment benefit. The Bank of England was still required to suspend the conversion of paper money into gold. The Labour government split in two, amid dark mutterings about a bankers' ramp, and speculative pressure switched to the dollar. That was the moment a US congressman pressed for the names of all banks receiving official support to be published. This created the fourth and final American banking panic, as depositors made a run on any bank remotely suspected.

The crisis was ended only by the new president declaring a bank holiday, a euphemism for closing the banks so that customers could not get at their money, and Roosevelt telling the people in his inaugural address that the only thing they had to fear was fear itself. This was a far from insubstantial fear since, between 1929 and 1933, nearly half of America's banks had failed. Naturally, no politician was going to accept any blame for this, nor any greedy customer accept that his desire for greater returns than those available on a deposit account exposed him to higher risk. Actually, since even innocent depositers had lost their all, and not just the buyers of bonds, shares and property, there obviously had to be villains somewhere. Bankers were the preferred option though they were equally convinced, with the politicians and their customers, that it was all the other fellow's fault.

Ferdinand Pecora, a former assistant district attorney for New York, had a reputation of accepting, and winning, all the politically dirty cases. When he took over the stalled congressional inquiry into the crash, he had two banks in his sights. One was Citibank, the most ambitious of the banks with the highest profile, and the other was J. P. Morgan, feared but respected. Morgan was unique, being the only bank in the world to have both a blue-chip commercial and an investment banking franchise. Pecora ruined its reputation by demonstrating that Morgans rewarded its friends, business and political, with profitable 'placings' of shares, of the sort that had originally enticed me into banking. None of Morgan's would-be investment-banking competitors had anything like Morgan's client list. Citibank's overzealous desire to compete made it an even easier target for Pecora.

Citibank, Chase and other Wall Street commercial banks used the bull market of the 1920s both to act as the sponsor to an issue – the Morgan speciality – and to distribute it, the role of the second-rank investment banks. Pecora's main complaint was that Citibank and its competitors like Chase, when they realised that their country loans were going bad, repaid themselves by making bond issues for Latin American governments. They then directed their investment salesmen to offload these dud bonds from the bank's own books and on to those of their unsuspecting and naive branch customers. These claims were never proven by Pecora, but they didn't have to be. Pecora, a Sicilian-born anti-party-machine Democrat, was tough, fearless and incorruptible, and his taunts and sarcastic asides soon had the bankers looking both crooked and incompetent.

For the next generation these would be labelled 'banksters', though the truth is neither in the high-minded but politically naive protestations of the bankers, nor in the shrill complaints of their customers. Investment transactions may seem very reasonable during an economic boom, but almost always look pretty stupid after the crash. Bankers are as gullible as any other investor, and investment hindsight is notorious for its 20:20 vision, especially when employed by those who have lost money. The nineteenth-century specialisation of banking was to ensure that the ignorant were protected from the conflicts of interest which are inherent within finance. The failure of American bankers to admit any responsibility for the crash meant that the banking reforms which it made inevitable would be politically inspired, rather than financially sensible.

Politicians, not only those of America, were determined that no such banking crash must ever happen again, even if this meant government guarantees, explicit or implicit, against banking failure. The American answer was the explicit one of government guarantees for banking depositors. That this would encourage bad bankers at the expense of the good was the fear of President Franklin Roosevelt, the Morgans and most Wall Street bankers, but he still signed the bill into law; Congress was importunate, for so many of its constituents had been ruined and considered the banks responsible, while Roosevelt was anxious to be off to his country home from a muggy Washington summer. The price demanded of American banks for their errors was that they should choose a basic function and, in future, either be commercial banks or investment banks.

The house of Morgan was divided, never to be reunited, and today Morgan Guaranty competes with Morgan Stanley, while Morgan Grenfell has become a department of Deutsche Bank. The irony of this is that Deutsche Bank was itself set up at the initiative of the German government to wrest some of the financing of German trade away from London-based banks, such as Morgan and Hambros, while Morgan Guaranty has changed its name back to J. P. Morgan and prevailed upon the US regulators to allow it to become again its pre–1933 self.

7

The Captain's Cabin

UNTERMEYER: Is not commercial credit based primarily upon money or property?

MORGAN: No, sir, the first thing is character.

UNTERMEYER: Before money or property?

MORGAN: Before money or anything else. Money cannot buy it . . . because a man I do not trust could not get money from me on all the bonds in Christendom.

Exchange between Pierpoint Morgan and
counsel for the Pujo Banking and Currency
Committee of the US House of Representatives
in 1912

DR HENRY KAUFMAN RECENTLY described the last four decades as 'an extraordinarily eventful and highly inventive period in financial history which has also yielded a number of disturbing financial mishaps, scandals and credit crunches'. Kaufman was chief economist for Salomon Brothers for much of this period, and became known as Dr Doom, for his stark appraisals of US credit policy had a wizardlike effect on interest rates and the price of US government bonds. Arguing that the financial world must necessarily be a continuous struggle between conservatives preaching stability and prudence, and revolutionaries emphasising the virtues of wider choice and greater efficiency, Kaufman identified these postwar years as the time when the maverick's triumph came at too high a cost.

In Kaufman's opinion, 'a badly fragmented and inadequately supported financial regulatory system, slow to recognise some of the more serious abuses of financial entrepreneurship and in urgent need of reform' led to 'a series of damaging tears in our financial fabric, characterised by huge losses to the American taxpayers . . . repeated scandals involving prominent institutions here and abroad . . . and a debilitating over-leveraging of our business enterprises, our families and our government itself.' Kaufman's conclusion is that 'whatever gains in economic growth were enjoyed as a consequence of this tilt towards unbridled (or at least loosely bridled) financial entrepreneurship are more than offset by the current and future costs of the excesses'. He identifies Wriston's development of the negotiable certificate of deposit, together with the concurrent development of the interbank markets, as the major break in the conservative bankers' defences. That was certainly my experience in London.

I discovered this new world during 1963, at a meeting with one of the new-style money brokers, when I was asked whether I had money to lend in the interbank markets or whether, to the contrary, I might like to borrow some. I was confused, for I had not even heard of these markets at the time, but also amazed that anyone would be mad enough to lend to us on an unsecured basis. I was embarrassed by my office at Whyte, Gasc & Company, which I described to friends as a down-market version of Scrooge's counting house. The business proclaimed itself 'private bankers' but, in practice, this was a money-lending operation. It was far removed from the banking and investment management business that I had envisaged. The only funds that Whyte, Gasc possessed, apart from its own capital, was an overdraft from its commercial bankers, which Whyte, Gasc used to lend to those desperate enough to pay the interest rates needed to cover the overheads of the business, the cost of the borrowed money, and a good profit on the owners' capital.

The borrowers were small-scale property developers and speculative dealers in shares, exactly the sort of business that was discouraged by the Bank of England. The cream of this, whatever the official lending guidelines said, was taken by the commercial bankers. The rest found its way to what would later be called the secondary banks, for, in truth, the dealing profits that could be made in those restricted times were so large that borrowers hardly noticed interest rates, except during loan negotiations. But Whyte, Gasc was exactly the sort of financial company that the money brokers were targeting. It seemed respectable, for it had become a quoted company in which the Courtaulds pension fund had invested £500,000, a significant investment for the time. My success in bringing this about had earned me a minority shareholding but, not for the last time, I was regretting what a golden tongue and imagination could achieve; the more I got to know them, the less I wanted to work with the industrialists who had established this bank-to-be.

I had met them after leaving Robert Benson, Lonsdale and joining the *Observer* London newspaper as their first ever City editor in 1961. This was an opportunity to write about growth companies for a larger audience than the investment committee of Bensons, and I spent much of my time visiting the smaller companies which, it seemed to me, showed the vitality necessary to reverse the seemingly endless decline of British industry. Another event, three years after Siegmund Warburg changed the City's ethos, soon persuaded me that I was more suited to be a participant than a spectator of this world, for 1962 witnessed another crack in the walls of the Gentleman Bankers' Club. The largest ever takeover mounted in London (up to that time) initiated an extraordinary battle between two British industrial heavyweights, and was another, and even more important, outing for the financial journalists who had first been blooded in the British Aluminium war.

Late in 1961 Imperial Chemical Industries offered to buy Courtaulds, a silk weaver founded in London by Huguenot refugees during the seventeenth century. By this postwar period it had become, as it remains, the core of the British textile industry. Both companies had resulted from interwar amalgamations designed to buttress British competitiveness against American and German challengers, and both were significant producers of chemicals. Neither had performed particularly creditably for their shareholders during the postwar period, and Courtaulds had just cut its dividend. After several months of discussion, the Courtaulds board had still not agreed a friendly takeover, so Morgan Grenfell pitched a hostile ICI bid at well above the market price for Courtaulds shares. Neither Barings, nor Courtaulds' chairman and chairman-elect, had any stomach for a fight. Most of the City, and all of the press, brainwashed into believing that 'big is beautiful', were convinced that amalgamation was the right fate for Courtaulds. Not only did the company appear to have lucklustre management, but the joint company would control over 90 per cent of Britain's output of synthetic fibres. This was an important growth business; it would be safer under ICI control.

Once the bid was in the open, the two banks, together with the chairmen of the two companies, agreed that the game was over, so our presence at the press conference was simply to hear the obsequies recited. But if in 1959 the great and the good had miscalculated on Warburg, then in 1962 another outsider, but an industrial manager rather than a banker, would upset their calculations just as badly. As the chairman of Courtaulds started his speech, Frank Kearton, a trained chemist educated at a free grammar rather than fee-paying public school, staged a boardroom coup. Shouldering his way forward to the front of the platform, he stated that ICI needed Courtaulds more than Courtaulds needed ICI, that the board would fight and the company would win.

Forcing Barings to produce asset revaluations, profit forecasts and critiques of the ICI figures, Kearton locked horns with Sir Paul Chambers, the chairman of ICI. But Kearton was not only a clever tactician, but also a great salesman. Though the financial weaponry that he first deployed quickly became common takeover practice on both sides of the Atlantic, he also flattered and charmed the press, including me. Struggling against Baring's reluctance to engage the enemy, he used financial journalists to second-guess market reaction to Courtaulds' initiatives, forced ICI to raise its bid twice, and still kept the Courtauld's share price above the level of the ICI bids.

The board, with Kearton as chairman, celebrated victory with a thanksgiving service; Kearton also carried a sample case for the next few years, to ensure that everyone in the company knew that the business of Courtaulds was selling product and earning profits, and not administering a corporate version of the British Empire. When Harold Wilson became prime minister, he appointed Kearton to head the Industrial Reorganisation Corporation, hoping that he would bite enough industrialists to infect them with his own madness. This was too big a task even for Kearton, although his IRC graduates have certainly strengthened manufacturing management within Britain. He was later ennobled by a grateful government for his services.

Kearton also mentioned that, should I ever go back into banking, he would like the company's pension fund to be given the opportunity to invest. This was the appeal of Whyte, Gasc, for its three founders claimed they wished to create a bank that would use their business and industrial contacts as its marketing base. Crucially, one of these controlled Triumph Investment Trust, a small company with a stock-exchange quotation. It was likely to lose this, and its tax exemptions, for it had ceased to invest in shares and simply held cash. By selling Whyte, Gasc for new Triumph shares, Triumph would be given a business, existing shareholders would have a larger market in which to dispose of existing shares, the bank would have the Triumph cash with which to increase its own capital, and I a vehicle with which to attract Courtaulds.

This was great as theory, but foundered on the character of Tom

Whyte. His partners had warned me that he could be difficult, but I felt sure that I could handle him. However, I had never before come across a Maxwell-style personality, and by 1964 I had had enough. This was partly exhaustion, for it was not sufficient to agree to a course of action on the grounds that Whyte controlled the business. I had to believe, really truly believe, that this was the right, proper and only thing to do. Not only did this mean hours of argument in the office, but even longer harangues on the telephone in the small hours of the morning. 'No, no, Russell, you still don't see' would be the inevitable prologue to another hour or two of talk, with my ear aching from the pressure of the telephone. Hard though I tried, my voice never had the right level of fervour when, desperate for relief and sleep, I would tell Whyte what he wanted to hear.

I became increasingly fearful that consorting with Whyte would destroy any reputation I might have, while still at the beginning of my career. Still under thirty, I reckoned I needed to get back among the blue-bloods before it was too late, and this time I used the traditional approach. Through Jules Thorn, an outstanding émigré industrialist whom I had come to admire as an analyst, I was given an introduction to Harry Sporborg at Hambros. Thorn strongly disapproved of Whyte, and asked me whether I wanted a career, which he could offer me, or to make money. When I sheepishly admitted to the latter, he remarked that the City was the only place to do that and, though he could promise nothing, he would talk to his own bankers. Sporborg asked me to come and see him, and he turned out to be an imposing figure.

Solidly built, and trim from fox-hunting regularly into his sixties, he had a sharp legal brain emphasised by the piratical eye-patch he needed to wear. A partner before he was thirty in Slaughter & May, the best known of London's corporate lawyers, he was asked to join Special Operations Executive, a wartime intelligence agency, where he became Sir Charles Hambro's deputy, refusing ever to wear uniform. Brain and eye-patch together enabled him to terrify generals and ministers, much as he frightened me. After the war, Sir Charles asked him to give up the law and join him at the bank, to which he brought many of his former clients. A week after the meeting, I was back to my first love of investment management. Just as well, for Whyte took advantage of those interbank market brokers, Triumph became a typical stock-market star and, in 1974, turned out to be one of the largest, as well as the most hopeless, of the secondary bank failures.

*

The English banking tradition, like that of Holland and France, concentrated on the sound and prudent management of money. Customers were already rich, and the job of bankers was to preserve that wealth. From 1970 onwards, English banking was an oligopoly of only four large banks and, of these, only the Midland had been established from the outset as a lender to industry. The others are predominantly amalgamations of private deposit banks, federations of those that failed to maintain their independence as population and business expanded exponentially during the nineteenth century. The underlying philosophy of English bankers favoured the lender to the bank, or depositor, rather than the borrower and, once the banking oligopoly was first established in the 1920s, exhibited just that financial conservatism which Kaufman condemns for it 'stifles economic growth, as well as social invigoration and renewal . . . makes it more difficult for fledgling enterprises to get started and flourish . . . with existing institutions favoured and supported, especially large ones, to the detriment of new business that may be more efficient and more promising.'

Citibank, followed by its New York peers, was a revolutionary within 1960s London, for lenders think differently from borrowers, and neither Thomas Jefferson nor his constituents minded a little inflation. This reduces the real burden of farm mortgages and business debts, though at the expense of their bankers, and was the policy issue argued over in the Federalist Papers during the early decades of the new American Republic. Should there be a Bank of the United States, a clone of the Bank of England, that would bank for the government, discipline the financial system, maintain sound money, and preserve the wealth of the already rich, or should banking be free – that is, with easy access to the industry by would-be bankers – so that cheap money and plenty of banks would exist to back America's farmers and artisans, the creators of future wealth? Citibank was the standard bearer in London of this alternative banking tradition, which developed in nineteenth century America and Germany. It emphasises the need to help customers get rich, for this approach developed within societies that were poor and capital hungry, and looked for a banking system that would support the business borrower. These were the two countries, also, that pioneered multi-national companies from the 1870s onwards, so it was also natural that American and German bankers came to regard themselves as the 'financial partner' of the manufacturing concern. Yet it was the English tradition which influenced Morgan, above all an Anglo-American house, for the Morgan business trusts were designed to protect corporate profits from excessive competition, and bankers and bondholders from loss.

Location, experience and policy had made Midland the banker to the businesses that turned eighteenth-century English wealth into nineteenth-century industrial might. The fragility of this after the First World War exposed Midland to considerable losses because, as the largest bank and the most business-inclined, it was hardest hit by the problems of the heavy industries of coal, steel and ship-building, and the decline in the textile industry's export markets. Midland was also the harshest critic of the Bank of England's monet-ary policy, which crippled industry with an uncompetitive exchange rate for the pound, and the most energetic of the commercial banks in identifying the financing problems of the fledgling business. By the 1950s, many of its large business customers were moribund, and Midland needed to return to its origins, relearning the infinitely more risky business of lending to new and growing companies. In the 1940s, and again during the 1950s, the senior management in Mid-land identified the policies that it ought to follow, if it was to resuscitate industry and rebuild its business franchise. That, unfortu-nately, was also the moment when its sense of corporate direction was lost, and a centralised and hard-driving leadership turned into baronial in-fighting.

Midland's failure was not inevitable. When acceptance houses found it hard to find any business at all, Hambros was regularly recording ever higher figures. Though Scandinavia was one of the largest of the UK's trading partners, Hambros faced all the protectionist, exchange-control and lending problems that others had. But using the commercial-banking skills entrenched within the British Bank of Northern Commerce staff – mostly themselves originally recruited from Midland – Olaf Hambro set out to proselytise smaller British companies to the benefits of acceptance-credit finance, for their internal as well as external trade. He also saw opportunities that were natural to high-street bankers, but to which their ossifying structures could not react.

The early years of war saw an influx of diamond traders from Amsterdam and Antwerp, fleeing the Germans with wives and children and with the tools of their trade – packets of rough or polished diamonds and their business contacts. Though these traders had both collateral and expertise, they needed credit and sympathy if they were to restart their business lives. More than most acceptance houses, Hambros prided itself on its language skills, and Olaf quickly dominated this new business, offering the refugees overdrafts and revolving acceptance credits of 70–80 per cent of the value of cut or uncut stones. By 1943, this new business extended from the dealers in Hatton Garden, London, to cutters in Birmingham and makers of industrial cutting tools throughout the Midlands, and the bank itself began to deal in diamonds. Real expansion came with peace. Before the summer of 1946, Olaf had bought various businesses which turned the bank into a major player as broker, trader and classifier of diamonds, and with entry to the annual 'sight', or sale of diamonds at the De Beers-controlled Diamond Trading Company.

This led to a major expansion of the banking business, served first from an office in a nearby building and then from a purpose-built branch in Hatton Garden. Before that happened, and in a rationed City where neither armoured cars nor taxis were much in evidence, staff members often carried diamonds worth £50,000, as collateral for loans, as they boarded the bus for the two-mile journey from the DTC to the bank in Bishopsgate. Not surprisingly, Hambros was soon known as the Diamond Bank: with the De Beers connection came the Oppenheimers, and with the Oppenheimers came Anglo-American, and with Anglo-American came that first use of the euromarkets. Diamonds and gold are natural partners, so trading and banking in diamonds led to Hambros doing the same in gold and, in the 1950s, the bank acquired Mocatta & Goldsmid, one of London's four gold and silver bullion brokers. Banking is about relationships and also opportunism; for, like the thread in the Minotaur's cave, a firmly anchored base can safely lead to unknowable, but profitable, encounters.

Diamonds led to gold, and both gave a considerable fillip to foreign-exchange-dealing profits, then turned into commodity dealing – a rather less successful venture – and of course created deposits, loans and payment needs. Hambros might as easily have become known as the Kipper Bank, had one of its trading initiatives been a little more successful, though this again was an opportunistic development of an existing success. The Bank of England, desperate to increase Britain's earnings of dollars, urged the acceptance houses to remember their trading origins throughout the late 1940s. Unfortunately, merchant blood had grown thin over the generations, and most attempts were fiascos. To be fair to the bankers, they tried hard and spent their own capital, for they could understand the Bank of England's urgency, but these would-be traders got little support from British manufacturers.

As Jocelyn Hambro remembers them:

> When they saw us coming, they were terrified, absolutely terrified, for they weren't very keen on exporting anyway, and the last thing they wanted was some young banker telling them how to go about it, and why they needed to change their designs, or production processes, or whatever, or giving them an order bigger than they had ever before seen in all their lives. They probably thought we'd take all the profit, as well.

The first time that Jocelyn saw action was in Normandy, where he was awarded a battlefield Military Cross. This was for successfully storming a hilltop strongpoint, commanding the road to Caen, which itself controlled the route to Paris. Against all military logic, for there was no possibility of infantry support within the time available, Jocelyn was ordered to attack alone. With his squadron of tanks, he succeeded both in capturing the position and holding it against enemy counterattacks until relieved by the late-arriving infantry.

It was similar baldheaded flair and inspiration that were needed, Olaf decided, if Hambros was to capture part of the American export market, and so he sent his son to the unexplored commercial lands of America beyond the Great Lakes. God knows what the mayor of Dallas and his fellow Texans thought when Jocelyn turned up with his tin leg, English drawl and MG sports car; but charm won them over, and the mayor consented to a grand tour through the town in this 1930s-design two-seat open-topped car. The publicity worked, even though the mayor later likened the MG to the first cousin of a malted-milk machine. For Jocelyn had appreciated what, several decades later, marketing gurus would sell for thousands of dollars. Britain could not satisfy American needs; it might, however, create some American wants. The MG was an adult toy, and fun to drive in the sun.

Of course, no US car distributor dared touch it, for fear of losing their own franchise with the major US car companies, so Jocelyn had to criss-cross America looking for go-getting Americans prepared to set up a distributorship for this Mickey Mouse motor. One certain advantage of war service for the English is that it breaks open social barriers. With six years of service behind him, Jocelyn had met all sorts of odd characters, some of whom would take him up on his wartime promises of backing. He developed an intuitive feel for winners and, though this didn't always work, it certainly helped him meet the merchant bankers' requirement to make more than they lose. The six MGs sold in 1948 had become more than 30,000 ten years later. There had been the usual failures and bad debts with the new distributors set up to sell and service the MGs, but these were dwarfed by the profits that were made. By the time that Hambro Automobile Corporation was bought out by the manufacturer – then the appallingly badly managed British Motor Corporation and now the Honda-influenced Rover company – it had a staff of 500 and covered the whole of the United States.

Hambro House of Design was to achieve for luxury Scandinavian and British goods, such as linen, china, glassware and food, the same success that was being realised with the cars. The opportunity looked equally good, because the average European supplier shuddered with horror when faced with the size of an enthusiastic American order. So Hambros bought goods on consignment, to sell to the luxury market through a specially designed shop. Jocelyn had proved himself a merchant, but he was neither the first nor the last to discover that merchanting and retailing are different businesses. The 'Queen of Scots' was a kipper that neither met the size and standard of succulence promised, nor endeared itself to American taste buds. The crateloads delivered became particularly odoriferous as arguments raged with the American authorities over safety and health requirements. The kippers finally had to be dumped at sea, while honey, stored in a warehouse where the refrigeration failed, fermented and exploded. Most other goods failed to meet the luxury levels promised, and the shop was closed at a considerable loss.

Not all new businesses succeed, whatever their early promise or the strength of capital behind them. Yet business, like nature, is a process of birth, growth, maturity, decay and death; if an economy is to thrive, the banker must be midwife as well as guardian, undertaker as well as nurse. This requires a competitive banking industry at the local, or community, level. This existed in British banking when branches had power, either because managers still remembered their past as independent bankers or, as was the case until the advent of the computer, because head office had control over branch activity only after the event, rather than before it. When the number of English banks contracted from seven to four in 1969, the authority of the branch manager was also usurped by the computer, which gave power to personnel and planning departments.

8

The Navigator's Table

'At a time of buoyant stock market activity more could have been done to determine the borrower's worth . . . yet it is not always easy to devise procedures that are completely foolproof against rogues, clever and cunning in their deception.'
Official history of Lloyds Bank, commenting on their Hatry losses of 1929

THE HAMBROS BANK THAT I joined in 1964 was as unusual as Robert Benson, Lonsdale, but whereas Bensons had chosen domestic issuing and investment management as their skill, and continued with this when they merged with Kleinworts, Hambros was exploiting the growing demand for asset-backed loans, and the euromarkets. Hambros and Citibank had more in common with each other than Citibank had with Midland; Rolf Dellborg and his Norwegian colleague Otto Norland were part of the new graduate generation of bankers that were being recruited by New York's commercial banks and London's merchant banks. Dellborg's first meeting with Olaf Hambro was typical. Olaf was intensely shy but Dellborg, a young Swede recruited in the early 1950s by the outgoing Sir Charles, and completely ignorant of banking, only knew that the chairman's age, gruff voice and great height made him a most forbidding personality. Sitting at the side of his desk, Dellborg waited for him to speak.

After asking whether Dellborg had settled down comfortably in London, and welcoming him to the bank, Olaf enquired: 'Know anything about merchant banking?' Dellborg said 'No'. There followed a 'humph' and a long silence, with the two looking at each other. 'Well, know anything about banking?' Again a 'no', 'humph' and even longer silence. 'Interested in money, then?' 'Oh yes, and I know something about that all right,' said Dellborg, relieved that he could at last say something positive. 'Good,' said Olaf after yet another long silence. 'That's all that merchant banking is, money.

But the secret, my boy, is to make more than you lose, for lose you certainly must. The skill is less about who to trust than how much you can trust them with, and just how far you're prepared to go with them. Remember this, though. If you don't lose money as a merchant banker, that's not because you're lucky or clever, it's because you're not trying hard enough.'

Dellborg remembered those words when, thirty years later, Rollatruc, a Swedish company with a £25-million contract with Maxwell's *Daily Mirror* newspaper group, asked him for his help. Maxwell was well known to anyone who had worked at Hambros, and rated a minus figure on any standard, so Dellborg agreed to do so only on the condition that he had a completely free hand. Rollatruc agreed; Dellborg was a director of its British subsidiary and, more importantly, £10 million had already been spent by them on an automated warehousing system, and Maxwell showed absolutely no sign of paying. Dellborg spent all one Thursday attempting to contact Maxwell, and was finally promised a meeting the following morning. This was cancelled at short notice, with no alternative time suggested, so Dellborg put his fallback plan into immediate operation. He knew that Maxwell got his way by bullying and lying, and that he despised those that he could either browbeat or flatter.

Calling together the Rolatruc managers, who were both running and installing the automatic stacking and loading equipment, Dellborg instructed them to be prepared to close down the warehouses the following Monday morning. Maxwell was advised later that Friday that unless Dellborg had a banker's draft for £12.5 million by 10 a.m. Monday at the latest, none of his newspapers or other publications would leave his warehouses the following week. The deadline came and went, for Maxwell always reckoned on outbluffing such threats and enjoyed the surge of adrenalin they brought him. But on Tuesday his warehouses were silent, which did surprise him, while Dellborg was as elusive as Maxwell had been the previous week. They finally agreed to meet that afternoon, and Dellborg went to the meeting alone, for he knew that more than toughness was needed. Maxwell needed Rollatruc but, unfortunately, the converse was also true since nearly half the contract was completed.

Alone in front of Maxwell and his subordinates, Dellborg reckoned that he had a chance of shaming or jollying Maxwell into paying the money, and without too much loss of face. Fortunately, Maxwell played into his hands. After the usual bluster and braggadocio about the Mirror Group, there was also much talk about his other public company, with its recent acquisition of the US-based Macmillan publishing group, and how Rolatruc could not afford to alienate him. 'Ah yes, Maxwell Communications Corporation, or MCC for short,' Dellborg mused, 'but this is hardly cricket, is it?' The room burst into laughter as the joke defused the tension and, though Maxwell initially scowled, he then led the laughter. Always feeling himself an outsider, Maxwell needed to show that he was anything but; so, with his defences now in ruins but dignity maintained, Maxwell passed over the draft, and agreed to pay for the remainder of the contract in advance of the original payment schedule.

Maxwell was initially financed by Sir Charles Hambro with an unsecured loan of £25,000, at least £375,000 in today's money. Maxwell had used his connections within military intelligence to obtain the meeting but, even with an introduction, this was still venturesome for a merchant bank. However, Maxwell, who had proved his courage by earning both a commission and a Military Cross on the battlefields of Europe, had great charm, enormous energy and a persuasive story. Maxwell had helped Springer Verlag restart its publishing business, by using his position on the British Military Control Commission for occupied Germany to get the necessary licences for them, obtain paper and recover book stocks trapped in the Soviet zone. This earlier help, his freedom to travel (still denied to Germans) and his fluency in several languages persuaded Springer that Maxwell was the man to restart their export business. The world's pre-eminent scientific publisher had been forbidden to export most of its publications ever since Hitler's accession to power, so there was an enormous world market waiting to buy the backlog. The banker could well understand the value of the contract that Maxwell wished to finance, which was the exclusive concession for non-German sales of Springer's scientific publications.

The good will of Springer and Hambro should have made Maxwell. But time and time again Maxwell's impatience, and his urge to prove how clever he was by reinterpreting his undertakings to his own benefit, would undermine all his considerable abilities. He played fast and loose with Springer and, though keeping their gratitude for restoring their export business, entirely lost their trust through his shoddy trading practices and crooked accounting. Pergamon, the company that was to be the centrepiece of Maxwell's business activities, would maintain such practices throughout its existence. Then, in 1951, Maxwell bought Simpkin Marshall with the help of Hambros. This was a company whose time was past, for it acted as a cooperative, through which publishers could wholesale their books to the retail trade. Business pressures, however, were forcing publishers to set up their own distribution networks to support their sales outlets, and Simpkin Marshall was badly managed, with an overvalued stock, and loss-making into the bargain.

Maxwell ducked and dived with increasing desperation, for he had bought Simpkin Marshall without any investigation into the stock position, precious few ideas of how to turn it around and none of the capital that he needed to save it. Sir Charles's partners became increasingly worried about the bank's association with such a dangerously uncontrolled maverick. Harry Sporborg disliked banking for anyone from the secret world, since he reckoned that their experiences had corrupted them utterly for honest business, and his worst fears were realised as the Springer relationship, and then the Simpkin Marshall business, both soured. By 1953, Sporborg had prevailed upon Sir Charles to give up his protégé, and the bank asked Maxwell to find another banker. Maxwell then defrauded Kurt Wallersteiner, a would-be financier, of the nearly £500,000 that he put into Simpkin Marshall, though few in the City cried over Wallersteiner's fate. As fraudulent as Maxwell, and an annoyance to the Rothschilds since his Liechtenstein-registered company used their name, he was rather less successful, and was ultimately jailed.

None of this was a state secret, and any competent credit analyst, enquiring among publishers or talking with bankers, should have been able to redline a loan request from Maxwell or any one of his innumerable companies. More onerous information requirements resulted from the corporate scandals of the 1930s, and the increasing use of the stock markets by institutional investors. Laws were passed that forced companies to inform their shareholders, and thus their customers and competitors, of facts that earlier businessmen would have regarded as trade secrets, and not even disclosed to their bankers. Analysing balance sheets, and checking with other bank lenders and trade creditors, can tell only so much about a company. It is people, and especially those in their marketplace – business managers, customers, suppliers, competitors – that create the mosaic out of which judgement grows. Knowledge, however acquired, has always been the bedrock of banking judgement.

This increased transparency of market information, to use the jargon, entailed the creation of a whole new world of credit and investment analysis. Theoretically, losses like those of Hatry, Maxwell and the Reichmanns should now be history, yet, despite this greater openness, banking losses become larger by the year. This is partly a question of judgement, for, however much information is available, it still needs to be properly assessed. Rodney Leach got to know this the hard way. He met Maxwell in 1969 when he was working for Rothschilds, trying to extricate an American client, Leasco, from its overhasty decision to merge with Pergamon. Remembering those experiences of twenty years ago, Leach has entertainingly reviewed Tom Bower's biography of Maxwell, remarking that Maxwell's efforts to suppress the book turned it into a best seller.

More seriously, Leach questions why so many blue-blooded bankers took no notice of the lessons the book held for them, for it was published in 1988, just when Maxwell was probably paying $1 billion too much with his $3-billion acquisition of Macmillan. At the very same time that the banks were most anxiously vying for Maxwell's business, Bowers was outlining the dangers of dealing with Maxwell. None of these surprised Leach, for his problem, when first investigating Maxwell, was the sheer blatancy of his frauds. The Pergamon accounts were those of a publicly quoted company, regulated by the stock exchange and audited by a reasonably well-known firm of accountants, yet they were a mere tissue of imaginative lies. There were trading links between the quoted and the private companies, always a danger signal for analysts, and much of Pergamon's profit depended on the value of back issues of scientific journals, and sales contracts to the private companies. Learning that these Pergamon sales contracts absolved the private companies from any loss on resale was one surprise to Leach; discovering that the stocks of the journals simply did not exist was the second surprise.

Rothschilds, on Leach's advice, advised Leasco to withdraw its offer to merge with Pergamon. Maxwell was not well pleased, nor was the American Saul Steinberg, for he was as much an outsider as Maxwell. Steinberg was the 1960s version of the 1980s 'rocket scientist' securities salesman. He had made a fortune in computer leasing, and his Leasco company had used the cash flow from this business to diversify into many other activities, including the acquisition of a sleepy, but large and reputable, insurance company. Success had gone to Steinberg's head and he had mused publicly about how his talents could improve the performance of Chemical Bank. Buying insurance companies was one thing, but raiding banks came too close to home, and Wall Street closed ranks in defiance of Steinberg.

The Leasco price fell, in part the response of Wall Street insiders to Steinberg's lese-majesty, but also doubts about the accounting principles which Leasco and other lessors used to calculate their profits. In 1989 this same issue would destroy the old-established

British & Commonwealth shipping company. When it was taken over by another financial whiz kid, and later used to purchase Atlantic Computers, shareholders in this FT-SE 100 company would lose their whole investment of £1.9 billion, while its lending banks would discover that their £1.5 billion of loans were equally at risk. Bower quoted Steinberg as saying: 'I always knew there was an establishment, I just used to think I was part of it', so he was vulnerable to an appeal to his vanity. This was to come from Maxwell, who was feeling equally unappreciated, for he had just been publicly humiliated by Sporborg and Hambros.

Maxwell had been offered by Rothschilds some 25 per cent of the share capital of the *News of the World*, a sleazy but highly profitable Sunday newspaper. Maxwell's long-time dream was to own a newspaper group, and so establish a reputation as an internationally recognised power-broker. This was his opportunity to parlay Pergamon, which now had a quote of its own, into the leading ranks of business. The shares came from a disaffected member of the controlling Carr family and, though the disaffection was partly personal, the paper's management was on weak ground. Circulation was falling, while Sir William Carr, the chairman, regarded the company as the personal fiefdom from which he could finance a life of considerable luxury, and pay for his drink; this was no small matter, as he was never known to be sober after mid-morning. Unattractive though 'Pissing Billy' was, he was a client of Hambros and there was no likelihood that Sporborg would allow Maxwell to achieve his ends.

After Warburg's British Aluminium victory, all the major banks had junked the niceties of the Gentleman Bankers' Code and rapiers were now carried unsheathed and bloodied. In consequence of the political complaints aroused by the sight of capitalist and competitive banks in full pursuit of their prey, particularly within a would-be egalitarian and supportive society, the Bank of England had stepped in with some self-regulatory rules. Regardless of the spirit of this takeover code, Sporborg played to the letter of the legal rules, bought shares in the market on behalf of the Carrs, extracted contractual pledges of support from other shareholders, and quickly amassed 48 per cent of the votes. Maxwell's advisers were outshot, outgeneralled and outmanoeuvred, but Sporborg had no intention of allowing Carr to continue in command. The next stage required some finesse. Carr needed persuading of the importance to the defence of Rupert Murdoch, the white knight from Australia that Sporborg had provided, while Murdoch himself had no intention of paying anything like the £34 million that Maxwell had offered shareholders.

Hambros, jointly with Morgan Grenfell, arranged for an increase of 40 per cent in the company's share capital instead, to be subscribed by Murdoch and satisfied by the sale of certain of the business interests of Murdoch's News Limited. Institutional managers were again outraged; once more they were being denied the market price for their shares, just as they had been in the British Aluminium affair. Furthermore, in buying shares in the market to support the Carrs, although with bank money, and then locking out other bids through the issue to Murdoch, Hambros had breached two major elements of the spirit of the new code. Sporborg might not approve of the secret world, but nor had he forgotten how to play by its rules; in banking as in war, winning is winning and the rest is nowhere. Murdoch disposed of Carr shortly after victory.

Warburg had commenced the killing of the Gentleman Bankers' Code, Sporborg had carried it forward, but Maxwell finished it for good. Steinberg, before taking advice from Rothschilds, had invested £7 million buying Pergamon shares, and Leasco needed the permission of the Take-Over Panel to withdraw its offer to buy Pergamon. There was a need to compromise, and Bower recalls Leasco's American lawyer suggesting that the agreement reached with Maxwell be recorded. 'The City, Mr Hodes, operates on trust' was the icy reply of Lord Shawcross, the chairman of the panel. Whether that was so beforehand is debatable, but it has never been so since. Leach remarks that Shawcross was silenced by his own impotence in the face of Maxwell's operating style:

> Before thirteen witnesses, including Lord Shawcross, several City grandees and a handful of eminent lawyers, Maxwell solemnly agreed to resign management control of Pergamon. Within five days he was importing the notion of 'implementation', a word whose orotundity was perfectly suited to Maxwell's plummy voice – 'this pledge will not, of course, be implemented until the appropriate time'. A week later came 'conditionality' – 'the implementation of this undertaking is conditional upon the endorsement of my board and the approval of shareholders'. By the time Lord Shawcross had returned from a brief holiday, Maxwell had achieved the total dematerialisation of his original promise – 'It is not in shareholders', employees' or customers' interests to implement the proposal in the form now suggested; the undertaking I proffered, from which it would be perilous to depart, and which my board will fully endorse, was that while I will resign as managing director, I will remain as chairman and chief executive.'

Mutatis mutandis, the same vanishing process could be applied to categorical assertions about sales, profits, working capital or seemingly open-and-shut matters like the availability of documentation to support the accounts. After a bout of such episodes, the most astute of financial advisers would be overcome by a numbing sense of stupefaction.

Leach believes that the Maxwell fiasco argues human fallibility, rather than Bower's suggestion of City incompetents protecting their own, or Maxwell's own belief that he suffered from the hostility and anti-Semitism of the 'Establishment'. The inimitable Maxwell style of later years is perfectly summarised in Leach's review of that earlier period, when Maxwell still thought he had a chance of winning, for he recalls that Maxwell

> asked me to visit him alone at Headington Hall. Perhaps he wanted to judge how much Rothschilds had discovered about his accounts. Alarmed by the underworld tales which had come to my ears about his years in the Berlin Control Commission, I agreed to the visit on one condition – that telephone calls would be put through to the house at specified times, and if I did not reply the caller had instructions to summon the police. Maxwell showed not a flicker of offence or surprise. Indeed, he seemed to view my precautions with some kind of respect, as evidence that I had at least some inkling of the realities of life.

My own view is that the centralised banking organisation, put laboriously and expensively in place during the 1970s, no longer buttresses human fallibility; instead, it exaggerates it. Banking judgement is a matter of organisation, and this is where banking has changed. The credit department once played the role of critic to the production activities of a bank; George Moore, though much more his successors, turned the credit analyst first into a supporter of the lending function, and later into its marketing arm. As lending officers came to be judged on the volume of business they wrote, they were also being made into judge and jury of their own loans. Quantity, not quality, became the essence of banking success. Yet company analysis is best done in the light of history. Benjamin Graham, the American accountant who fathered investment analysis in the 1930s, recognised that fashion plays all too great a part, however unconsciously, in our immediate reaction to company news.

Bankers, whether lenders or investors, need to support their judgement by maintaining files on all companies that they are interested in, and check any new decisions against their earlier judgements. Banking relationships, just like businesses, grow and change; it is always the little point, easily forgotten, that destroys the hard graft of analysis. People always say more than they mean to, which is why bankers ought to, but often don't, keep records of all meetings with company officers, summarising what was said about business conditions, what facilities the company needed, and what had been promised by the bank. It is not only how that bank account or share price has behaved that is interesting, but also what the company has to say about its competitors and what they say about it. This policy has certainly kept Warburg safe throughout the vicissitudes of the last three decades.

Banks have always had credit departments, for, as Moore says, the credit department of a commercial bank is where you learn to be a banker, just as a newly qualified doctor learns what medicine really is by serving time as an intern in a hospital; investment analysis does the same for investment bankers. Midland's high fliers went into the bank's centralised credit department just as soon as they were able to distinguish themselves from the ruck of their contemporaries. From one complete floor in the bank's palatial Lutyens headquarters building in Poultry, London, the credit department was able to monitor the exposure of the bank as a whole, by industry, by geographical districts, and by types of loan. Branch managers had to pass loan proposals to this department for review and recommendation, and to be appointed to it was a test of courage as well as ability.

Managers were well-entrenched local figures, who had probably already committed themselves in principle, for a Midland requirement was that no proposal be made without the manager signing off with 'I unreservedly recommend that the Midland Bank grant these facilities'. Managers who attempted to strike out this clause had their proposal thrown back at them, with instructions not to waste the bank's time in future, while opportunities of future promotion were blighted by this 'lack of moral fibre'. The analyst's comments on the manager's proposal, his assessment of the risk and his recommendation would be passed up to the general managers, who would give the 'yea' or 'nay' to the request; proposals would be signed off by all concerned within twenty-four hours, calculated as being the time most normal customers would expect their manager to take, before coming to a conclusion on their requirements. It is always easy to be negative as an analyst, for if no loan is made it is not easy to prove a credit decision wrong. Midland was a lending bank, however, and expected its best people not only to make loans, but to make them profitably, and to get them back when they went wrong.

Credit analysts, once they proved themselves, would be promoted to a branch, where they would learn to temper the purity of credit analysis with the practicality of commercial life. Whether the loan turned out to be a disaster, or was refused and the businessman went on to become a great success with another bank, the judgement and names of all concerned were there to be seen ever after. This formalised bureaucracy of a branch-based bank contrasted with that of Citibank, organised historically as a one-branch bank on a pattern similar to that of Hambros or Morgans. An American commercial bank 'vice president' was equivalent to an English merchant bank 'senior clerk' or 'manager', depending on time and bank. The authority of these was based on the 'authorised signature', updated lists of which were regularly sent to correspondent banks. Appointment as a 'signature' entitled bank officers to commit the bank, either on his own or with a colleague.

Commercial banking signatures had direct lending authority as well; when Moore became a vice president, he could lend $500,000 of the bank's money with just two other signatures. With a 'senior initial' among them, that figure was doubled; two senior initials together could lend up to Citibank's limit of 10 per cent of its capital, together with its reserves. This would have been equivalent to about 1 per cent of the bank's total assets. American commercial banks did not have partners' rooms, but a few had separate offices, and bank officers sat together on a raised platform overlooking the banking hall and the tellers' positions. There they could see, and be seen by, their customers and each other, and be overheard by the juniors in their department. Banking is doing; if the best way to learn is by doing, the second best is to watch and hear what others do.

By the time he was twenty-eight, George Moore was acting for his chairman in recovering Citibank's multimillion debts, which included not only the lending horrors of the 1920s Florida land boom and the bankrupt affairs of Citibank's investment banking affiliate, but also the loans made to Citibankers. These were encouraged to buy Citibank shares as the bank drove for growth through the 1920s boom, and the shares, driven up by Citibank's own securities salesmen, had reached $500 a share in early 1929, only to fall to $20 by 1933; few of these debts were ever repaid in full. The importance of personal responsibility for loans is that credit judgement needs to be more than a calculation of the security margin. It is also about intuitive judgement or, as it was known in Hambros, 'whether you liked the colour of the fellow's socks'. While Lloyds was lending to Hatry, many others were lending to Ivar Kreuger, the Swedish match king.

As Jocelyn Hambro tells the story:

> Kreuger was wonderful at softening up bankers. He would take out a box of matches, open it up and say to them: 'Now, how many matches do you think are there?' The banker would say: 'Oh, about fifty, I expect' and then Kreuger would take one match out and ask again. Of course, the banker would still say about fifty and then Kreuger would reply: 'Ah, but that one match is worth so many millions extra profit to the company, and you can't tell, any more than anyone else, whether I put in or take out that extra match.' That was magic, pure magic as a way of getting banks to part with their money, but we were saved because my father looked down and saw that Kreuger was wearing bright-yellow socks. He just didn't think that any serious businessman should wear socks like that, so we were one of the few banks not to lose money when he went bust.'

As it happened, neither did Citibank, but they claim this was due to their friendship with the Wallenbergs of Enskilda Banken, so it is equally possible that Hambros had other reasons for refusing Kreuger.

Moore was known to his subordinates as 'three-way Moore' because he remained alive to the fact that there is no such thing as a one way banking bet. He always wanted to know that, if his borrowers' plans went wrong, they had other ways to repay – by cutting back on expansion plans, by selling surplus assets or property or, if matters were that desperate, disposing of a branch of the business. Banks need to diversify the way that they hope to be repaid, as well the loans and investments themselves, for bankers' must remember that the future can never be known, however convincing analytical reports appear. Walter Wriston argued that countries can't go broke, which is true enough; history shows that governments default on their loans and break their banks instead. Collateralised loans are fine in principle, except that courts often reduce bankers' rights, and retail stock can't be sold at anything near its market price, if the shop has been closed down by the bank. While it's also true that God no longer makes land or oil, the banks that lent to Olympia and York are now discovering that you can't sell what nobody wishes to buy.

Other banks, knowing the problems of realising such notoriously illiquid assets, structured their property loans to be serviced by rents. This cash flow analysis, though better than most, still assumes that there is someone out there to pay the rent. Unfortunately, if the recession is bad enough, that ceases to be a valid assumption. Bankers then find that they have to pay out more money, in property taxes, heating and security costs, just to preserve the current value of the asset against which they have lent. The best bankers, says Moore, should follow their customers closely, catch trouble early, not panic but keep their borrowers going, while finding ways to help them pay. After all, most borrowers want to survive and repay, just as much as the banker hopes for repayment. But this relaxed approach is helped if, as well as the proposed source of repayments from the sale of finished product of airline seats or whatever else has been financed by the loan, the banker can see alternatives.

Lending, as Moore knew from the 1930s, is a high risk business which needs judgement, good documentation to ensure that the collateral is sound, and a price that gives sufficient reward for the residual risks that still remain, after all possible precautions have been taken. The weakness of banking analysis, whether for loans or investment, is that there are no absolutes. All values are relative to time, place, and each other. Len Mather, a booming extroverted northerner and Midland's general manager in the 1960s, tried to resolve this with his concept of the 'gone concern' valuation. Using Midland's voluminous statistics, he calculated the likely percentage that the bank might collect on the various items of a company's balance sheet, from factory and finished stocks at one extreme to raw materials and office furniture at the other. By using these industry percentages, and the company's own valuations, lending officers could ensure that the bank had a margin of security, even assuming that Sod's Law did its worst.

Great in theory, Mather's approach had several drawbacks in practice, including Midland's own very un-English tradition of supporting customers well beyond the margin of security. However, it certainly avoided mistakes of fashion or carelessness, and Midland was the only one of the English clearing banks not to be sucked into the 1974 secondary banking crisis. Unfortunately, both the principles of Moore and the calculations of Mather were forgotten as the 1970s progressed, and banking judgement became institutionalised around Wriston's optimistic assumption that inflation would always bale out lending mistakes. Sovereign debt losses and collapsed property values are again teaching bankers that intuition, which only comes with personal responsibility, must be a key component in banking judgement.

Yet, when Maxwell drowned himself in 1992, Midland joined many other banks at creditors' meetings, wondering where their share of Maxwell's £2 billion of borrowings had gone. Brian Goldthorpe, the bank's deputy chief executive, gave me no direct answer when I asked how Midland, with its history and traditions, could have found itself in such company, saying instead: 'At the last meeting, I saw an old friend from Lloyds, and asked him how he had come to be involved, "Market share," he said, "and meeting the target for loan volumes in the departmental budget. And what about you?" "Snap," I said.' It is inconceivable that the traditional credit departments of the English commercial banks, had any survived beyond the 1970s, would have allowed their banks to lend to Maxwell. This is not because their judgement would have been any better than it was with Hatry or Kreuger, but because the 'proposal-counterproposal-agreed proposal' system would have thrown up the weaknesses of the Maxwell loan requests.

The experience of those dealing with Maxwell, and there were many more than just Hambros and Springer, would have been one warning sign, but the decline in the authority of credit departments went hand in hand with the decay of banking memory. For another responsibility of those credit departments was to ensure that the bank took 'good security', which is what the banks do not have today. Many thousands of Maxwell company pensioners have had their life savings stolen; of the £700 million looted by Maxwell from his pension funds, about half is held by the banks as security for loans to Maxwell. Much of the direct collateral, such as the assets of the private companies or the shares of the two formerly quoted companies, is now of little value. But there will be argument about the ownership of the supporting collateral offered to the banks by Maxwell, for this was stolen by him from the pension funds. The 1986 Financial Services Act may stamp roughshod over the common law, but it does not entirely supersede the duties of trustees nor of agents, however browbeaten they may have been by Maxwell, or confused by contradictory legislation.

The pettifogging bureaucracy of credit departments was designed to make sure that banks lent only against property to which they had unquestioned title. Banks may sell money, but credit officers also know that they sell time for, ignoring interest costs, 70–80 per cent of banking overheads are staff and property costs. Time spent in court, as well as in the internal, and interminable, management meetings which attempt to recover bad debts, is as much a loss as the loan itself. Insisting on seeing the relevant corporate statutes, having documents attesting signatures and signing powers, receiving copies of the minutes of meetings, and expecting authorisation under the relevant corporate power to grant security to the bank, was designed to make sure that the bank spent time *before* it lent money, rather than *after* money had been lost.

The general embarrassment of government, banks and regulators alike is evidenced by the unwillingness of any of them to address the issue of the pensioners, several months after Maxwell's death. None of Maxwell's professional advisers, colleagues and subordinates, nor the government and its regulatory authorities, are willing to ask themselves the classic questions. 'What did he know; what should he have known; when did he know?' would expose the reluctance of the government to legislate for pension schemes, despite recommendations from government and City committees going back decades, and the greed for business shown by all who dealt with Maxwell. Even Maxwell could not do what he did without going through certain bureaucratic forms, for the financial services industry is spending well over £100 million a year, supposedly regulating itself against such fraudsters. All the parties involved, not least government ministers, much prefer to mouth the traditional excuses to the police – I wasn't there; if I was, I saw nothing; it certainly wasn't me, even though I was there; it wasn't my fault, it was an accident that could have happened to anyone. In the meantime, tens of thousands of completely innocent people worry, thousands are forced to do without the income on which they depended, and hundreds are losing their homes.

After the debacle of the Leasco affair, Maxwell regained complete control of Pergamon, and continued to milk the scientific community to his great profit. His basic idea had come from working with Springer, for Pergamon segmented science into as many separate slices as possible. Then it exploited the academic community, arranging conferences and publishing their proceedings. From these came regular publications, covering that speciality. These consisted of expert papers, for which Pergamon paid virtually nothing, knowing that leading scientists had to be published if they were to build their reputations. Equally, Pergamon gouged university and research libraries for large subscription costs, knowing these had to maintain comprehensive cover of the literature. This business made Pergamon profitable and cash-rich, and Maxwell was able to develop a new hobby. He became an active dealer in shares and currencies, while waiting for the opportunity to restore his reputation.

This came when in 1980 he bought just under 30 per cent of the British Printing Corporation. It was a mixture of packaging and printing companies, most fundamentally profitable, but the company's management had a hopelessly damaged morale, the result of the costly frauds perpetrated by Wilfred Harvey, the creator of the company. Furthermore, like nearly all its weakly managed competitors, BPC was also in thrall to the printing unions, whose corruption was hardly less than that of Harvey. By 1980, National Westminster was owed £17 million by BPC, and looked like losing much of it as it contemplated calling in the receivers. Maxwell's appearance on the share register brought no joy to the management, whose earlier experience with him in an encyclopedia partnership had been an unmitigated disaster. But it opened up the options before the bank, particularly after Frank Kearton then approved Maxwell's rescue plans, saying that he thought that the Department of Trade report into the Pergamon accounting practices had been a bit harsh.

Stimulated by the chance of a return from the wilderness, Maxwell excelled himself, and the unions were out-negotiated or outflanked. Within the year, he had turned monthly losses of £1 million into profits of a similar level, and was being hailed as the wonder-worker who had done what even the Canadian owner of *The Times* and the *Sunday Times* had failed to do – he had tamed the printing unions. Within another two years, Maxwell had taken on another horror story – a printing plant from Reed, yet another large and messy printing conglomerate – and two years later finally achieved his life's ambition. Reed sold him the Mirror Group of newspapers. The share price of BPC went from 12p to over £2, banks were competing to work for him, the Mirror Group was floated off as a separate company, BPC became Maxwell Communications Corporation, and bought Macmillan. The man described by the Department of Trade report as 'not a person who can be relied on to exercise the proper stewardship of a publicly quoted company' now had two public companies, together with his mass of private interests and finely honed negotiating techniques, with which to befuddle his bankers and advisers.

The banks had nothing to oppose him or any of the Maxwell lookalikes of the 1980s, except their annual sales targets, departmental budgets, and target lists of companies. Personal responsibility and critical credit departments had melted down in the heat of lending competition. Credit analysis and evaluation became the responsibility of lending officers, and their accountability was subverted by centralised lending and budget directives. Banking numbers had expanded, memories grown dim, and nobody even tried to guard against Maxwell and his like.

9

Promises for Performance

'Do you sincerely want to be rich?'
Bernard Cornfeld's rhetorical question to
IOS sales recruits during the 1960s

EMILY BRONTË IS BEST known as the author of *Wuthering Heights*. As impoverished middle-class ladies, the Brontë sisters had no matrimonial prospects and could only look to a future as governesses for a yearly salary of some £20–30. The yield on the most secure stock of the time – British Government Consolidated Annuities (Consols) – varied between 2.5 and 3 per cent, so their aunt's legacy of £1,500, divided among the four children, scarcely made them wealthy. Nevertheless Emily, the most fey of this brilliant but ill-starred brood, with the aid of her local banker improved the family's meagre financial prospects by successfully investing in the bonds of the new railways. Three years later, in 1845, the *Economist* weekly magazine could celebrate the railway age and the changing function of the stock markets by writing: 'Everybody is in the stocks now. Needy clerks, poor tradesmen's apprentices, discarded serving men and bankrupts – all have entered the ranks of the great monied interest.'

Remembering this helped me make a name in Hambros. This was through a joint venture with the Westminster Bank, to sell their customers unit trusts. Set up in 1966 at a capital cost of £10,000, Hambros' stake of £2,500 in this mutual-fund company was bought out for £500,000 less than three years later, having in the meantime made Hambros a power in the investment world, and ensured that the 1960s equivalents of Emily Brontë had another chance of entering the great monied interest.

In 1969, Jocelyn Hambro ventured £1 million on the unit-trust salesmen, who were beginning to replace bankers as financial advisers. This enabled Mark Weinberg to leave the Abbey Life Assurance Company, which he had founded a decade earlier, and set up the Hambro Life Assurance Company. Hambros' profit from this was £158 million, probably London's most profitable banking deal this century. It certainly saved the bank, since these profits enabled it to survive the crisis of the mid 1970s when tanker prices plummeted. While Olaf Hambro was exploiting commercial-banking opportunities and his son the retail-investment market, the Midland Bank, which also needed to rethink its role and its business, was forgetting that the surest source of banking profit comes from banking for those that need you, and not those that you need.

The Westminster-Hambro joint venture helped push Midland into buying Montagu Trust in 1967, offered to them as far back as 1960; for, after nearly a century of dealing with the biggest and the best of British companies, Midland's base was under a double threat. In the takeovers of the 1960s, the bank's traditional borrowers had all too often been on the losing side, and the euromarket-energised London branches of the New York banks were attacking what remained with American-style loan offers. Montagu Trust was a sensible response, since its main operating business was Samuel Montagu, a profitable competitor of Hambros in gold and foreign-exchange dealing. Samuel Montagu belonged to both the acceptance and issuing houses' committees, and its reputation was good enough for it to be successful as a domestic issuer, were it to be fed by Midland's branch network. In addition, Montagu Trust controlled two of the country's most successful insurance brokers, which were of growing importance as sales outlets for newly developing tax and investment advisory services, together with a profitable and very Swiss private bank in Zurich.

The prospects were more than promising, for the Midland could become, on a very large scale, what Hambros was in miniature, and replicate, though more safely, the fast-growing Citibank structure of the 1920s. Yet the Midland created no new retail-investment business from its own deposit base, ignored its own origins as the banker to fledgling industry, and failed to use its branch structure to fatten Montagu's skimpy issuing business. Nor did the Midland rethink its own private banking traditions, and so failed to appeal to its mass of rich and successful customers. This could have been of interest to all three banks within the group, as well as the two insurance brokers, for high personal tax combined with rising prices was making these desperate for investment ideas that could protect their wealth. The potential of this 1967 purchase was wasted and, when the Midland faced its moment of truth after the disappearance of many of its remaining manufacturing customers during the recession of 1980–82, it had neither the new businesses nor the dealing income that might have rescued it.

Instead, from 1980 onwards, the Midland Bank advertised itself in newspapers, on television and in the cinemas as 'the listening bank'. This was a classic example of displacement activity by a dying organisation: recognising what had gone wrong, while loudly proclaiming that the quality which had been the essence of its previous success still survived. Midland was much slower to use the euromarkets than Citibank, or other London banks, yet its senior management still treated the interests of its small depositors in as offhand a fashion. Its management had become increasingly inward-looking during the postwar decades; hindsight would show that, while most of its strategic initiatives were superior to those of its competitors, the Midland's unwillingness to address its own management weaknesses ensured that most of these would be unprofitable and, in the case of alliance with the Crocker Bank, disastrous.

Their hubristic disregard for their customers' interests would bring as destructive a denouement to the commercial banks as any envisaged in classical Greek tragedy. One of the avenging furies was Mark Weinberg, a South African lawyer whom I had first met at Oxford. He had come over, looking for opportunities to take a senior law degree, and the next time I met him he was at London University. He was already thinking of the ways he could use his South African experience to shake up the staid London financial world, and I well remember a conversation over coffee in my kitchen:

'I've got to go home to finish my thesis, and check up on a few more business ideas, but I intend to return and set up a life-assurance company.'

'You must be out of your mind! No one sets up life companies these days; just look at the size of the competition, for God's sake, the entry cost makes it impossible. Anyway, looking at the results of the quoted companies, the returns don't seem very attractive. If you want to do something in the City, why not banking or investment management?'

'That's just the point. There's more opportunity in life assurance than in banking, because most people react just like you. With a capital of £50,000, which I reckon that I can raise from among friends back home, I can be in business. You forget that I know something about this, for my father was one of the country's best insurance salesmen. Life assurance, just like banking, is about savings and investment but, while everyone says the British don't buy enough life assurance, no one says they don't have enough banks.'

By 1963 Weinberg was back, Abbey Life was in business, and I was on its board as a nonexecutive director. South African friends and colleagues, together with the successful Liberty Life of South Africa, for whom Weinberg had worked, had subscribed more capital than the Board of Trade minimum. This was just as well, for breaking into the British market turned out to be more difficult than anyone had envisaged. Abbey Life was extremely efficient, for Weinberg is an organisational genius, and he had brought some very bright expatriate South Africans to work with him. In 1964 two of the industry's best-known actuaries used the industry's professional journal to describe 'best practice', and what this would mean to a life company's running costs; Abbey Life, less than two years after its foundation, was already well inside those ratios.

The trouble was that there were only two ways of selling life assurance, and Abbey Life was too new and too small for either. Weinberg was maddened by the defeatist attitude of the insurance brokers, with whom conversations would always end: 'These are very exciting policies, and I reckon that our clients would love them. If only you were one of the major companies, we'd put these at the top of our list and get everyone pushing them . . . but as it is, selling through bank managers and to a generally conservative market, I don't think we can do business together.' The other established sales channel for life assurance was a direct salesforce or 'the man from the Pru'. These working-class equivalents of the middle-class life broker or commercial-bank manager were the industrial life companies, such as the Prudential and the Pearl. Their salesmen collected premiums door-to-door, on a weekly basis, for life-assurance policies which covered such basic needs as a cash payment on retirement or for death and accident at work and, of course, money for a stylish funeral.

The difference between insurance and assurance is between possibilities and certainties, and death comes under the latter heading. British policy was to support overseas allies by allowing them access to the London stock market, with its cheap and abundant capital. Life companies stimulate long-term savings, and are the institutions that traditionally buy the bonds of government and companies, so governments, ever since the days of William Pitt and the wars against revolutionary France, have encouraged both life companies and the provident by granting tax exemptions to those who save to provide pensions for themselves or capital for their dependents. Abbey Life took advantage of higher taxation, better-policied share markets and improvements in technology to offer simpler policies. The investor's premiums were directly invested into unit trusts (mutual funds), so policy holders could see that their savings were not being used to fund the riotous living of life-company executives, while Weinberg emphasised contracts that would pay out while the saver was still around to enjoy them.

With the majority of its funds invested in property and shares, Abbey Life also promised better returns than other companies. Weinberg was not entirely altruistic, for unit linking meant Abbey Life needed less capital and reserves than if it had invested these premiums in the traditional way, through the company's own capital and reserve funds. Furthermore, by allowing policy holders to follow the growth of their savings through the increasing price of their units, which were quoted daily in the newspapers, Weinberg also encouraged the salesforce to push the company's regular savings contracts. These paid out much more commission, thus helping recruitment, encouraging the investment manager with a steady flow of funds, and locking the customer into a lifetime relationship with the company.

A handful of Canadian companies operating in Britain bridged the divide between the traditional life policy and 'the man from the Pru'. These companies sold to the middle classes, just like the brokers, but their salesmen had to find their own customers, for they could not break into the local professional 'mafias' of bank manager, lawyer and accountant, and were paid no salary but only commissions on the policies they sold. The salesmen were interesting, too, for these were also a reflection of British class divisions. In America, most would have been investment bankers or stockbrokers; these careers in Britain, at the time, were not open to those whose parents had not paid for a public-school education. Abbey Life, and after it Hambro Life, would tap this unexplored stratum of talent. The ability of such people to make good, and in such a spectacular fashion – for many of these salesmen became millionaires – would change the ethos of the City just as much as Warburg's attack on the Gentleman Bankers' code.

The Canadian company salesmen immediately saw the attraction of Abbey Life policies for themselves and their customers. What these potential sales recruits needed from Weinberg, and what he could not give them, was a first-year guarantee of earnings. Life-assurance salesmen live entirely from commissions, and today companies pay out more in commission than has strictly been earned but, back in the 1960s, the position was very different. The Canadian employers held back some 20–30 per cent of what their salesmen earned. These retentions officially covered cancellation of policies contracted by customers, and so discouraged overzealous selling, but they equally discouraged salesmen changing employers. Anyone who left, also left these unpaid commissions, so joining Abbey Life meant a considerable investment through this sacrifice of past earnings.

Reluctantly, Weinberg decided that the only way that Abbey Life could procure its future was to sell out to an American suitor, a strange partnership between Georgia Life, a small but successful life company, and International Telephone & Telegraph. ITT, the international mirror image of 'Ma Bell' or American Telephone & Telegraph, had become an acquisitive conglomerate during the 1960s and, vital for Weinberg, owned the British Standard Telephone & Cable company. This would be Abbey Life's initial hunting ground and its tens of thousands of employees offered those Canadian company salesmen sufficient prospects to guarantee them a good return on their investment. The combination was an amazing success. But the more that Abbey Life produced, the more ITT demanded, and it was this that persuaded Weinberg and his closest colleagues to leave Abbey Life, and set up Hambro Life.

The success of mutual funds attracted imitators. Property is as much a real asset as a portfolio of company shares, though amateur investors believe they understand property investment better than the share markets. That misconception was put to the test by real-estate investment trusts, which raised billions of dollars during the 1960s from American, and some European, private investors, and then lost nearly all of it during the early 1970s. The banks did almost as badly since, whether they were promoting in-house REITs or simply supporting those of customers, they were lending heavily to them. Hope springs eternal in the investment breast, for REITs were a close relative of the highly borrowed share trusts of the 1920s; the most famous of these was the Goldman Sachs Trading Corporation, whose share nosedived from $104 to $1 in less than two years, worse even than the performance of Citibank shares over the same period. Much the same happened to REITs after 1974 and, even with inflation helping out, the banks lost heavily on their property-secured loans.

Europeans escaped no more lightly. During the 1960s Bernard Cornfeld, together with his chums in Investors Overseas Services, raised $2.5 billion (at least $10 billion in 1992 money) from Americans serving in Europe and from European investors. Initially British investors were protected by a simple law, called the Protection of

Depositors Act, which made the sale of securities illegal, except by recognised dealers such as banks, or others granted a licence by the Department of Trade. Furthermore, British individuals could not invest overseas, except by going through a complex and expensive bureaucratic process. On the other hand, there was no control of insurance services and in Britain, as in many other countries, life-assurance policies were a mixture of protection – against early death or accident – and long-term savings. Moreover, since London was a world insurance centre, insurance companies had investment rights that were denied to the ordinary company, or investor. IOS set up a pair of British and Luxembourg insurance companies to bring their own brand of international investment to the public.

Like most IOS schemes, this was a great success for the salesmen, if not for the investor, and in 1969 a list of the 'great and glorious' underwrote the $110-million offering of IOS shares. Neither Hambros nor Warburgs were to be seen among the underwriters, nor even the London Rothschilds, though Banque Rothschild was there among the six principal sponsors, as was Drexel. Less than two years later, IOS was seen for the bankrupt pyramid-selling shell that it was, and a clean-cut young American businessman wrested control of IOS from Cornfeld in 1970. Much of the investment money that IOS collected had been squandered through self-indulgent investment policies, luxurious living for senior managers, investment-banking deals that made no sense, and the pyramid-selling techniques that made over 100 of the salesmen into millionaires when they cashed in their shares on flotation. Enough was left to attract Robert Vesco, the would-be rescuer, for he gutted the company of what was left, and has since enjoyed spending it in Costa Rica.

The IOS scam put German investors, among the most enthusiastic buyers of the IOS story, off the equity markets for another generation. The Italian government stepped in to rescue their investors; the result of that rescue was Fonditalia, still the largest Italian mutual fund. The success of Cornfeld's Dover Plan, as it was called, taken together with Weinberg's more solid success, made all British life companies attempt the emotionally draining management of direct salesforces. As a consequence, the level of commissions on savings plans has increased significantly, while returns have declined, and today's Emily Brontës get skinned alive.

The banks, in divorcing the interests of the monied classes from their own, and throwing them to the mercies of aggressive and commission-hungry salesmen, misread their own history. The very wealthy have always been able to establish their own income-producing investments, but the more modestly rich need help, and investment interest has always been widespread. It was small investors that fuelled the 1627 Dutch tulip boom (actually a market in futures), and then drove stock markets to unprecedented highs in 1720, the first international stock-market panic. This was the year of the 'South Sea bubble' in London, and the collapse of the Mississippi Company in Paris. Both stocks were quoted on the Amsterdam stock market, together with many other international issues. There is nothing new about 1929 or 1987.

The importance of the banker to the investor was that the nineteenth-century company promoter supplied the seed capital but looked to the stock market for loan capital: theoretically this was secure, and would be repaid, because the real risk was being taken by the equity of the business founders and managers. In practice, as investors repeatedly found, their loan capital was just as much at risk as the owners' equity – and often more so. This partly reflected the laxity, or even complete lack, of company law which allowed the 'robber barons' to flourish. These were American industrialists such as Jay Gould and Cornelius Vanderbilt, all experts at 'watering' company stock so that they as promoters took large profits from the company before it had even begun to trade. Their like were as common in London, Paris and Vienna as they were in Wall Street or Berlin, whose rapid growth and free and easy financial ways earned it the name of 'Chicago-on-the-Spree'. Company promoters succeeded because stock markets were happy for them to do so.

During the 1870s first a select committee of the British House of Commons and later a Royal Commission questioned the ability of company promoters and investment banks to use the London stock market to raise money on obviously fraudulent prospectuses. A senior stockbroker testified at the time: 'The Stock Exchange is a channel, not a filter. It argues no fault in the construction of an aqueduct that the water it conveys is often dirty. The people who made the aqueduct did not supply the water, and never undertook to clean it.'

As the Industrial Revolution progressed, and some of the new wealth began to percolate downwards, the need of the growing numbers of these monied classes was for such a filter, and they found it in the information networks of the banks. And since they also looked to their local banker for help with regular savings, advice on the safekeeping and deployment of capital, as well as the execution of speculative business, the relationship was fruitful for both. Whether the 'stagging' of a railway issue (then) or a 'privatisation' (now), the hopes of the investor remain the same – to invest safely and make a little money as well. The banks acted as administrators for these investors – running the accounts, instructing the stockbroker, taking possession of the security before parting with money, and collecting and crediting dividends. It was always the transactions and savings of the small investor that constituted the vitality of the security markets and the deposit base of the banks. This dependency of financial firms on the middle class is not surprising, since banks and security markets were, and are, designed to bring together those with money but no business ideas, and those with ideas but inadequate capital.

Bank deposits attract the cautious, while securities markets appeal to the 'get rich quick' mentality, at least as common among private investors as it is among market professionals. An analysis of the dividends paid on Consols in January 1852 shows that a third of the recipients had holdings of less than £200 (£8,000 today), nearly half owned £400 or less, while less than 20 per cent had capital of more than £2,000. This combination of safety and risk is what made the Hoare style of private deposit banking attractive to the rich, while the not so rich found equal comfort in the manager's office of the local bank. The nature of commercial banking allowed bankers to be impartial, since they were bound to earn regardless of what their customers chose to do, and their customers knew it, too. By the 1970s the growth in world prosperity, as well as a levelling of income differentials, meant that many more had joined 'the great monied interest' but the commercial banks had lost interest in their concerns and their problems.

The most difficult of these was inflation, and the way it was eating away at the value of savings. These customers became the fundamental base of commercial-banking profitability, for profit from the deposits and commercial transactions of the middle classes increasingly subsidised most of their other activities, as commercial lending became more competitive and less profitable. The banks ignored the needs of these customers, lest by attempting to help them they would harm their own profits. Others solved their problems instead. The American mutual funds offered money funds that invested in bank CDs, Treasury bills and other short-dated money investments, which drained deposits out of the banks, for they offered significantly better rates and made much of the transparency of their dealings. The European insurance companies used their reputations, and a cleaned-up version of IOS sales techniques, to increase their market share of the savings markets, offering better returns by investing in shares and property, as well as financial assets.

Then, in 1977, the computer supplied the mutual funds with the ultimate weapon for the attack on the business base of the banks. Merrill Lynch, a commission-based stockbroker with the largest US mutual-fund-management business, introduced the cash-management account. This is a mutual fund investing just in bank deposits and CDs, but it offers credit cards and loan facilities, and is simply better than any account the banks offer. Cash haemorrhaged from American commercial and savings banks, and the regulators had to act to save their charges. Their removal of regulatory controls on the interest that could be paid to depositors exposed the banks to full competition, and removed the only source of subsidised profit that they had left. A McKinsey study reckoned that this was a body blow to commercial-banking profitability; $28 billion of earnings in 1981, subsidised by these deposits, had turned into losses of $10 billion by 1986. The same process is now at work within European banking, and 1986 earnings of $12 billion are expected by 1992 to have become losses of $8 billion. The turnround will be slower but the effects as grave.

As monopolists, both of function and information, banks never used to concern themselves with competitors, only with other banks. In a business where the customer always paid, banks ceased to enquire into the profitability of their various activities. Cross-subsidisation became the normal approach, and banking worked on a pool system: the total of what was earned in interest was offset against the price of deposits, and the difference between the two covered all costs and services. The two great costs, other than staff salaries, were also the two that kept competitors out. These were the branch networks and the correspondent-account relationships. Neither is necessary to survival, especially now that technology has destroyed banking skill. What remains essential is offering customers what they need, and this has always been a method of keeping safe and administering family and company money.

Because payment services grew from the safekeeping services, and banks discovered that they could make money from other peoples' money, these payment services became a banking freebie. This was not a problem while banking retained its monopoly of information and function, because bankers could adjust their deposit rates easily enough to cover these costs. It is not a problem as long as banking services remain personal. C. Hoare & Company was founded in 1672, remains today an unlimited-liability banking company, but has expanded in recent years. The original Fleet Street office has now been joined by another in Knightsbridge. Hoares paid interest to customers on their current accounts in the eighteenth century but, as banking expenses rose during the nineteenth century, stopped doing so. The reasons for that decision – the cost of banking payments and other services – remain as true today as they were then, but late-twentieth-century competition has forced them to pay interest again. But, as Henry Hoare explains:

> Whenever we consider increasing fees, we worry about the effect that it will have on our business, and whether we will lose our best customers. But always, in the event, it goes much better than we fear. Of course, we always explain our reasons, and give the customers alternatives. If they don't like paying fees, they can always increase the interest-free balances they keep with us; if they want market rates of interest, then they pay fees. It's their choice, and we don't seem to have problems.

The Hoares have been in business a long time, but the same policy works for Edmond Safra, one of the most successful of modern postwar bankers, who has built up an enviable business by remembering that a safe and convenient home for money is the most important characteristic that people expect from their banks. Safra's banks do little lending, but offer a service instead, and make their profit by charging fees, for the bulk of the bank's deposits are invested in reserve-type assets, such as Treasury bills, CDs and short-term trade bills of companies of undoubted worth.

Safra understands the insecurities of banking customers, for he is a Sephardic Jew. These were the people who, expelled together with the Moors from Spain five centuries ago, made new homes for themselves in the lands surrounding the Mediterranean. English bankers once shared Safra's insecurities, for most were either immigrants or Dissenters from the Church of England, such as Quakers, and, being ineligible for state employment, they were forced into business instead. That world changed during the nineteenth century, and these outsiders prospered but when it changed again the banks had become complacent in their size and strength, and did nothing to prepare themselves for a new challenge. By the 1970s banking costs were rising precipitately, as their incomes were beginning to fall. Though Hambros recruited partners from its auditors, to act as finance directors, most banks believed they had no need of accountants, for they themselves were financial experts. Midland was the first, and so far only, English commercial bank to recruit an accountant to its board, and that was only in 1983.

Midland's failure was symptomatic of commercial banking as a whole. It was not only that banks such as Hambros exploited commercial-banking markets, while commercial bankers chased investment banking's will-o'-the-wisp profits. Savings banks on both sides of the Atlantic initially benefited from commercial bankers' disdain for their private depositors but, in the long term, also failed to derive any lessons from the mistakes of their commercial colleagues. It was the mutual-fund industry in America, and the insurance companies in Europe, that made the real gains. The losers were not only the banks; their customers lost just as heavily.

10

Fast Steaming

'It's easy enough to lose a £million, but hard to make it back
again. With lending margins only 1 per cent, and the float a
fading memory, loans no longer make banking sense.'
        Jocelyn Hambro, chairman of Hambros Bank,
                in conversation with the author in 1969

'THERE ARE ONLY THREE important men in the world – the
 Pope, the King and the fellow who owes you a lot of money'
goes an Italian proverb, and that's the voice of experience, I thought,
as early in 1972 I waited apprehensively for a delegation from
Zastava Yugo Automobili. I had reason to worry. The company
manufactured cars and trucks under licence from FIAT, and I knew
the Serbs expected me to lend them $7 million for at least ten years,
to buy equipment with which to modernise their production lines.
That was the total extent of my knowledge of them or their business,
except for the unwelcome fact that I was required to lend them this
money at a margin of ¾ per cent over what it would cost to
buy in the London money markets. Banks need an average margin,
between the cost of money and the interest on their loans, of at least
1–1½ per cent just to break even. This is before making any pro-
vision for the inevitable bad debts, and bad debts is what Italian
International Bank could expect. This was my first ever commercial-
banking loan, and IIB was a new bank without any natural source
of lending business.
    Nor was I happy with our meeting place, a squat black metal and
glass building which, with its taller companion building, makes a
plaza off Leadenhall Street in the City of London, one of the very
few developments within the City to have any pretensions to archi-
tectural merit. But bank was hardly the correct description for the
hangar-like space of 5,000 square feet in which I and Zastava were
to have our discussions. Until a month or so earlier, this had been
used for low-level clerical functions, and the evidence was still there

in the disconnected telephones which littered the cheap carpeting, stained from coffee spills and showing the marks where partitions had once stood. The lease had been signed only the previous week, and there was no staff, no furniture and no facilities – just me as the general manager of London's newest bank-to-be.

There was, however, a properly formed English company with a paid-up capital of £5 million, subscribed by four Italian banks. There was also an understanding that, once various formalities had been completed, the Bank of England would recognise this Italian-owned company as an English bank authorised for the purpose of foreign-exchange dealing, almost the highest grade of approval given by the regulatory authorities at that time. And at least the meeting would not have to take place with us all sitting cross-legged on the floor, which, I idly thought, would not go down well with a people that had suffered Ottoman rule for most of its history. Instead, I had persuaded some decorators working in the building to lend me some paint-spattered kitchen chairs, and acquired a table from one of the other offices. The IIB was just about ready for its first customer.

The Zastava meeting had originated in a conversation some nine months previously when, during the spring of 1971, the telephone operator of Hambros Bank rang to say:

'Mr Taylor, I'm sorry to interrupt you but there is someone who insists on speaking to you, but won't give me either his name or his company. He is some sort of foreigner, and I can't fully make out what he is saying, except that he claims he knows you.'

That was too much of a mystery for me to refuse. A few minutes later, I was even more mystified as I mulled over what my caller had said to me in heavily accented English:

'Mr Taylor, this is Alfredo Novarino. You remember we met in Athens last year. Please say nothing now, and don't mention this call to anyone in the bank, but just give me your home telephone number, and a time when I can speak to you. It is most important that we speak privately, and that you mention the matter to no one, as you too will understand after we have spoken.'

We had agreed to speak that evening, and I spent the afternoon wondering what it could be about. Novarino was obviously Italian from the name and accent and, though I had nothing to do with them, Hambros had strong Italian connections. I had certainly passed through Athens in the previous year, on my way back from Cyprus, where I had been setting up a joint-venture leasing company, and remembered that the bank's representative in Greece had given a lunch for me with a few Greek and foreign bankers. I could vaguely recall an Italian, but the conversation had been very general. Novarino was not only that banker, but also the chief foreign manager of the Bank of Sicily. His mission, however, had nothing to do with Hambros, but much with the changing nature of London banking. Novarino represented a Luxembourg holding company grandly entitled Anciennes Institutions de Credit Italiennes, which was to be the vehicle for the international ambitions of the four banks that owned it.

AICI's name was a statement of fact, for the Monte dei Pascei di Siena is the only bank in the world with unbroken written banking records stretching back to the 1450s, and the Istituto Bancario Sao Paolo di Torino is only a century or two younger. Piedmontese and Tuscan history and attitudes differ sharply, yet both had more in common with each other than with Banco di Sicilia and Banco di Napoli. Apparently modern foundations – for both had been formed after the reunification of Italy under the Savoy monarchy in the nineteenth century – their origins certainly went back to the Bourbon kingdom of the Two Sicilies, and maybe even to the earlier Spanish suzerainty over the whole of southern Italy. Though among the oldest, none was considered to be in the top rank of Italian banks, nor had any of them much international business even though the two southern banks had been 'banks of issue', printing and circulating their own currency notes until well into the 1920s.

Nevertheless, AICI intended to establish a bank in London, had already obtained permission from the Bank of Italy, and expected to have the agreement of the Bank of England as well. There was an elegant appropriateness about IIB's shareholders and their return to London, for medieval Italian bankers were the forerunners of today's international bankers. Though neither popes nor cardinals were renowned as prompt payers of banking debts, the Italians had little choice but to lend to them. Six hundred years ago, Rome was the centre of the financial world and bankers, then as now, had to dance to the tune of those who had power and needed money. These bankers managed the flow of wealth as tithes, or church taxes, flowed from every part of Europe to Rome.

This money had to be recycled, as bankers would do with Arab petrodollars in the 1970s, for economic life would grind to a deflationary halt if the papal vaults were allowed to demonetise Europe. English wool, the finest available, was the essential raw material for this banking process. The medieval equivalent of a petrodollar economy was England, as this wool was essential to the fashionable furnishings and robes that were required by the well-connected papal courtier, and the whole process of collecting, remitting and then reinvesting the cash flows of this trade was handled by Italian bankers. It was Italian banking partnerships in London that financed the collection and purchase of wool in England and then exported it to the spinning houses of Belgium. The London branches cooperated on this with their opposite numbers in Bruges, who financed the transformation of the raw wool into cloth. The Bruges banks then worked with their parent banks in Siena and Florence, and consigned this cloth to dyeing and tailoring firms throughout Italy. The final sale of the finished goods, to the cardinals and bishops who thronged the papal court, was financed by Roman bankers, or the Roman branches of the Tuscan banks.

The elegant head office of Monte dei Pascei now incorporates the palaces of two of the greatest of the Sienese banking families, both of whom were bankrupted by this trade. For England also became the Latin American borrower of its time, once the Plantagenet kings of England turned from diplomacy to war in the pursuit of their centuries-old dynastic quarrel with the Capetian kings of France. From the early 1300s, these monarchs were always in need of loans, and had perfected the art of political greenmail long before Japanese politicians and stock-market operators showed their mastery of similar tricks. Banking loans were the necessary grease for political favours, which, for Italian bankers, were licences to export English wool. So, half a millenium after the destruction of Italian banking dominance and fifty years after its own humbling by New York, London had regained its nineteenth-century power as the centre of the financial world. To bankers' surprise, this was the place where banks now had to be.

The delicacy of Novarino's approach was due to Hambros' high reputation among Italian bankers. The matter that he had to explore was whether, were the Italians to ask me to become general manager of their new bank, I would accept, and if my answer was 'no', would I please keep silent about the approach? Somewhat unfairly, the chief general manager of one of the English commercial banks referred to these four banks as 'nice enough homebodies but more like sun-drenched building societies than banks'. Furthermore, most London bankers assumed that the Bank of Sicily, with its head office in Palermo, had to be in thrall to the Mafia. (I was to discover that, like everything to do with Italy, that was much too simple an assumption.) Nevertheless, it took me no time at all to decide that I had been made an offer I could not refuse.

I did not make that too obvious, instead questioning Novarino about why the banks wanted to own a London bank, and what business they expected to do with it. The answer was that they did not know, which was why they were approaching me, an investment banker, rather than hiring a soon-to-retire general manager of one of the major English banks. I should tell them what to do. Whatever the chances of sharing Italian lending business with other London banks, my experience at Hambros persuaded me that there was a niche for the IIB, and that I could carve out a profitable business in London with these Italian connections. Even if I had not thought that, I would still have said 'yes' to Novarino. The appeal to my vanity and the challenges to my business imagination were much too tempting for me to contemplate refusal. The banking world was in ferment; the arrival of the US banks and the growth of the euromarkets had fertilised the stagnant pool of London banking, and I was ready to try my luck. What others had done, I also would do; my experience of working with the exceptionally young directorate of Hambros had persuaded me that nothing was impossible.

'Say nothing, just listen, but this is Rome. Can you come out next week? A ticket is on its way to you.'

The four Italians that I was to meet were neither the chairmen of the shareholding banks nor their general managers. They seemed to have no particular power base, yet they were important and influential, and would be the alternate directors to their chairmen on the board of IIB. Though they controlled, or influenced, the foreign department of their banks, they were not necessarily the nuts-and-bolts foreign managers. They were all university graduates, very different from the senior managers of British commercial banks, most of whom had left school at fifteen or so and gone straight into banking. Life is complicated for Italian bankers. Banks must be in Rome, because that is where political power resides. They have to be in Milan, because that's were business is done. And they dare not forget head office, because in such a particularist country as Italy, bankers who do not pander to the pride and interests of the home city do not last long. Office politics are a curse in British and American banks; in Italian banks, they have developed a centuries-old virulence. Not for nothing do senior Italian bankers fear to be side-lined as 'general manager in charge of the chairs'.

So these were also men of the world, with super-political antennae. After several months, I finally figured out that their chief function was to act as advisers to their chairmen and general managers, and to bridge the often yawning political chasms that opened up between the head office, Rome and Milan. It was not a tidy arrangement to an Anglo-Saxon mind, and it took me some time to understand it. But, as in much of the apparent chaos in Italy, underneath the surface confusion is an efficient and functional system. Except for the unfortunate connotation, the role of these four in each of their respective banks was not unlike the *consigliere* role of Tom Hagen in the film *The Godfather*.

The Novarino meeting had set me thinking furiously about the possible lines of business that could be created with an Anglo-Italian base, so I had prepared myself with some care, but, in the event, there were only three questions that mattered. The first was where to house the bank, the second was what to call it and the third was how much I wanted. These were all discussed over lunch, and that was that. All my carefully prepared policy papers, budgets and timing schedules were waved to one side.

'Thank you, and just leave them with us. You are the expert, of course, so we will take your advice and if we have any questions, we will come back to you after we have looked at them. Now that we have met, let's go for lunch, as there are matters we must agree immediately.'

One was the wine. I should have been alerted when we went to one of the few Roman restaurants that ape the French manner. Normally, Italian restaurants are about good food, of course, but also theatre. This is where they differ from the French: the main purpose of going out to eat in Italy is to allow the host to cut a good figure. The arrival of the menu, the description of the specialities, the inspection of the food, the chit-chat with the head waiter, the ordering of the meal, the discussion of the choice, the reconsideration of the order, and the final instructions — these are all much more important than the food itself. Dinner in Rome, I later discovered, was best enjoyed after a very late lunch. This was different — very quiet, very discreet, indeed very English except for the quality of service and food. So when asked whether I preferred French or Italian wine, I should have known better than to try to curry popularity. I have never seen four faces drop so sharply.

'Well, yes, Italian wine can be very nice,' said my host. 'You are no doubt right that some is very good, and the wine waiter will certainly have it. But, you know, even for me, an Italian who loves his country, it's difficult to say that any of our wine is as good as good French wine, and this restaurant does have some excellent burgundy. Are you really sure that you wouldn't prefer that instead?'

Spirits lifted, once that problem was out of the way, and serious discussion could take place on the bank's home. This was much more difficult. Space was at a premium in London, and the changing banking scene was typified by the building off Leadenhall Street. This plaza had been jointly developed, as their world headquarters, by the Peninsular & Oriental shipping company and the Commercial Union insurance company. They were examples of companies grown great and rich through London's stranglehold on world trade. That was slipping away for, with the decline of sterling, companies were quoting each other in dollars, and much of the ancillary business that lived off London's financing of world trade, like shipping and insurance, was also heading towards New York, where business denominated in dollars had to be settled. As those service companies declined, foreign banks were coming to London to take advantage of the new eurodollar markets and American banking ideas and deals. Now P&O had discovered that housing banks was more profitable than running ships, and were moving out their clerical staff to make room for bankers.

The Italians liked the P&O building, as I did, but this was in London's EC3 postal district. Blue-blooded banks had always had an EC2 address; it was shipping and insurance companies that slummed it in EC3, just a few minutes' walk further away from the halls of the Bank of England. There was space available in EC2, but neither so modern nor so attractive as that of the P&O Building. And there was a catch; the address was Love Lane, EC2. What did I think; could an Italian bank, with the British perception of the Italians, possibly have such an address? We chose the P&O.

A similar issue was the new bank's name. Would it be better to have a bland, anonymous name, or should the bank proclaim its origins and, if so, how? I was in no doubt in my own mind. Italians had created many of the techniques of international banking. There were plenty of anonymous London banks; we should be the first Italian bank in London – the Italian International Bank. Over coffee, I was discreetly asked how much I wanted and when I could start. I asked for £30,000, or nearly 50 per cent more than the £18,000 I was earning at Hambros, and kicked myself for not asking for more when it was immediately agreed.

My research was poor. Although what I was earning at Hambros was good for English banking, and the figure I had asked for was about par for American bankers in London, only when it was too late did I discover that Italian bankers were the highest paid in Europe. They also had pension arrangements that, as befitted the country that was home to Vatican City, were out of this world; if not spiritually, certainly as far as practical British actuaries were concerned. We agreed that I would start working for the IIB from January 1972, and that the key working relationships would be between me and my hosts. They promised to find some business to get the bank off to a good start, and this was the Zastava loan. The money would enable Zastava to buy some second-hand FIAT car-making machinery, and FIAT had offered this to Istituto Bancario San Paolo di Torino, its local bank and one of the four IIB share-holders. But I was far from happy at the thought of lending money to Zastava, particularly if this was an indication of what the Italians thought was a good start.

Zastava was a Yugoslav company, but that description of 'company' is the only thing it then had, or has now, in common with its Western equivalents. The enterprise manufactures outmoded FIAT models as the Yugo marque, and is owned in some strange way that I never fully understood by the Serbian part of what was then the Yugoslav Socialist Republic. But its workforce was also involved as managers and owners through Yugoslavia's co-partnership compromise between communism and capitalism; this in turn involved the local bank, also part of that same co-partnership arrangement. What was certain was that Zastava's accounts, which I had not seen then nor was likely to see, would be quite meaningless to a Western banker. I had no objective way of judging how likely it was that Zastava could pay the interest on the loan, let alone repay the principal. Anyway, the nature of 'socialist property', even though Yugoslavia was independent of the Soviet bloc, meant that bankers had little hope of redress from the courts if things went wrong. Should Zastava choose not to repay its loan, there was little that I or anyone else, including FIAT, could do about it.

My expectation that my knowledge of Serbo-Croat would be only slightly worse than the Zastava team's knowledge of English was quickly borne out by the initial introductions. But the business had been introduced by Cesare Romiti, the general manager of FIAT, and, since the Agnelli family who own FIAT had certainly replaced both pope and king in the financial affections of Italian bankers, that was a name of some power to my shareholders, and therefore to me as well. There was an Italian minder with the Yugoslavs, which was just as well, and he did most of the talking. It became apparent very early on that the Serbs knew what they wanted, had been promised that they could have it, and were not going back to

Belgrade without it. However eloquent I waxed about ten years
being much too long a maturity for a London banking loan, the
unattractiveness of non-repayment loans to banker and borrower,
or the economic cost of money, my only answer was four glassy
stares and a grunt. The grunt meant 'no', and Serbs obviously needed
no lessons from Soviet diplomats in how to say it.

The loan I was about to make is called a 'bullet' loan by American
bankers, an appropriate name for the damage they could do and
had, indeed, done to medieval Italian bankers. This was something
that I thought the Italians would have appreciated. The maturity, or
life of the loan, was much too long, and in too risky a part of the
world, for a deposit-taking bank. There was no certainty when, or
even if, the IIB would ever see its money again, while those who
lent to us would need to be repaid on time. True, provided that
things remained the same, we could be sure of renewing those
deposits by 'rolling them over' from another lender within the interbank markets. Yet one of the key lessons of banking history is that
bankers should never make such assumptions, for banking is always
changing.

As the negotiations progressed, I had been thinking of Zastava's
ties with its local bank. One of the easiest ways for a bank to make
money is by borrowing other people's and not paying for it. This is
known as the banking float. For centuries, it had been one of banking's secret gold mines, and I already knew that Zastava's Yugoslav
bank was going to be very slow in remitting interest to us every
three months, even assuming that they themselves got it on time
from Zastava. This quarterly payment would undoubtedly get 'lost'
in someone else's bank account as it made its way across the world,
for, since the loan was in dollars, the interest payments had to go
through the New York bank clearing system. Banks need bank
accounts, just as much as companies and individuals, and for much
the same reason. Bank accounts are the only satisfactory way of
holding cash, and it is the 'correspondent' accounts that banks hold
with each other that create the domestic and international payments
system – the mechanism by which manufacturers, trader and individuals pay each other.

Banks are prompt enough to debit customers when instructed by
them to pay out money, but are somewhat more lackadaisical when
it comes to crediting their accounts with money received. This is
the banking 'float', the interest-free money that banks create for
themselves. Zastava's bankers would have a field day with us because
they would argue, first that they themselves had not been paid by

Zastava, then that they were still awaiting authorisation from their central bank to send foreign currency abroad, and last that it had been sent to their correspondent bank in New York and they really could not understand why we had not been credited – but they would check the transfer and notify us. Such slow receipt of interest was going to cut into our lending margins, without even counting the staff and telex costs involved in chasing Zastava and its bank, and their correspondent banks, as we tried to track down the interest due. I was already thinking how we could modestly increase the money-market quote in order to claw back some, or even all, of this lost margin, when there was a final twist of the knife. As we agreed the terms of the loan, the Zastava spokesman asked about the reference bank. I expressed surprise, saying:

'Reference bank, what do we need a reference bank for? The price of money is clearly established in the London money markets, and published in the newspapers. Don't you trust the IIB to get you your money at the best price?'

Too damn right they don't trust us, I thought, any more than I trust them.

'Of course, it's not a matter of trust, but the bureaucracy back home. They don't understand these things too well, and one has to spell them out simply. It's so much easier just to say that we are borrowing at the Midland Bank rate. They know that bank, and that it understands the business of international banking.'

The name put paid to any hopes that I had. Midland, with the world's largest correspondent-banking network, could borrow at the very finest rates. We would have to be at our sharpest to match their reference rates, let alone make anything on them. Such mundane considerations of profit, however, were not going to stand in the way of Italian bankers doing business with FIAT, even if the relationship was at one remove.

'No, no, Russell – you worry much too much about profit. You know that we are public-sector banks, and that most of our profits go to charities, so what's a little more or less? We want IIB to be a prestige bank, and do business with the right sort of companies, and not worry about showing profits immediately. Anyway, it's a good interest spread, and once you've done this for FIAT, think of all the other business you'll get from them.'

The trouble was, I simply could not think of what the IIB could do for FIAT, and felt pretty sure that FIAT had no idea either. And though I could accept that the Italian banks didn't mind about profits – or, at least, not initially – I knew that the London banking community would be nowhere near so generous. Actually, I had not really expected profit considerations to get me out of the Zastava deal, but hoped instead to achieve this through a question of banking principle and the risk to the bank. I had recommended that the IIB follow US banking regulations and not lend more than 10 per cent of its equity capital to any one customer, whether that be a single company or a group of related companies. For IIB this meant a maximum loan of £500,000, or approximately $750,000 – far removed from Zastava's $7 million.

Another proposal was that the IIB should make only self-liquidating loans. At least with these, even though the loan is made over a period of years, the bank's cash flow is helped by the regular repayment of part of the capital as well as the interest on the loan. Also, the bank knows that it is getting repaid, rather than hoping either that the borrower is rich enough to repay on maturity, or that the money markets are buoyant enough to allow them to renew the loan with someone else. The Zastava loan was all that I most disliked – an unknown borrower a long way away, long-lasting and with no repayments, and no ancillary business. Also, the margin was too small to cover the bank's costs. My arguments with the Italians got me nowhere.

'Of course, Russell, you're the expert on banking in London, but you're looking at this too much from the London angle, for we know FIAT and you don't. They aren't going to let us down, and Zastava depend on them for their business. They'll see that Zastava make money and repay the loan. And there's bound to be some other business that comes from this. Even if you get nothing from Zastava or FIAT, think of what this will do for IIB's reputation in Italy. There are plenty of smaller Italian companies, but very good ones, that want to expand abroad and, when they see what you have done, they'll come to you. Anyway, we've told FIAT we'll do this, so it will be embarrassing to let them down, but you're the general manager, so you must decide.'

That last sentence meant that there was no way of avoiding the loan, which, though this would come to look like good business in later years, at the time was exceptionally generous to the borrower and particularly risky to the lender. Of course, the IIB was there to enable its shareholding banks to participate in the revolutionary changes that were taking place in banking, and the most obvious of these was medium-term lending, but I certainly reckoned that my shareholders had taken too deep a breath of London's revolutionary air.

*

It was American competition that was forcing change on London. European bankers considered that medium-term bank loans ought to be secured on a profit-earning asset, such as a ship or machine tool. There were, though, a few multinational companies sufficiently powerful, and with a good enough credit rating, to persuade any bank to lend to them for three to five years on their name alone. This lending was based on an analysis of the borrower's profitability, its ability to service the loan from cash flows, and the bank had to rely on the standing of the borrower for repayment, rather than tangible security such as a mortgage on property, or a legal charge giving the bank preferential rights to the company's assets in a bankruptcy. Most such companies were American, and these were rapidly becoming satiated with lending offers from their New York bankers.

Those that were not American were now becoming the target of Citibank, and its aggressive marketing upset not only Europeans, but also the US Mid-western and Californian banks. As American banks sent out marketing teams to solicit the larger British companies, this reduced both the volume and the profitability of Midland's domestic business, for between the late 1960s and the early 1970s some 30–40 per cent of British corporate lending would be captured by American banks. Since its unhappy experiences in revolutionary Russia, Midland had clung rigidly to its belief that bankers did best by sticking to their last, so Midland refused to compete with banks in their domestic markets. Instead, it considered itself to be 'banker to the world's banks' and, in consequence of this unique and single-minded policy, Midland dominated correspondent banking with some 20,000 banks within its network. This is the management of international banking relationships, in which each bank is responsible for creating international business from its own domestic customers.

Howard Thackstone, the general manager of Midland responsible for rethinking Midland's ideal of cooperative banking, once the euromarkets released the expansionary instincts of Citibank, developed the idea of consortium banks. Each of the shareholding partners could use these to defend itself and its customers from predatory American tactics, for the network of consortium banks was designed as a framework within which the partners could identify and strengthen their business relationships with the most important of their friends, while the jointly owned banks would each develop speciality services, not suitable for a commercial bank. Midland would thus be tied into those banks and countries that it considered essential to its future, while still not competing with them domestically. Midland and International Banks Limited (MAIBL) cemented the links between the banks and countries of the former white empire in 1963, while various partnership banks, ultimately linked under the umbrella of European Banks International Company (EBIC), were designed to do the same for Europe.

No one at that time believed that the single European market would take another two decades to come about. The genesis of IIB was the shareholders' fear for their domestic markets and their own future, and a consortium bank in London was an insurance policy against such competition. When I first started talking to the Italians, a dozen or so consortium banks were already working in London. Western American Bank, with Hambros as a minor shareholder, was one of the more interesting. It linked several of the leading Californian banks, who hoped to use WAB and London to protect their domestic American business from the American money-centre banks, and even to pre-empt their financial advantages and image with a London base. What WAB hoped to do to the New York banks, I thought IIB could do to the three big Milan banks.

Banks normally proclaim their function by their names, such as commercial or investment banks, private or savings banks, but only consortium banks were defined by the nature of their ownership rather than their business. In truth, no one really knew what they were for, except that everyone else was doing it. The imprimatur of respectability was given by the creation of Orion Bank in 1970, which linked six of the world's top ten banks together – including some of the Midland partners, for such is the incestuous nature of banking – and the stage was set for frenetic expansion. Over the first two to three years of the 1970s, consortium banks would more than double in number and, at their peak by the end of the decade, total over forty. Hand in hand with this went a corresponding increase in bank branches and investment banks. In 1960, London had 70 foreign banks, mainly American or the London stock-market-registered Commonwealth and British overseas banks. By 1970, and including the consortia, these had doubled to 158. When 1980 dawned, London had 358 foreign banks and 96 foreign-owned investment banks.

Loan syndication and consortium banking became the latest and hottest of London's banking fads. It appeared that the banking equivalent of perpetual motion had been discovered. The American banks in London created loans which they were prepared to share, or syndicate, with others, while the money markets supplied deposits of almost any size and maturity. Theoretically, banking simply required telephone, pen and ledger, and profits came automatically. Since banking nirvana had arrived, everyone wanted a share of the action, though no one was willing to bet their job on it, for the London banking scene did look just a little too good to be true.

This was all the justification needed for opening in London and, as I was to discover later, consortium banks were set up to 'test the water' at the prompting of the international-banking divisions of major domestic banks. Mercenaries were brought in to run them, because these could easily be discarded if things did not work out, with no loss of face to the managers of the shareholding banks. Equally, if the results were promising, the shareholding banks could benefit directly later, either by buying out the other partners of the London bank, selling out and setting up a London branch instead, or even having a branch and participation both. With this attitude, none of the partner banks suggested that I use their London representative office to hold my Zastava meeting. It took me some time to understand that, in setting up the IIB, there was safety in numbers for the bankers involved; sitting in with me on the Zastava loan, should it go wrong, would link them into my judgement. I was being paid to take risks, so I should do it on my own.

In the meantime, knowledge was being gained, and staff were being trained, and all at less cost than by acting alone. This was a sensible low-risk strategy for large commercial banks, and especially for their senior managers. By joining with other banks, the general manager of the international division protected his back, since, when many are responsible, none is accountable. As nearly all were to say in the years to come: 'It looked right, and everyone else was doing it. My God, look at the partners that were in with us, and who else had done it. How can anyone possibly blame me for the fact that things went wrong?'

Consortium banks were always a small minority of London's banks – which today number nearly 600 – but their influence was out of proportion to their numbers. Hundreds of bankers would learn about international lending through their service with the consortium banks, and their 'slam, bam, thank you, ma'am' approach to lending business. These banks, set up with no apparent function other than to make money by buying business, first established the idea that 'banking' could be divorced from underlying business reality, and that 'transactions' rather than 'relationships' were the bankers' objective. This was the hallmark of bank lending in the 1980s, for, by then, seconded staff had either returned to influence the loan policies of their parent banks, or consortium banks had been absorbed back into the international division.

Commercial banking should be simple, safe and profitable. Everyone, business manager or individual, faces timing gaps between receiving money and spending it. Commercial bankers act as intermediaries between those who have money and are not using it now, and those needing it now and not having any; they simply recycle this money between known customers. Since every trade has its own particular pattern of cash movements, the bank lends the money of those customers temporarily flush to those that are short, and commercial banks, provided they have a good mix of business clients, can finance their lending from their customers' own funds. This lending is reasonably secure, since most banks only lend to companies whose accounts, over the year, they know will go from the black to the red and back to the black again. This recycling process is helped because individual customers, and service businesses like lawyers and accountants, generally deposit much more money with the bank than they ever borrow. Little, if any, interest is paid on these deposit balances. Once, only those with a fair amount of money were welcomed as customers. Service was both personal and good, and this is the business that has kept C. Hoares & Company safe, profitable and family-controlled for over three centuries.

The medium-term loan was imported into London by Citibank. After the 1930s crash, many large US corporations shunned their commercial banks, traumatised as they had been by intemperate demands for repayment during the crisis. They concentrated on the bond markets instead, now denied to commercial banks, so medium-term loans were an opportunity for commercial banks to calm their customers' fears, and compete again with the investment banks. The Fed agreed, in 1935, to rediscount formally contracted term loans, and no longer to categorise these as 'slow' or nonperforming loans, thus making them more liquid and more attractive as assets. This made eminent sense, for commercial bankers fool themselves to some extent about the self-liquidating nature of their loans. Contractually, nearly all loans are repayable on demand or within one year, but, practically, lending banker and borrower alike accept this as whitewash, designed to keep the credit committee and board of the bank happy that they are not committing banking's original sin of borrowing short and lending long.

This maturity pattern had always been true of much American

and German lending, but became more obviously so in Britain when, during the interwar years, industry became larger and more capital-intensive. More and more, bank loans were rolled over from year to year, for they no longer financed working capital, but capital investment. Postwar reconstruction, combined with the freeing of international trade, gave a boost to this market, while Wall Street banks saw medium-term lending as the way to regain lost business more profitably. Bankers could ask for a higher interest spread – or gross profit compared to the cost of money – for medium-term loans, which, like bonds, could have a life of up to ten years. Business liked these loans, too, for repayment terms were tailored to the income that the borrower would create from the investment, and they were quicker and cheaper than borrowing in the securities markets.

American lending practices began to colonise London from the 1970s onwards and, had Zastava been a normal borrower, I would have whipped the Serbs along to the bank's lawyers, who would have produced a medium-term loan agreement, running to twenty or thirty pages. Though many of these paragraphs might have been otiose – boilerplating is the trade name – all derive from those unfortunate occasions when banks have lost money as a result of omitting them, or not even realising that there was a risk. The resulting documents are weighty and impressive, and give the lenders considerable power over the manner in which borrowers conduct their financial affairs. Should the borrower then do something that the banks don't like – such as spending the borrowed money in unauthorised ways, giving other lenders better security or just losing too much money as a company – then the banks can declare an 'event of default', and demand immediate repayment of the loan.

Some far-sighted London Americans, mainly Morgan bankers, were expressing doubts as early as 1970 about London's ability to understand the philosophy that underlay the credit assessment of American medium-term credits; with my experience at Hambros, I could only agree with them, since Zastava failed on every count. Loan agreements assume a commercial borrower, of course, and commercial courts in which to pursue execution of a legal contract, neither of which I had with Zastava, and these were equally absent from the East European-country loans that had become all the rage in London. So, rather than wasting the bank's money on lawyers – the Serbs had already refused to pay the bank's costs – the deal was done on slim English banking lines, which meant a letter from the bank to the customer, covering the germane points in a few succinct paragraphs.

Zastava needed medium-term finance, but the normal route via the bond markets was out because neither shareholders nor bondholders were recognised by Yugoslav law, and so would have no legal rights. The same was true for any foreign bank lender, which was why I was so unenthusiastic about this Italian present to the IIB. Yet a foreign bank loan was its only hope, for its own bank was no good, since it could only lend Yugoslav dinars while FIAT wanted money that it could use, like American dollars. There was a safe way, and this was the business that I had suggested that the IIB do in partnership with its shareholders. Investment banks everywhere were exploiting national policy to sell the country's capital goods more successfully than anyone else. This had, as always, come down to finance; for example, if Britain wanted to sell its ships to Norwegian shipowners, British yards had to offer not only competitive prices and delivery dates, but also attractive financial terms. So all governments, including America's, had schemes to subsidise and guarantee medium-term loans to finance export orders.

Cheap finance was the essential bribe that persuaded customers to buy European, and not American, machine tools or British, and not Swedish, ships. This had been a godsend to London merchant banks, which had immediately used their contacts and skills, and other people's money, to make such loans to the politically risky countries of Eastern Europe, or the financially risky ones of Asia and South America. This expertise was not as lender to the buyer, as was intended for IIB, but as financial arrangers to the manufacturer of the goods. The merchant bank took a handsome fee for negotiating and arranging the loan; the government guaranteed – and generally subsidised – the commercial banks who actually did the lending. These in turn were grateful to the merchant bank for being given risk-free business that made them look good in the eyes of their exporting customers. The taxpayer, theoretically, gained from the extra employment created by these exports.

Hambros managed such Export Credit Guarantee Department funds for British shipbuilders, and the fees it earned were a very handsome return on the detailed, and occasionally risky, paperwork that this entailed. I wanted to establish a similar business base for the IIB. FIAT had already made one profit out of the equipment it was selling, so it could have financed its sale to Zastava itself, either from its own cash resources or by borrowing further money in its own name. Italy had a similar system of export guarantees, and FIAT could undoubtedly have arranged such an export-credit guarantee. There might have been a problem with Italian government guarantees, since FIAT was getting a second lease of life out of this outdated manufacturing plant by selling it to Zastava, and ECGD-type money was usually available for new equipment. There are always ways to do things, however, if the willingness is there; investment bankers are paid to find the answer. FIAT could have worked with IIB and the shareholders to find a more elegant solution to the Zastava loan, but the truth was that it had no confidence in any of us, and was not prepared to make the effort.

True, IIB was specifically intended to be different from its shareholders as a consortium bank, but FIAT just wanted someone else to take the Yugoslav credit risk. IIB was the chosen innocent, being assumed to know no better, and more than willing to roll over for FIAT. Amazingly, and compared to the deals that were later done in the London market, the Zastava loan was quality business. The borrower existed, had been in business since 1853, and was making a product that people wanted. The loan bought actual machinery, which was used to make cars, while FIAT's involvement meant that little, if any, of the money went walkabout into the Serbs' Swiss bank accounts. Finally, the Italians were right about FIAT, and Zastava did repay.

11

Going for the Riband

'The pursuit of fashion to the point of mania has indeed been
the hallmark of financial institutions – and especially banks –
throughout the ages.'

Sir Kit McMahon, deputy governor of the Bank
of England and, later, chairman of the Midland Bank.

'I DON'T KNOW WHAT you, or the Italians, think that you can
do with this bank, but I will give you whatever help I can. This
may be more keeping them from each other's throats, and off your
back, than anything else, but one thing I must make clear. I'm too
old to risk my reputation, and I don't want anything to go wrong,
so I expect you to follow a very cautious approach.'

Lord Cobbold, who had been ennobled for his work with the
Bank of England, had called me to the office he maintained there as
a former governor helping with its history, and explained that he
had accepted the chairmanship of the IIB because of his liking for
Italy and Italians. He had spent several happy years in Milan during
the 1930s, when he had been sent by its British shareholders to
rescue a small Italian bank. That was a fair enough attitude, so I
willingly acquiesced, though my real feeling was that his reputation
had been made, while mine was still to make. If anything was to go
wrong – and I was determined that it would not – it would hurt me
more than him.

We both agreed the need for caution, particularly with the new
medium-term loans, and his practical experience and my theoretical
knowledge meant that both of us regarded country lending,
especially to Latin American countries, as well-proven banking
poison. But both of us were living in a dream world, for bankers, even
central bankers, are affected by general economic conditions. Though
banking controls had restricted the super-boom of the 1950s, the
emergence of the unsecured money markets during the 1960s
enabled bankers to sidestep central banks while the opportunities to

profit from the reconstruction remained exceptional. This was another decade lost to British industry, as politicians spent five years arguing about an overvalued currency, but everywhere else the pace of economic growth quickened. The financial bubble went international and gained in strength, and its bursting in 1974 would blow us all away.

Naturally, the Bank of England had taken a close interest in my appointment, since they were about to consign the reputation of a former governor to my care, and James Keogh had already called me for an interview. I knew him from earlier discussions about Hambros' finance-company subsidiary for, as head of the Bank's Discount Office, he was responsible for monitoring the health of the money markets. Among many other duties, this meant supervising the dozens of new banks setting up to take advantage of the euromarkets. The Bank remained extremely jealous of its control of the domestic banking market, but it took the view that well-established foreign banks knew what they were doing. This ensured, in the words of a senior American banker, that 'London was a very warm place for doing business'. Keogh certainly felt warmth towards IIB, for his limp came from a wound taken during the 1944 Italian campaign; he loved Italy, spoke the language well, and delighted in telling me that the IIB shareholders were the older-established *bancos* rather than the parvenu *bancas*.

Renowned for his dry wit and convivial nature, Keogh assured me that IIB, like all the other major international banks which he supervised, could do what we liked provided only that it was not specifically prohibited by the law and that, whatever we did, we 'shouldn't do it in the streets and frighten the horses'. Keogh's attitude towards IIB was perfectly understandable. A considerable number of new British banks, emerging by the dozen during the 1960s, were simple moneylenders of the Whyte, Gasc type. Keogh, with a department of only fifteen in total, was too occupied with these, and the few recalcitrant banks that he described as his 'slum properties', to have much time for the new international banks. Rightly, he considered the share-owning banks, and therefore their offspring, as 'undoubted for their obligations'.

Other consortium banks might have a board of directors consisting of senior bankers from the parent banks and an English banker or two, but the IIB was different. Machiavelli was an unsuccessful Florentine civil servant whose clear-eyed description of how men actually behave, as opposed to how they say they do, or believe they ought to, has made him a byword for devious thinking. But complex political manoeuvres have always been vital for personal and institutional survival in Italy, which, more often than not, has been divided not only by its own fundamental differences, but also by the ambitions of a variety of foreign rulers. So the IIB had to have a board that could infiltrate every nook of British life and chosen, wherever possible, from those who had already proven themselves as successful survivors.

Banking was represented by Cobbold, a man as close to God as the Italians could find, for he knew the Italian central-banking establishment through the meetings of the Bank for International Settlements. This is the Basel-based 'bank for central banks' and is, as the Italians well knew, the world's most exclusive banking club. But I reckoned that Cobbold was of considerable practical value to IIB's image, for forex (foreign exchange) success would be essential to the IIB, and would enable an Italian bank to be taken seriously. Foreign-exchange dealing is the London banking skill *par excellence*, and success would ensure that the IIB would have no funding problems. This was vital, and the close connections between the forex market and the eurodeposit markets would resolve any problem. So, as I listened to the Italians outline their plans for the board, I expressed no objections. My only concern was expense, for the Italians do things in style and the people they had chosen knew how to spend money, but I kept those views to myself.

There had to be a business representative, for the IIB was, after all, a bank, and business introductions from board members, though not mandatory, could be useful. There could only be one choice. Charles Forte, not yet ennobled, was the leading if not the only internationally known Anglo-Italian businessman. The Trust House Forte group was, and is, one of the largest hotel groups in the world, with substantial investments in America as well as Europe. Forte was proud of his Italian and Scottish ancestry, and delighted to help the Italians. However, neither banking nor business connections were as important as politics, for, in Italy, banking and politics are Siamese twins. The positions of chairman, board director and general manager of hundreds of Italian banks are the gift of particular factions of one or other of the main political parties. So the IIB had to have a politician, if for nothing else than to keep company with the chairman of the four shareholding banks, and the choice was James Callaghan. As it happened, Callaghan had some banking experience, and was to get more.

Sir Julian Hodge, once known as the 'usurer of the valleys' for his success in anticipating the consumer society, with its demand for credit, had recently sold his finance and personal-loan business to Standard Chartered Bank, and was then negotiating with the First National Bank of Chicago to achieve his dearest wish – a proper bank for Wales. Hodge was an important supporter of the Labour Party machine in South Wales, known to irreverent journalists as the 'Taffia', and Callaghan was one of its senior members. Callaghan joined the board of this new Commercial Bank of Wales, which is now, after some vicissitudes, an independent subsidiary of the Bank of Scotland. However, his real importance to the Italians was as a former home secretary and chancellor; though still in the future, the election of a Labour government in 1974 would make him foreign secretary and later prime minister. Such promotion justified even more, to Italians, the original choice of Callaghan.

There were four Italian directors, so there had to be four Britons, and a court connection would obviously complete the envelopment of British society. Such an appointment was important for *bella figura* and, who knows, the introduction of fashionable Britons needing mortgages with which to buy their Tuscan villas, but there Italian charm failed. A senior courtier had been sounded out, and had shown interest, but finally refused the appointment. Another Briton was needed, so Cobbold came up with a more appropriate candidate. Rather than the court, Rupert Raw represented bureaucracy, much the greater of the two powers today. After some years with the Organisation of Economic Co-operation and Development in Paris, Raw had joined the administrative staff of the Bank of England at Cobbold's request. Disappointed in his hopes of becoming one of the four executive directors of the Bank, Raw was promised the IIB succession by Cobbold; the latter had made it clear that he intended to resign on his seventieth birthday.

Raw, who had been parachuted into Yugoslavia during his service with SOE, was typical of the 'British imperial servant' and a true Mr Buggins. Small and wiry, he never wore, as I remember, anything but a pinstriped suit and an old Etonian tie so faded and dirty that it looked more like a bootlace. After one long day with the Italians, and before going out for dinner, Raw asked me whether the party was to be formal or informal. Informal, I said, and an hour later Raw came down the stairs, dressed exactly as he had been all day, but with black shoes exchanged for brown suede, almost as ancient as his tie. Raw's attempts to understand the foreign-exchange markets and the changing nature of London banking risk drove nearly everyone mad, for he had the true bureaucrat's approach. The letter was everything, the underlying reality of no importance. Whenever he came into my office, waving one of my draft reports, I knew I was in for several hours of detailed analysis of where exactly the coma should go, and should there not be a semicolon there, rather than a full stop?

Raw sometimes caught me smiling secretly at these sessions, but I could never tell him that he reminded me of the jaundiced comment of an industrialist friend whom I had helped in his takeover of a quoted competitor. He had remarked of the company secretary, with whom he was stuck by his American minority shareholders, that 'he's someone who needs an important job, and where his penchant for details will be invaluable. I have just the thing. The Bertram Mills circus needs someone to walk behind their elephant, cleaning up after it with a mustard spoon'. Privately, I wondered what value any of the board other than Cobbold might be, for what IIB needed was business introductions, and these would come from the shareholders or from nowhere.

The bank was already paying well over £100,000 in rent and property taxes, and staff costs would come to much more than that. The board, much good though it did my ego, wasn't cheap either. The IIB was committed to paying £8,000 a year to each director and £12,000 to the chairman. Since the salary of a Member of Parliament was only £4,250 p.a. at this time, IIB's contribution to offsetting the effects of inflation was welcome to all the English directors, particularly since, with the help of AICI, we were also able to pay much of this abroad, and so tax-free. London was a tax paradise for nonresidents, and US bankers had even better arrangements to avoid British tax, so I felt no compunction in arranging IIB's affairs in the most tax-efficient way, even if this was costly in professional fees.

There were other expenses, too, such as first-class airfares to and from Italy. London, together with Harrods, had an irresistible fascination for the Italian psyche, so, what with one thing and another, we ended up with board meetings, or meetings of the executive committee of the board, every two months or so. As a friend, a senior manager with the Royal Bank of Canada, remarked to me much later: 'We bankers are great at building up the overhead fat, but find it almost impossible to slim when conditions change and profits are hard to earn.' That remark was all too close to my own experience and soon, whatever my initial intentions, the IIB had to lend, if it was to cover its overheads.

The Bank of England considered itself a supervisor, rather than a regulator based on banking law. Supervision had developed out of the Bank's historical experience, which saw banking as a particularly attractive self-supportive business club, whose members were linked by school, university, regiment and family ties. New members, like the IIB, needed a proper family background, and their managers had to be accepted by their peers within the banking community. Bankers were assumed to know correct behaviour and, within these limits, were allowed to do whatever they wished. The discount office was the club secretary, ensuring that members followed such rules as there were. Those who transgressed, by attempting transactions outside their skills or doing too much on their capital, were politely, but firmly, told to mend their ways. Repeated failure to follow the advice of the Bank once had grave consequences, for its displeasure would be communicated to others in the market. These would then become reluctant to deal with the offender since, if and when a financial crisis hit the market, its securities would no longer be accepted by the Bank as 'good security' for rediscount.

Relationships between banks, or between banks and their customers, were based on the English common-law principle of 'buyer beware', but also backed up by the strict responsibilities laid on banks through the law of agency. Should neither this nor the warnings of the Bank suffice to stifle the greed of club members, then other bankers, to protect their own good names, would effectively destroy the offending business by blackballing its principals. The Bank's supervisory authority had little effect on the commercial banks, for their financial strength made the Bank's threats an irrelevance, but the Bank exerted its control through various laws designed from 1914 onwards to protect the currency and restrict the total of bank lending. Supervision worked with most foreign banks; Americans were overawed by the Bank's history, and confused by its urbane and indirect remonstrations, while the Europeans and Japanese were convinced that this apparent lack of rigour hid draconian and terrifying powers. Either way, the Bank was able to achieve its aims, for it was dealing with institutions that were long-established and important banks in their own countries, and that knew the foibles of their own regulators.

These institutions found the supervisory approach in London a refreshing change from the regulatory attitude of their domestic authorities. Originally based on the state-centred approach of continental European capitalism, regulation had received an enormous boost with the 1933 American banking reforms. Banking liquidity within the American banking system comes from the 'money centres', of which New York was by far the most important, and the major Wall Street banks insured each other against failure through the New York Clearing House. This, like the Bank, protected only members in good standing within the club, but banking reform changed all that. Rather than relying on banking common sense and 'buyer beware', the law established barriers between different types of banking, and what business was permissible for each type. Regulation says: 'Unless the law specifically says that banks can do this, you can't do it, even if technology, customer needs or competition have changed since the law was first written, and we will ensure that you comply by inspecting your business, and your books, at times of our choice.'

The intention of regulation is to protect the public from incompetent or dishonest banks, and bankers from themselves. At some stage, the Bank would have been forced to take a closer look at the books of the foreign banks it was supervising, and become more of a regulator. Freedom from their own banking laws, together with the overflowing cornucopia of the money markets, made most foreign bankers in London a trifle dizzy. Just as much as the euromarkets undercut the interest-rate control of America's Fed, they also weakened the authority of the Bank. Who would care about its displeasure, if the euromarkets ignored it and British banks were run by people who were quite unclubbable? Indeed, the secondary banks were doing exceptionally well because the Bank, by refusing to recognise banking qualifications granted by the Department of Trade and Industry, ensured that these escaped the lending controls that were hampering the competitiveness of British banks.

Keogh perceived that these secondary banks, though not recognised by the Bank as such, were trading on the name of 'bank', using this illicitly borrowed reputation to borrow unsecured from the money markets. Any failure on their part was bound to reflect badly on London banking, for it was not only banks that used these markets; overseas governments, British local-government authorities, multinational companies and, indeed, any organisation with spare cash were now active dealers. Refusing to supervise these distasteful interlopers, the Bank had no choice but to eliminate them, if it was to preserve its delicate political balancing act. Its own constituents were becoming restless, as these new banks stole their profits, but the Bank had no authority over the DTI. Their authorisation was extremely limited, simply freeing new-style money lenders, such as car-finance companies and the like, from the simple but effective restrictions of the nineteenth-century Moneylenders Act.

But, once bank status had been granted, no one could prevent these firms from proclaiming themselves 'bankers'. Even today, this is a valuable image to have, and then it was truly powerful.

The Bank could not appeal to its political masters, since its policy was based on denying that it had any. The Labour Party had never forgiven the Bank for its part in the series of mishaps and misunderstandings that had split the 1931 Labour government, but remembered instead the Sicilian saying that 'revenge is a dish best eaten cold'. The first action of the victorious 1945 Labour government was to exact payment for that earlier humiliation, by nationalising the Bank in 1946. Since it had been at least half a century since the Bank had shown any concern for its shareholders' interests, a little thing like nationalisation wasn't going to faze its management. Finely honed bureaucratic techniques immediately saw off the Treasury, its new master, by terrifying ministers.

The Bank argued that only it really understood banking, that the 'invisible earnings' of the banking industry were an important component to running a surplus on the country's trading account with the rest of the world, and that this was central to the successful management of sterling. The war had left as its legacy a vast overhang of sterling debts, and Britain was like an illiquid bank. Given time, the country could pay, but without successful management of the currency, and confidence that there would be no devaluation, there would be a run by the holders of sterling balances. The country, just like a bank, would be forced to renege on its international debts, and admit to bankruptcy. The events of 1931 were too sharp a memory for any Labour minister to disregard that warning. So, unlike virtually every other country in the world, Britain allowed its banking policy to become insulated from politics. The Bank decided what would happen, when and why, and ministers were informed after the event, if at all. This suited everyone, except ambitious Treasury officials, and in 1971 the Bank completely rewrote the rules of the banking game.

The Bank of England's policy known as 'Competition and Credit Control' swept away virtually all the banking controls, which had been first introduced in the crisis of 1914 and had been developed and strengthened over the following decades. The only major restriction that remained was exchange control, which restricted banks' use of currencies other than sterling. The Bank voluntarily gave up its direction over how much domestic banks could lend and to whom, and decreed that in future only cost-efficiency would count. The issue of banking efficiency, to which CCC was a response, had first arisen in the early 1900s, and the English answer then was the same as Citibank was following half a century later – increase the range of banking services offered, widen the geographical base or, even better, do both. Banking cannibalism had ceased to be an option for the English banks in 1920 but, fortunately, beneath the breast of every banker beats the heart of a moneylender.

When, rather against his better judgement, Cobbold allowed banks to buy hire-purchase companies in 1958, there followed an orgy of branch expansion and personal lending. Even Hambros bought a West Country finance company, and the fight for market share that followed had lessons for the future, though none of us bothered with them at the time. Midland's own tough credit controls and efficient administration stood it in good stead, as competitors pushed for market share by passing out signed, but blank, cheque books to second-hand car salesmen. The consequent multimillion-pound losses which surfaced from 1960 onwards did no good to English bank rankings, though they certainly justified Cobbold's misgivings, nor did the building-up of two distinct banking distribution networks do much for banking costs.

Citibank, like other American banks, regarded car finance as basic commercial-banking business, to be done by the branches rather than through separate finance companies. Head office dealt with the manufacturer, encouraging the use of the bank's new computer for payroll services, and persuading employees to be paid by cheque rather than cash. The branches lent money to the dealers, so that they could fill their showrooms with the new models, while the individual branch customer was encouraged to take out personal loans and buy a new car with the money. Even this virtuous circle of banking business was threatened by technology, and the American equivalent of the British car-finance debacle was the credit-card wars of the late 1960s.

The plastic credit card is the computer's substitute for the current account and the bank clerk, so bankers were bound to regard it with some ambivalence. But whatever its long-term impact on banking's future might be, its immediate promise was large new volumes of highly priced consumer loans. Citibank's plastic general was Thomas Wilcox, then battling for the succession to Moore's crown with Walter Wriston. As in Britain, credit control and administration collapsed under the weight of enthusiastic marketing programmes, as unsolicited credit cards with pre-set spending limits of several thousand dollars were mailed to all and sundry; for America's small and not-so-small crooks, Santa Claus arrived early and stayed late in the 1960s.

By the 1970s, the answer to banking profitability was greater professionalism, not wider coverage and, with CCC in place, the Bank had every expectation that its charges would utterly destroy the DTI-registered banks. This was good theory, for it had worked in Canada, and it might have worked in Britain, had bankers ever needed to analyse their internal profitability. But analysis was something the Bank was good at, not its charges, for bankers still operated within a business oligopoly protected by a functional monopoly of skill and knowledge. The new policy was introduced by the Bank's first governor to be promoted from its own ranks, an example of meritocracy by the Labour government in power at the time which is only now being repeated, and it ignored the practical warnings of bankers. Jocelyn Hambro protested that the new banks, and the market, needed time to digest the changes brought about by the euromarkets. While supporting the principle, he recommended that the reforms be eased in over a period of time, rather than as a 'Big Bang'.

These were well-based warnings, for Hambros was close to some of the more successful of these new banks, all of whom would fail during the coming crisis. The Bank also failed to take account of the possibility of a financial bubble, financed through the euromarkets, or to think through the effect of an earlier change in its policy which might encourage such overexpansion of lending. In 1970 the Bank had insisted that the commercial banks disclose their true profit and reserve figures, in return for being allowed to merge the last nine English commercial banks into four. Midland discovered it was no longer top of the heap but only slightly above Lloyds, while Barclays and National Westminster were well placed to challenge each other for the top spot. Three of the banks that disappeared – Martins, District and Williams Deacons – were headquartered in the North, and their loss would weaken still further the English banking commitment to industry and small and medium-sized businesses.

The result of CCC was quite unintended, and certainly not expected by the Bank; supervised banks outbid the DTI-authorised moneylenders in their enthusiasm for property lending, as they unleashed a competitive frenzy for league-table dominance. The 1974 British banking and property crisis was part of a worldwide bubble, and it not only swept away many of the new banks, but also destroyed the Bank's mystique. Keogh was sacrificed to the enraged politicians, and exiled from an institution that he loved, but even this failed to save his superiors from their own mistakes. The

Treasury moved in, the Bank was forced to adopt the 1979 banking law, and the politicians required the Bank to become more of a regulator than a supervisor.

Turning the IIB into a bank meant impressing other London banks and persuading them to lend IIB the money that it needed, if it was to lend to others. Of course, it was possible that the shareholders would borrow in their own name, and pass the funds on to us. Several banks in London operated in this way, but it seemed unlikely that IIB would. The Italians had stressed to me that: 'Of course, Russell, we'll help you all we can, but, with your experience, you'll know how to use the London markets much better than we do.'

I had, correctly, as events were to prove, interpreted this as meaning: 'You're on your own; if we've got problems of our own, don't expect any help from us if you can't fund yourself.'

Actually, this attitude of the shareholders did not break my heart, I had very definite ideas on how IIB was going to raise its money, and I reckoned that using the money markets was going to be significantly cheaper than borrowing directly from another bank, particularly if it was a shareholder. My years in the City had made me rather cautious about relying on shareholder good will, even though Italian family feeling might be stronger than the English variety. The importance of money, and its cost, was that the maximum IIB could lend would be £50 million; though I hoped to gear the bank at 20:1, I intended to keep at least half of that in quickly realisable assets. This interbank lending would make something, and I had ideas on how to make it a worthwhile something, but it would always be a speculative and variable source of earnings, and not one that I could rely on.

The bank's only certain income would come from its capital or its loan portfolio, and for that I could only assume a margin of 1 per cent. I could not rely on any earnings from the capital, for much of this was bound to disappear into necessary, but definitely non-earning, assets like furniture and office partitions. The cost of the office would be more than averagely expensive, since forex dealing-room equipment was expensive even then, and we were going to buy the best. The only way to establish IIB as a borrower in the money markets was to establish it as a forex dealer, which also meant opening correspondent banking accounts in New York and Milan, for, since we would specialise in the dollar/lire markets, we needed clearing accounts in both places. Such 'nostro' and 'vostro' accounts – the names given them by the Italian bankers, such as the

Medicis, at the time that they first developed international forex dealing – do not pay interest, and do require substantial credit balances and were thus very profitable to banks, like Midland, with a substantial correspondent banking connection.

Little enough of that £5 million would be left free after fitting out the office, paying initial expenses, covering the initial revenue losses, opening a non-interest-paying account with the Bank of England, and holding the low-yielding reserve assets required by the central bank. That was tough enough, but what neither I nor most other bankers of the time recognised was the effect of inflation on banking balance sheets. The pricing of international loans assumed that banks had no cost problems whatsoever, yet this was not true of banks in an inflationary world. Inflation averaged 15 per cent during the 1970s, which meant that the value of our capital was halving every four to five years. The best solution was to develop a substantial fee-earning business, requiring no banking capital, or to increase the capital base. IIB's capital was doubled to £10 million in 1974, but the problem persisted for banking generally, and its after effects would influence banking policies throughout the 1980s.

If bank gearing remained the same, together with earnings on the assets, every year salary and property costs would swallow up a greater proportion of this. Bankers could either emulate the jujube bird, running around in ever decreasing circles until we disappeared in a puff of smoke, or increase gearing and lending. Since bankers needed a new supply of borrowers, country borrowers appeared on cue. Few could contemplate banking default in a world of Cold War and euromarkets, and Citibank made sure that its syndicated loan was redesigned to suit the vanity of politicians and the needs of eurobanks. Such loans, which totalled less than $5 billion in 1970, increased to an annual demand of $133 billion by 1981. They seemed a banker's dream in size and simplicity; in 1982, when the major borrowing countries of Mexico, Brazil and Argentina defaulted, that dream turned into a nightmare even as loans hit a record total of over $220 billion.

Citibank was exceptionally well placed to negotiate such loans, for it owned large commercial and savings banks in many Latin American countries, and acted as the New York clearer for the central banks and treasuries of nearly all of them. Though increased banking capacity had forced lending margins down to inadequate levels on good corporate business, better margins could be obtained on these country loans. The modest lending spreads of the loan originators were boosted by their negotiating fees, while the banks that bought them took equal comfort from the thought that, if Citibank was putting name and money behind the loan, then the borrower must be good. The 1974 crisis was appreciated as an opportunity by Wriston, and Citibank quickly became the foremost bank in developing country lending. It suited US foreign economic policy, because the quintupling of the oil price was as grave a threat to the prosperity of the world as anything that had happened since 1930. It was a tax by the undeveloped – and therefore low-spending – Middle East on the developed world, for oil had already become the basis of all industrial costs, affecting transport, energy creation and manufacturing equally.

The oil-price increase was like an unexpected and enormous tax hike, and was highly deflationary. It was essential that these enforced savings be recycled for the benefit of Western industry but, rather than increasing official aid to both developed and developing countries hit by the price hike, US politicians and officials alike encouraged the banks to recycle these petrodollars as the quickest and least contentious way of maintaining prosperity. No government wished to upset its constituents by increasing aid to the Third World, but loans would do as well as grants, since either would be spent on Western goods. Nevertheless, banks still faced a catch–22 situation, and one that I endlessly discussed with Jinx Grafftey-Smith, a banking friend who had left Samuel Montagu to run the Wallace Brothers Bank. The latter was theoretically better placed than the IIB, for Wallace resulted from the merger of the financial activities of a substantial nineteenth-century Indian merchanting house with those of the similar and equally long-established Sassoon Banking business, but in fact we both had the same problem.

Neither of us had much experience of, nor any liking for, commercial lending, and each was attempting to build a typical London merchant bank. Traditionally, these exploited family or business connections to develop specialist markets, some based on lending or guarantees, some on dealing and others, such as advising the rich, producing fees and relatively cheap deposits. Once such a business was developed, we would both have a deposit float from this business base, as well as some cheap current-account balances. This would equalise our competitive position with long-established banks, who could reckon on a spread of some 2–3 per cent between their internal cost of money and what their marginal needs cost them to buy in the markets.

Though Wallace could not initially deal in foreign exchange, its bills were accepted by the Bank of England as 'fine bank bills', a market status equivalent to that of an acceptance-house credit. Wallace was a century-old customer of the Bank of England. With this reputation, it was able to build a profitable sterling-dealing business in trade bills and sterling bank CDs. While IIB was developing its forex business and a Channel Island-based private banking operation, Wallace was creating a London sterling-dealing and investment-management business. Both dealing and advisory activities take time to become profitable and, with staff and property costs representing the bulk of our non-interest overhead costs, we needed a source of immediate income, for inflation was crucifying both of us. The worst year was 1975, when the year-on-year increase in prices was 25 per cent, but over the decade as a whole the annual rise averaged 15 per cent.

Compound interest normally works in favour of bankers, and a 15 per cent compound rate can double capital every four years or so. But inflation is a negative rate of interest, and banking has no 'product' on which it can raise the price, but only money-denominated capital which determines how much a bank can lend or deal. Compounding inflation on to a purely financial business turned this into banking's death by a thousand daily cuts. Until our businesses were established, we had to buy every penny of our money from the money markets, and each of us reckoned that, if we were to lend, we needed a spread of at least 1 per cent to cover our basic costs, another 0.5–1 per cent to cover likely bad debts and show a profit, and another 0.5 per cent to account for funding risk, or the times that we would find it difficult to borrow in the market at the planned rate. But the market rate for syndicated loans was less than 0.75 per cent and falling, and with no fees for anyone except the originating banks, like Citibank for Latin America, or the big German banks for the Soviet-bloc countries.

Whatever the conditions in the market, we had to lend, for additional income was essential to staunch the capital bleeding and, despite our investment-banking backgrounds, both of us accepted the common assumption that banks are there to lend. Yet loans that yielded 2–3 per cent over the cost of money were, by definition, dangerous loans, so if we lent and lost, we worsened our capital position, while if we didn't lend, inflation would so erode it that the lending alternative would become impossible. Our shareholders expected it, our balance sheets needed it and, by the time our other activities meant it was no longer necessary to lend, our loan losses made it essential to continue to do so. The same problem was faced by our longer-established competitors, and additional loan volumes seemed essential to survival. All major banks were faced by an inexorable growth of overhead cost, and the answer was to stretch capital further. In previous decades, this would have been considered folly, but now times had changed.

Banking practice, certainly until the 1960s, was that a bank could borrow £10 for every £1 of capital, but would be unwise to lend more than £6–8 of this. The rest needed to be kept in reserve assets, short-term lending through the discount market, or the purchase of easily realisable assets, such as three-month acceptances, Treasury bills, prime bank bills or CDs. This theory was based on the assumption that banks try not to lend where they cannot be sure of getting their money back, but always needed plenty of 'high-powered money' on hand with which to repay depositors, lest a run develop. It also assumed that banks need a reasonable base of shareholders' money with which to repay depositors, should their lending decisions go disastrously wrong. But the need for this base was being questioned. Less than twenty years earlier, the idea of any bank gearing itself more than 10:1 would have had regulators reaching for their examiners, and Cobbold would occasionally arch his eyebrows at our own 20:1 gearing, and wonder what was happening to London bankers.

I would reassure him by showing him some of our competitors with balance-sheet ratios of up to 50:1. Many needed this, because they were lending on a marginal-cost basis. This is fine as a means of gaining market share, but assumes a base of profitable business. Branches could afford such aggressive pricing, for their parent bank argued that this was part of the cost of London representation. For a separately capitalised bank, however, doing all its lending at marginal cost meant that it could never cover its overheads; these banks did not perceive this as a problem, and as fast as they increased their gearing, lending margins fell. Overgearing became a problem in the 1980s, not out of concern for depositors but through competition.

Nationalised European banks, and Japanese banks supported by the booming stock markets, were raising gearing to unprecedented levels, or getting new money extraordinarily cheaply, or doing both. The Anglo-American banks cried foul, for they could not compete on lending margins, and finally the world banking community, through the BIS, agreed that banks did need a minimum capital base. The Basel agreements on solvency require banks to have at least £8 of capital (as defined) for every £100 of liabilities.

Since neither IIB nor Wallace could afford the majority of syndicated loans, that left only property or small-company lending. Grafftey-

Smith had recruited merchant bankers for his credit department, while I had looked for commercial bankers, but we both ended up with property loans which, however carefully checked at the time, turned out to be uniformly disastrous; only Midland of the English banks, and Morgan Guaranty among the Americans, escaped relatively unscathed from the 1974–6 disaster. Banks had traditionally been wary of property loans, because most failed George Moore's 'Three Ways' test; property developers could not pay the interest on their loans, let alone repay the principal, except through the sale of the property, and property values fluctuated as wildly as share prices. Furthermore, property is an unattractive asset to repossess. Taking possession of the quoted securities backing a borrower's debt is relatively painless, except for recognising the loss, but holding or owning property costs money in taxes, maintenance and insurance, and sometimes rental payments to freeholders or superior landlords.

Citibank and other American banks had learned this lesson in the Florida land boom and bust of the late 1920s, and the English banks, indirectly, rediscovered it in the deflation that followed 1931; the property assets that secured the borrowings of their foundering industrial customers turned out to be valueless, because they could not be sold. But postwar inflation seemed to change the equation. By the 1950s the value of the private mortgages, which had almost bust the Bank of America in 1933, had recovered their original values, while the consumer society created an apparently never ending demand for new offices and houses. As memories faded, mainline bankers began to look with envy on the profits being made by the savings and mortgage banks. From 1960 onwards, Citibank became an aggressive property lender within its domestic market, building its portfolio over five years from virtually nothing to some $167 million in 1967, or 2 per cent of its loan portfolio.

What made sense in America seemed even more attractive in London, and the American banks led the way in offering competition to the secondary banks. The Bank of England's squeeze on domestic-banking balance sheets, combined with the generally uncompetitive practices of the English banks, assured large lending spreads and high fees, for the profitability of property development was sustained by government restrictions, and arcane and corrupt planning regulations. These property loans were the icing on the cake – the high-risk but high-return business that justified the otherwise dry and tasteless nature of the international-lending cake itself. Without a branch network, or a long and costly build-up of a specialist reputation, City banks could not compete for small company business and, as I expensively discovered, most that was available came with problem companies.

But London banks could easily outperform the branch manager or secondary banker in property lending, both in their understanding and structuring of complex problems of security and cash flow, the size of the loan they were willing to contemplate, and their speed of decision. City office rents, in consequence of inflation and the surge of banks into London, reached their peak in 1973, and were not exceeded in real terms even in the latter years of the 1980s property boom. After the event, it was easy to see how the euromarkets, the Bank of England's CCC policy, and cost pressures encouraged the London banks to create a speculative bubble. Between October 1971 and June 1973, the sterling CD and interbank markets almost trebled in size from £3.8 billion to £11.2 billion; the participation of the London clearing banks in these markets, as they moved to make up for lost time, increased tenfold to 50 per cent of the total.

At the time, I just enjoyed the bidding for the IIB's old offices, for, as the speculative fever reached its peak, the insurance company that occupied the mezzanine offices of the P&O building was taken over. These offices were drab and failed to make use of either their street entrance or the large, light floor that overlooked the plaza. Such a public position was much prized by bankers and the IIB was able, through the cleverness of its Italian architects and without paying a premium rental, to acquire a Leadenhall Street entrance, a large and elegant banking hall and an efficient and modern dealing room. The bank still occupies those offices. Better still at the time, I was able to recoup much of the cost of the move from the sale of the remaining two years of the existing lease. I had always considered the P&O lease to be expensive, but the Italians' judgement was more than vindicated by the excitement generated by its proposed sale. Though the time to renegotiation of the rent was short, and this was already high, so many banks wanted the premises that we ended up with a sealed-bid auction between the three most enthusiastic, which showed up the contrasting national attitudes of the new London bankers.

The English bank obviously disapproved of such blatant commerciality, and rather huffily offered an extra 10 per cent of the asking price. The German bank doubled the price, though this came with five pages of conditions. The Japanese bank simply wrote a one-sentence letter. Since this read 'We offer £10,000 more than the highest bid you have received', I suppressed any doubts about the slyness of this approach and accepted the £250,000 on offer.

12

Worsening Conditions

'It takes a lifetime for a broker to get together a connection and to keep it . . . it needs an expensive establishment of clerks . . . expensive offices near the Stock Exchange and other necessary outlays' to earn a commission of ½ per cent, or only ¼ per cent when this has to be split with the bank introducing the client, complained Charles Branch, partner of the London stock-brokers Foster & Braithwaite and market specialist in US railway stocks, whereas the marketmaker 'with no necessary outgoings except his subscription to the Stock Exchange, makes two, three, four or five times the commission which I make.'
Evidence to the Royal Commission on the
workings of the Stock Exchange in 1877

THERE ARE STILL ONLY two sure ways of making dealing profits, and these remain the same as those used by dealers on the Amsterdam exchange four centuries ago. The best is to have a large customer base, and to know more than they do, and this is what IIB aimed to achieve, for it has always been greater knowledge that has enabled bankers to make money when no one else could. The other reasonably sure source is to follow a definite trend within the markets, upwards or downwards doesn't really matter, provided it lasts and the dealer recognises it before it changes. This is much harder to do than to say. Naturally, the uncertainty of dealing profits gains few political brownie points and, until the 1980s, dealers were generally despised by their banking colleagues; these feelings were reciprocated.

Nor should John Gutfreund, the chairman of the board of Salomon Brothers, and his four most senior colleagues have been surprised by their dismissal in 1991, for it was Wall Streeters who re-minted the lore of the markets as 'bulls and bears may prosper but hogs are always slaughtered'; attempting to corner the US bond market, the world's largest, was bound to upset a fair number of influential people. The hoggishness of the 1980s Salomon traders in their New York and London dealing rooms is described by Michael Lewis in *Liars' Poker*, and one of its quotes summarises the age-old fears of investors about market professionals:

> While most of America imagined that Wall Street meant the stock market, our bond market was setting the tone and pace of Wall Street in the 1980s . . . I once walked through the bond trading floor when the firm was attempting to sell the bonds of the drug-store chain Revco, which later went bankrupt and defaulted on those very bonds. The voice boomed out of the box: 'C'mon people, we're not selling truth.'

All banks are dealers, and must be dealers if they are to meet the contradictory requirements of their customers, and also protect their own capital from unexpected changes in the financial environment, But good dealing rooms – and Gutfreund had clawed his way to equality with Wall Street blue-bloods such as Morgan Stanley and First Boston through the excellence of Salomon's dealing skills – are not directly about money but about building world-beating teams. I learned that lesson within three months of opening the IIB when Ron Brett, who was IIB's head of treasury, asked for my agreement to dismiss a dealer. Brett and I, together with Alan Wiseman, who was head dealer, had been out for lunch that day, wooing a potential dealing counterpart, for we were promoting ourselves as London's dollar/lire specialists. During this time the duty dealer had entered into a transaction which, though outside his authority, had made the bank a $50,000 profit.

> He's got to go, Russell. It's partly that he ignored some very clear instructions, and I've been worried for some time that he's got the wrong attitude to discipline. But now it's dangerous, for this success will go to his head, he'll convince himself that he's a genius and, if we don't get rid of him, his next deal will probably cost the bank ten times what he's made today.

The dealer cleared his desk and was gone within the hour. This was not macho behaviour, of the sort that thrilled personnel directors as they sacked bankers by the busload at the end of the 1980s, but was designed to build morale within a new dealing room. The same reasoning makes crack regiments, such as Special Air Service battalions, 'return to unit' any recruit who fails to meet regimental standards, and at the very moment he does so. Such instant dismissal emphasises that group standards are not easily met, ensures that no one has any doubt about the consequence of failure, and develops the self-esteem and team spirit of those who survive. The survival of the IIB today, when nearly all its competitors have disappeared, is a tribute to the success of Brett and Wiseman in developing the IIB's dealing esprit de corps. Physically, the two could hardly be more different, though both came from east London, a generator of excellent forex dealers, bookies and car salesmen. Dennis Weatherstone, the first Englishman to be chairman of J. P. Morgan, comes from that background, and Wiseman is now managing director of IIB.

Brett was a gentle giant of a man who had joined an Austrian bank as a fifteen-year-old in the 1920s and, as head of Manufacturers Hanover's London dealing function in the 1950s, became one of the founders of the eurodollar market. He was my 'minder', wished on me by the Bank of England to ensure that neither deliberately nor accidentally did I exploit the foreign-exchange regulations. These were designed to protect a country's balance of payments, and ensured that a nation's stock of gold, dollars and other convertible currencies, like Swiss francs, were kept for officially approved spending, such as buying raw materials and machinery, rather than squandered on riotous living on the Côte d'Azur. Nearly fifty years in London's forex markets meant that Brett knew every dealer, as well as all the American and European banks of any importance in these markets. Together with Cobbold, he gave the IIB an enormous initial advantage but, to achieve my aims, I needed a dealer, and one with a very different philosophy from that of Brett and Manny Hanny.

Like nearly all American banks at that time, Manny Hanny only acted for customers, used the markets for funding only, and never took a dealing position. That policy would never work for IIB, since it was my intention to get the business of Italy's 1,500 banks, and to do that I had to offer a better service than their existing counterparts. Those were either Hambros or Morgan Grenfell in London, or the Milan dealing rooms of the three state-owned Italian commercial banks. Once Brett was aware of my ambitions, he pooh-poohed my tentative suggestion of advertising the post, and put the word around his friends within the dealing community. To my great pleasure, and within less than a week, Brett's fishing hooked the small and wiry figure of Alan Wiseman. I had known him as second dealer at Hambros but Charlie Hambro, in one of his moods, had degraded him for some footling reason, and Wiseman had left.

Hambros were one of the most macho of the London dealing banks, so Wiseman was bored out of his mind as head dealer at Security Pacific, since his superiors in Los Angeles hardly seemed aware that other currencies than the dollar existed, or that the function of a dealing room was to deal in these, and not to be an elegant pendant to a London branch. I was all too aware of Hambro dealers' penchant for playing chicken with their Scandinavian commercial banking counter-parties, most of whom had several times the capital of Hambros. This meant that dealing-room income fluctuated alarmingly month to month, from profits of hundreds of thousands to losses of the same level, and I wanted the profits, but IIB certainly could not afford the losses. Between us, we agreed that IIB would act as marketmaker in the lire markets, but would never expose itself to losses by taking positions in currencies. Instead, we would hedge these by using the forward markets and, luckily for the IIB, Brett and Wiseman were two of the cleverest users of these new markets.

To borrow dollars, or any other currency, as a sterling-based bank or company, is to take a tremendous risk, because if dollars are borrowed, dollars must be repaid. If, between the borrowing and the repayment, the pound sterling drops in value against the dollar, then many more pounds will be needed to repay the same amount of dollars. This does not matter so much to a company with a US-based subsidiary, or one exporting its goods to overseas buyers and being paid in dollars, for it is generating the dollars to repay the loan. But without such dollar or other currency earnings, borrowing in another currency, however cheap the interest rate seems to be, is the financial equivalent of Russian roulette. Banks always account in the currency of their domestic market, which is the same as that in which shareholders' capital is designated. Banks and companies can borrow sterling or dollars, but if they have the one and need the other, then they must sell sterling and buy dollars.

If a bank borrows or buys foreign currency, it runs the risk of an exchange loss, and these are just as painful for shareholders as any other banking loss, such as losing money from unwise loans or a badly timed investment of the bank's capital in the bond markets. But using commodity-market techniques, and the forward markets in foreign exchange, allowed banks to insure against this risk – 'hedge' is the technical term. Forward contracts are about transactions at today's price for settlement in the future, and are much used by commodity dealers, who call them 'futures'. The difference between forex and commodity markets on the one hand and the securities markets on the other, is that in the latter it is possible to sit out the dance. Investors do not have to buy bonds or shares; they can hold cash, and all they forgo is the opportunity profits they might have made.

This option is not available to business. A manufacturer either buys the raw materials he needs for a contract, or waits until later. But if the contract has been priced against current raw-material costs, the waiting is a gamble on the future; prices may stay the same, fall or rise. Whatever happens, the profit margin on the contract is at risk, and the risk is compounded if the raw materials have to be bought in a foreign currency, or if the contract itself is expressed in the buyer's currency, rather than that of the seller. A chocolate manufacturer either has cocoa or doesn't. If it hasn't, and the price rises, it's in trouble, for the price of chocolate bars in the shops is pretty well fixed, so the extra cost of the raw material comes out of the manufacturer's planned profit. But the position can be almost as embarrassing if the raw material is bought and the price falls, for then competitors, if they choose, can compete on price. The use of forward markets allows manufacturers to control these business risks.

The object of commodity dealers is to ensure that their manufacturing employers have physical stock when it is needed, and yet have it at a price which is not significantly above the spot price, or the cost of delivery today. This requires active dealing, to average out the regular ups and downs of market prices; dealers buy some stock now, buy some at today's price for future delivery, and then deal in these spot and futures markets to average out the price of their total contracts to as close to market levels as possible, while ensuring they are always covered for the supply of physical stock, as and when wanted for the manufacturing process. This is the function of forward foreign-exchange deals also, for a manufacturer can destroy hard-earned profit margins, if unaware of the movement of currency prices and the effect these can have on the cost of raw materials and the value of the contract.

The cost of insuring manufacturing profit against foreign-exchange mishaps is small, compared to all the other costs involved, and only banks deal in currencies; since these kept market rates secret, this was a very profitable business, and remains so today, especially at the retail level. A study recently carried out within the European Community, just changing money into successive currencies as the twelve borders were crossed, showed that a starting £100 ended up as only £37. The IIB had no trading customers, but we could act as forex wholesalers to banks, who did have such customers and needed to balance the forex exposure that they had undertaken on their behalf.

Using the forward markets enabled the IIB, Hambros-style, to carry out whatever currency transactions our banking customers put to us, but to square off our positions every night, Manny Hanny-style. These forward deals took place between spot, or today, and a specified date in the future, while forward-forward deals took place between an agreed future date – say three months hence – and another date three, six or nine months later still. In effect, we doubled up on every forex deal; when we bought lire and sold dollars in the spot market, we would immediately undo the deal by selling the same amount of lire in the forward market against the same number of dollars. In currency terms, the IIB was 'square'; since it had no 'long' or 'short' position which would cost us money if the exchange rate between the dollar and the lire changed.

Using these future markets helped the IIB to raise money efficiently, for it was often cheaper to borrow Deutschmarks, and swap them into dollars, than to borrow dollars directly. More importantly, it enabled us to handle all the myriad commercial transactions that Italian banks were undertaking for their manufacturing and trading customers. The use of the forward markets meant that IIB was taking a view on interest rates, which reflect market expectations about currency movements, but not gambling on those adjustments. Additionally, all three of us agreed that IIB should pattern itself on the Midland, and act as a London 'bankers' bank' to smaller Italian banks that had a need of the London forex market but were terrified of approaching it because of its reputation. Forex contracts are verbal, made on the telephone, and innocents are given very short shrift within any complex marketplace. We resolved to act as nurse-maid, and show these inexperienced dealers how to achieve the best result for themselves and their customers, by acting as their guide to London forex dealing. This wasn't altruism, for the more customers we had, the greater the odds that we could match their requirements over time, and the more we matched, the more certain our profits.

Dealing is the art of recognising and controlling short-term risk; if you can't do it, not all today's electronic wizardy will help you, which is why banks still make horrendous losses during those rare occasions when all is favourable. Generally, however events turn out in retrospect, good market dealers never give hostages to fortune, and always assure each other that things have never been so bad.

History proves them right, yet the twelve years of rising prices and volatile markets from the mid–1970s onwards fooled many bankers into thinking that dealing is a safer business than it really is.

For much of the time, markets go nowhere except sideways, as happened to London share markets during the 1960s while much the same happened in Wall Street, though with greater volatility. There, share prices failed to break the psychologically important barrier of 1,000 on the Dow Jones Index during the 1960s, and spent some seventeen years – from 1965 to 1982 – violently going sideways. That was because the early 1960s had been so good for American business that Wall Street was carried away by enthusiasm, and priced the shares of the major American corporations on levels comparable to those of Wall Street in the 1920s, or Tokyo in the late 1980s. Believing that these companies were on course to take over the world, they lost some 90 per cent of their customers' capital as the share prices of these 'nifty fifty' companies crashed back to reality during the 1970s. Fortunately, long-term bear markets are even less frequent than super-bull booms, and catastrophic collapses rarer still. The two most famous are those of 1720 and 1929 and, though the 1974 crash had similar potential, inflation bailed out bankers and governments alike.

The financial process that turns a financial crash into an economic disaster was outlined by the American economist Irving Fisher in the early 1930s, but it can be studied first-hand today in Norway, Finland and Sweden. Such crisis years are hard for dealers. So convinced were professional investors that neither politicians nor bankers would allow so obvious a catastrophe as a debt deflation to happen, that they plunged heavily into Wall Street in 1931. But Fisher and other analysts were wrong, which is why 1929 ranks so high in banking demonology. Amateur speculators and overborrowed investors had been wiped out by the initial crash in October 1929, but no one worried unduly about this. Securities markets separate the men from the boys, and the mark of the professional is the ability to operate the bigger-fool system, which is that it is perfectly proper to buy securities at a stupid price provided only that you can be sure that the market will supply a bigger fool to buy from you at a profit.

By 1931 the bigger fools had bought and been wiped out, prices were sensibly low, and it was time for analysts and market professionals to act. All moved in to clean up, but got cleaned out instead, for Fisher's road map was ignored by politicians and bankers alike. Debt deflation inexorably ground down business activity, and Wall Street prices fell further and faster between 1931 and 1933 than they had from 1929 to 1931. Market dealers have always accepted that they can only guess the future, and never predict it. The function of dealing, as Wiseman taught me, is to respond to *what is*; this gains more reward than to plan for *what might be*. As an investor, I looked too far ahead to be a good dealer, for though numerate – and many bankers aren't – I use figures analytically; dealers use them comparatively, forever figuring the odds, for dealing is like betting, which is why bright East End kids who don't become forex dealers, become successful bookies.

Charles Branch was a London stockbroker who acted as an investment banker for US railways in the 1860's, introducing these to British investors, as well as making a market in their stock. He was concerned that the proposed reforms of the London Stock Exchange, designed to separate the function of making money as a principal from that of earning commission as an agent for investors, would cramp his style. It did, of course, for a passive client base had always been a useful way of turning a bank's short-term dealing mistakes into the long-term investment policy of clients. These days 'front-running', or buying for the bank's account before executing large institutional orders, is an additional help. Unlike London, New York never had 'single capacity', or the legal separation of function designed to reduce the conflicts of interest that are inherent in financial markets. Nor has London since 1988, for the Big Bang did away with this protection of the investor.

Although New York once had a similar practical distinction, that has also gone, for Morgans and its 'dusty money' competitors concentrated more on supplying issues to the markets. Their less well-connected hangers-on, financed by Citibank and other Wall Street commercial banks, would buy the securities and trade them afterwards, while the 'our crowd' banks invested more of their own capital in trading the product that they supplied. Both are necessary functions of an efficient securities market, though the interests of 'issuer' and 'investor' often differ, while those of 'trader' always do so. Yet if bonds and shares (stock, in twentieth-century American and nineteenth-century English parlance) cannot easily be traded after their initial offer, the banks soon lose investors for future issues, however illustrious their name or that of the company issuing the securities. So one way or another, all issuing banks have to find ways of working these secondary markets – sometimes called the aftermarkets – either by trading themselves or by paying specialised houses to do it for them through the underwriting system.

Just like commercial banks, investment banks have a tiny capital compared to the size of the securities markets or even their own trading commitments. Trading technology came to the rescue, for there has always been a timing gap between striking a bargain – the contract – and paying for it at the settlement. Though more easily done within the securities markets, similar opportunities exist within the forex and money markets. Robert Maxwell extracted some £100 million from the banks by 'teaming and lading', as it is known. He bought currency from one bank, having it credited to another, but did not pay for it within the working day, as is the custom. Instead, he repeated the exercise, though in bigger quantities, and used those proceeds to pay the first bank. Having played this game with most of the world's major banks, over a period of three to four weeks, even they grew suspicious, and refused to deal without seeing Maxwell's money first; the game stopped then, as Maxwell's companies had run out of money to use, assets to pledge or credit to exploit.

Life is easier within the securities markets, where settlements stretch from New York's five working days to London's two- and three-week accounts. Dealers sell short but, if prices do not fall sufficiently fast to show them a profit, rather than closing their contract at a loss, they borrow stock, deliver it to the buyer, pay the lender for the privilege (so improving the owner's income return on the stock), wait a better time to buy in the borrowed stock, and then repay the lender. The 'stock lending' of the Maxwell pension funds is a perfectly respectable activity, except that the self-admitted incompetence of the regulatory authorities enabled Maxwell to pervert the system, and so siphon money out of the pension funds into his private companies. Equally, bulls who do not wish to take delivery of purchased securities, probably because they lack the money to do so, can find other dealers willing to accept delivery, provided they pay them interest on the money expended for the settlement. Dealing in the derivative markets, not for today but a date several weeks or months in the future, influences immediate prices upwards or downwards, and benefits dealers by turbo-charging their likely profits (or losses) by reducing the amount of capital needed for dealing.

The options market, for a small percentage of the cost of the security, gives dealers the right, thought not the obligation, to buy or sell the security in question some time in the future, but at today's price. An option also 'gears' the dealer; rather than speculating 1,000 to gain 100, an option costs 100 to purchase 1,000 in the future. The appeal to the dealer is that the hoped-for profit of 10 per cent remains the same as an absolute number, but becomes a return of 100 per cent on an investment of 100, rather than of 10 per cent on an investment of 1,000 in the underlying, or cash, market. Dealing in futures produces the same result, though with a higher risk, for the option is a 'right' but a futures contract is an 'obligation'; the dealer in futures has dealt, whatever happens to market prices afterwards, and must settle the contract. Amsterdam dealers used all these tricks, though they were more brutal in their terminology; not for them the mealy-mouthed 'derivative' markets to describe these markets in 'options', 'futures' and 'forwards', but *'windhandl'*, or 'trades in air'.

Dealing opportunities were enhanced by the 1971 collapse of the Bretton Woods system, as President Nixon cut the dollar free from any link with gold. The foreign-exchange markets went mad and the euromarkets expanded tenfold over the decade and, in time, euromarkets developed for all major currencies. The expansion of institutional investment funds fed the expansion of the eurodollar markets, for these attracted depositors, since they were outside the regulatory system and could offer better rates. Normal bank deposits were more expensive to the banks than simply the rate of interest they paid, for central banks required the banks they ruled to keep a percentage of their deposits in something that could easily be turned into cash, if the need arose. These 'reserve assets' were generally non-interest-bearing deposits with the central bank or approved types of, naturally, low-yielding securities issued by the Treasury or another government ministry.

Prudential controls reduce the rate of interest that banks can offer, but regulators only regulate the banks of their own country and deposits in the national currency, so no reserve assets are needed against deposits that do not officially exist. Citibank in New York, like most of its competitors, hardly knew what foreign-exchange dealing meant in 1971, though it had taken a couple of multimillion dollar losses out of its Milan and Brussels offices during the late 1960s. But it had a most impressive forex business in London and, by 1974, Citibank was making 60 per cent of its profits from international banking. Since many of its branches were relatively new and loss-making, the great bulk of total bank profits must have come from its London treasury – i.e. forex and money-dealing – activities. Forex dealing was easy money in those first few years, as business came to terms with floating rates of exchange.

Banking regulations were posited on a world of paper currencies. The world after 1933 replaced national currencies exchangeable into gold for one in which only the dollar had a gold parity, and all other currencies were measured by their exchange value against the dollar. This dollar-exchange system, established in 1944 by the members of the prospective United Nations Organisation at a hotel and conference centre in Northern Vermont called Bretton Woods, had served the world well by encouraging trade but was crumbling by the late 1960s. The wealth of the US consumer attracted larger and larger flows of goods from the revitalised industries of Europe and Japan, but Bretton Woods was finally destroyed by the spiralling costs of the Cold War, and President Lyndon Johnson's attempt to fight a hot war in Vietnam and a social war on poverty at home, all without raising taxes.

The result was a crowding-out of American savings by government spending; Kaufman's figures show the US deficit doubling geometrically over the decades from 1 per cent of gross national product in the 1950s to 2 per cent in the 1960s and 4 per cent in the 1970s. Mercifully, the increase slowed in the 1980s, with the deficit averaging 5 per cent, otherwise the boom and bust of that decade might have been even worse. Something had to give, and this was the American balance of payments. As the US trade deficit increased, so European governments accumulated dollars. They needed the euromarkets, if they were to earn a return on such enforced savings. There was no alternative 'store of value' since the pound sterling, the only other international currency, was the weak reflection of a sick economy, forever flirting with devaluation. The Germans and the Swiss discouraged the use of their currencies by every means in their power, which included charging interest to foreigners who held deposits in Deutschmarks or Swiss francs.

Gold was another alternative, but it paid no interest and, as long as the Americans held its price to its 1936 dollar value, there was no chance of capital appreciation either. When the gold/dollar link went, the answer for national treasuries was still not easy. Currencies from then on had no absolute reference value, so their values were determined by the words and actions of politicians – although all denied any intention to print money to resolve domestic difficulties, their actions generally belied their words – and those of foreign-exchange dealers. Foreign-exchange dealing rooms became the arbiters of comparative currency values, deciding among themselves which currency seemed least inflationary and was the one to be bought in preference to others. Whether or not this is a good way to determine currency values – and there is no best way – it is a splendid source of profits for a well-run foreign-exchange department. This was the world into which IIB ventured but, given our size, we carried a rifle with telescopic sights, rather than a shotgun.

The effect on our competitors was all that I had hoped, and it was reinforced when, in June 1973, Reuters news agency introduced its Forex Monitor for the first time. Shortly after this, I was at lunch with the foreign managers of the Midland and, not entirely innocently, asked them what they thought of Reuters.

> It's bad enough having people like you around, queering our pitch, but Reuters is the end. What's the point of having decent dealers, if a television screen gives all the world the buying and selling prices from every Tom, Dick and Harry of a bank that thinks it ought to be a forex dealer. We used to take a good point out of any deal we did with a continental bank, even Deutsche Bank, for God's sake, and now we are lucky to get a fraction of that. And as for your Italian shareholders, Russell, I'm surprised they haven't hung you yet but when they get around to it, tell 'em I'll join them.

For us, the Monitor was a godsend as, for Reuters, it was a gold mine. When it was first introduced there were five banks contributing prices and another seven subscribers as information recipients only; by the end of that first week the number was up to fourteen contributors and seventeen takers. The takers included banks as well as finance companies, commodity brokers and corporate finance directors. A year later, and there were signed contracts for 52 contributing banks and 194 takers in seven countries, with negotiations under way in another two countries. Now it is an indispensable tool for dealers. My Midland friend was mad at me because, although the theory was that contributing banks would update their prices and deal at those screen prices, no one had any intention of destroying the secrecy surrounding forex prices. The major banks signed up as an insurance policy, not believing that Reuters would work, and simply updating their prices once or twice a day and otherwise continuing as if the Monitor screen did not exist. But IIB had nothing to lose and everything to gain, so we priced aggressively to the screen, dealt off those prices, and let everyone know what we were doing.

We had already developed a good customer base amongst the plethora of small Italian banks, because they had discovered that we acted on our stated policy of one price for all, however big or small the business, however unsophisticated the dealer. Citibank and other like-minded American banks in London used us because they found our service so much better than that of the Milan dealing rooms, or those of our shareholders come to that. Now, through the Monitor, we became price setters and, as it advanced through the world, so did our lire forex quotations. Everyone started to use us, our prices got keener still, and even the big three Italian banks gritted their teeth, and dealt with us too. Banks turned to their dealers, to make good the losses they were incurring on their loan business, and as the 1970s progressed these service functions became profit making 'treasuries'. The London forex market exploded; from a daily turnover of tens of millions, forex dealing first became hundreds of millions, and then billions. The Bank of England's snapshots of the market shows a daily turnover of $90 billion in 1986 – the first ever enquiry into its size – doubling to $187 billion in 1989, and rising to $303 billion in 1992.

The relationship of forex trading to the actual needs of business became so out of line that, for most banks, forex dealing became entirely speculative. But it was profitable, because it took time for out-gunned central banks to learn how to mislead and ambush the banks' dealing departments. It remained safe for those dealers, like the IIB, whose customer base was other banks, because the other great change in this market was that it ceased to be driven by the movement of traded goods. The forex market was influenced, instead, by capital flows as the investment decisions of investment institutions replaced the 'hedging' and 'covering' of manufacturers protecting their profits; 'speculation' and 'investment', and 'hedging' of investment positions became the vital engine of growth. This institutionalisation of dealing, and the reduced role of the individual dealer, destroyed the influence of the contrarian thinker in dealing markets, leaving the field free to bank dealing rooms and the sensible bureaucratic desire to be all right, or all wrong, together. The resulting markets tended to be more volatile, and more dangerous.

Dealing profits are high but volatile, and need to be balanced by something slower and more solid. Since lending was not a long-term option for the IIB, it had to be management and administration, the third of banking's triangle of income. The way ahead was shown by the three major Swiss banks, which had all been savagely mauled by the 1930s crisis, and returned to their 1920s level of profits and assets only in the 1950s. Postwar economic controls badly hurt their traditional international corporate lending, but with the easing of exchange controls in the 1960s, borrowers and depositors began to flock to Switzerland, and these three banks took off on the course that would take them from modest-sized banks to among the world's biggest and most profitable. The interesting thing to me about Swiss banking strategy was that instead of chasing after corporate business, they concentrated on aggressively building up personal banking activities.

In 1967 Union Bank of Switzerland entered the Swiss domestic market for the first time, and was closely followed by its two competitors, all offering home mortgages and small savings accounts as a counterbalance to the flood of short-term foreign money attracted by banking secrecy and the price stability of the Swiss franc. These banks, whether dealing with domestic or foreign business, improved the natural profitability of their business by spending heavily on training and thinking hard about automation. Indeed, just as the English banks began to ignore their depositors in favour of international lending, the big three Swiss banks, who had made their original reputation as international commercial banks, switched direction. They took on many of the attitudes of the prewar English commercial banks, in their attention to the service needs of the rich and successful and their families.

It was this strategy, so distinct from what was accepted as banking gospel, that first aroused my interest. While at Hambros, Rolf Dellborg and I had discussed bringing together the Channel Islands branches, the Pall Mall branch and Hambros' own rich customers into a private banking operation to compete with the Swiss. We knew from Channel Islands experience that we would have no staffing problems, for the commercial banks were full of well-trained trust bankers, desperate to get away from their stultifying employers and turn their ideas and contacts to good account. What would have worked for Hambros would work as well with IIB, for private banking, the service that most banks are now desperately peddling since so few of their other activities make money for them, is the traditional core of commercial banking. It is simply the management and administration of the wealth of the monied classes – the 20 per cent of the population that are either rich, successful or connected to those that are one or the other. For European banks, however, political risk made private banking a little more complicated than it was before 1914.

Jinx Grafftey-Smith and I would swap essays, when our social life got in the way of the needs of our Oxford tutors, and remained in touch as we both became bankers. While I was developing a mass retail-investment business for Hambros, he was the Hong Kong representative for Samuel Montagu. From there he would direct the growing wealth of expatriates and the Chinese to the safe haven of

Swiss private banking in the shape of Guyerzeller Zurmont. Like all private bankers, Jinx offered discretion and personal loyalty, which was sometimes tested to breaking point.

> I'd had a very successful trip to Taiwan, and, as the plane gathered speed, treated myself to a thanksgiving slug of whisky. When the pilot suddenly aborted the takeoff I was a bit nervous, more about physical safety than anything else, until I saw this jeep, full of armed police, haring out to the runway. That's when I began to shit bricks, for I had several hundred thousand of 'illegal' foreign currencies, for new investment accounts, hidden in my luggage. Could I hold out while they pulled my toenails out, or should I turn state's evidence and drop my customers in it? That would destroy my banking career, of course, but I wasn't sure that Samuel Montagu would still want me, even assuming I survived a few years in a Chinese jail. After all, private banking is much like life itself – everything's forgiven except getting found out. I was too frightened to turn around when they came on board, though my heart began to slow when I heard them man-handling some poor Chinese bastard behind me, but I wasn't breathing properly until we were out of their airspace. It's true, by the way, that if you're sufficiently terrified, alcohol has no effect whatsoever. I could have been drinking water, for all the effect that a bottle of whisky had but I certainly remembered the promise I made myself. That was my last trip as a courier.

Jinx certainly persuaded me that neither I personally, nor the IIB, should be involved in the courier trade. There was no need, really, for the Vatican Bank was always prepared to help the well intro-duced, for a commission of 10 per cent, to get their money out of Italy. Vatican City is a sovereign state and, though lire is the currency of use, the Vatican Bank ignores Italian forex regulations. And there were plenty of others in the same game. Couriers would take money across the frontier for less than 10 per cent, though this option was not always such a bargain. One unfortunate, whose large and unclaimed cardboard box looked all too like a bomb in those nervy days, saw it blown up in front of him, just a few miles from the frontier. The Italian market for private banking looked absolutely right, for the cost of Swiss banking services was going up even faster than the Italian lira was depreciating against the Swiss franc.

The political scene was certainly confused, for there was a pandemic of financial kidnappings – orchestrated by the police, according to the more paranoid of my colleagues – bombings and assassinations, and coups and rumours of coups. The most serious, called off at the last moment, took place just before I joined the IIB.

This was planned by Prince Paolo Borghese, a right-wing politician and a general in military intelligence, in cooperation with Operation Gladio agents; this was a secret army funded by the British and American intelligence services, and trained for resistance activities should Italy fall to the communists. What with rumours and counter-rumours, and real enough outrages, Italians were desperate to get their money out of Italy. I had no qualms about this business, for the loyalty of a banker should be to his customer and, provided he follows the letter of his own law, he need not be too nice about its spirit or, certainly, anyone else's laws.

State theft is still theft, and UK marginal tax rates were 98 per cent until 1980 although, during the 1970s, the value of money was falling by over 15 per cent a year. The Swedish tax authorities in 1976, to gain publicity for themselves, falsified a tax accusation against the director Ingmar Bergman, arrested him on the stage of Stockholm's Royal Dramatic Theatre in the middle of a rehearsal, and so drove one of the country's greatest artists into exile. Rome emptied one weekend when the rumour went around that two members of the Italian financial police had penetrated Banca della Svizzera Italiana and, after several months working there as account clerks, were on their way back to headquarters with lists of names and numbered accounts.

Once out of the country, such money needs to be managed. This is what the IIB did, setting up and managing discretionary trusts so that the owner, if ever charged with possession of illegal funds, could deny ownership on oath, for ownership had indeed passed to the trustees. The former owner's relatives remained beneficiaries, of course, but civil-law countries did not understand such English niceties, since this piece of archaic European church law had been abolished by the French Revolution. This has now changed, for even the Swiss have given up Liechtenstein in favour of trusts, most civil-law countries have case law which recognises it, and French lawyers are agitating for the full incorporation of trust law into French legal practice. In his use of Liechtenstein, Maxwell was as old-fashioned as his frauds. The IIB, despite advice to the contrary, never had any problem in persuading rich Latins that an English trust was an elegant solution to their need for financial privacy and security.

Midland reorganised its trust operations to work with its Channel Islands branches but, whatever was said, the reality was that the Swiss banks wanted personal business, while the Anglo-American banks wanted corporate loans and were not prepared to make the service effort necessary to secure a reliable source of deposits combined with a fee-paying business. Midland made no attempt to make money out of the unique private banking hand that it had dealt itself when it bought Samuel Montagu, and even today the managers concerned don't understand what they missed. That loss still weakens the commercial banks today; of at least $2 trillion of assets held outside their owners' country of residence, more than half is managed by Swiss banks and, in terms of importance, the ratio between Switzerland, Luxembourg and the Channel Islands is 100:10:1. Yet those funds pale into insignificance when counted against the funds looking for management within their domestic markets, but the commercial banks still have organisational problems in handling such business.

Nevertheless, the boring business of looking after the individual's affairs, even if very high wages need to be paid for the efficient handling of customer accounts, can be very profitable. Credit Suisse was to prove that to the world in 1977, though not, perhaps, in the way it would have chosen. Chiasso is a small, charmless town in the Ticino, the Italian-speaking canton of Switzerland, but the surprising number of banks proclaims its position as the first Swiss town north of Milan. For several years, the Chiasso branch of the Credit Suisse was one of the best performing within this rather staid banking group controlled by the Protestant *haute bourgeoisie* of Zurich. Though Chiasso's German-Swiss manager had little rapport with his predominantly Italian clientele, his performance belied that fact. Indeed, his success was used as an example, encouraging other Credit Suisse managers to maintain the bank's comparative ranking with the equally staid and federally structured Basel-headquartered Swiss Bank Corporation or the parvenu, ambitious and centralised Union of Swiss Banks.

There had been mutterings about the behaviour of this branch, even from its two competitors, but Credit Suisse in Zurich, like all good Swiss, did not feel disposed to enquire too closely into what was going on. Banking confidentiality works well for Switzerland, and what is sauce for outsiders is considered equally so for insiders. Occasionally, however, this relaxed federal approach is abused, and finally Zurich was forced to recognise that its well-regarded manager had been running a bank-within-a-bank, and not a minnow either. Since the manager did not always agree with the bank's fuddy-duddy credit guidelines, especially as they related to relaxed and imaginative Italian businessmen, he decided to make the loans himself, using a Liechtenstein company called Texon as the lender and investor. Over fifteen years Texon grew and grew and, by 1977, it controlled Italy's largest wine and food business, exported 40 per cent of Italy's wine, owned a major international transport business, several luxury hotels and a variety of smaller businesses. One of these was a well-respected Swiss engineering company, which Credit Suisse were proud to have as a customer of their Zurich branch.

Texon was financed by some 2 billion of Swiss franc fiduciary deposits, guaranteed by the Chiasso branch in the name of Credit Suisse. The Swiss have always regarded cash as at least as important an investment sector as shares or bonds, so the tax authorities naturally levy stamp duty on changes in deposits just as they do on the sale or purchase of securities. To avoid this stamp duty, levied every time monthly interest rates are confirmed or changed, Swiss banks place their clients' deposits on account with other, foreign banks. These fiduciary accounts do not normally carry the guarantee of the placing bank, though clients certainly expect to have its moral guarantee. Rich Italians fleeing the political uncertainties of these years wanted good rates, which Credit Suisse could not offer them, for the Swiss authorities were determined to halt inflation, and were doing their best to discourage flight money by charging interest on new foreign-owned deposits. They also wanted good security, so Chiasso offered them Texon for the rate, and a Credit Suisse guarantee for their security. The combination was irresistible, and Italian business flocked to Chiasso.

The failure of a neighbouring bank panicked depositors in the Ticino, and finally burst the Texon bubble. As the full story slowly trickled out, Credit Suisse accepted responsibility for the 2 billion Swiss franc Texon deposits, as well as another 350 million Swiss francs of credits extended to Texon companies by Italian banks. The bank wrote off $500 million of the Texon debt to its inner reserves, and unblushingly revealed little change in the bank's 1977 profits, compared to the previous year, while shareholders received an unaltered dividend. The Swiss banks had reconstructed themselves for the modern world, ignoring the popular fashion and concentrating instead on doing business with those that needed the bank, rather than those the bank needed.

This policy kept Credit Suisse safe when it hit its iceberg, just as, in the 1980s, Citibank would successfully use a private and consumer banking strategy to keep itself afloat. The Midland crew, or those that remained after most were thrown overboard in the wake of Crocker, would simply play the same old tunes faster, as the slope on the *Titanic*'s deck got steeper.

13

Heavy Seas

'May God preserve me from my friends; from my enemies I can protect myself.'

Sicilian folk saying

THE ESSENCE OF BANKING lies in the two ideograms that make up the Chinese word for 'risk': these are said to be 'crisis' and 'opportunity'. The attraction of IIB to me was that it had no history, so I could do what I liked, and I was full of ideas, for I had spent much of the previous couple of years analysing the inner workings of Hambros Bank. While not adding to my popularity, particularly as I extracted more and more information on comparative profitability, it convinced me that small banks could be profitable, and find profitable niche markets for themselves. The Italian political situation was certainly in crisis, but such conventional thinking ignored the opportunity – however badly managed the country was, its people were imaginative, hard-working and successful. There were plenty of business possibilities to be exploited.

Size is the enemy of flexibility, as Machiavelli well knew, since

there is nothing more difficult to take in hand, more perilous to conduct, or more uncertain of its success than to take the lead in the introduction of a new order of things. The reason is that the innovator has for enemies all those who have done well under the old conditions, and lukewarm defenders in those who only may do well in the new. This coolness arises partly from fear of the opponents who have the laws on their side, and partly from the incredulity of men, who do not readily believe in new things until they have had a long experience of them. Thus it happens that whenever those who are hostile have the opportunity to attack, they do it like partisans; whilst the others defend lukewarmly, in such wise that the prince is endangered along with them.

This is the real banking problem today, for all banks have

increased immeasurably in size since 1960, the commercial banks from thousands to tens of thousands of employees, and the investment banks from hundreds to thousands, or sometimes even tens of thousands. This is the danger of being a protected species; with no predators to keep the banks fit and lean, and to destroy the inefficient, the banks have become self-generating bureaucracies. Lowell Bryan is a senior partner of McKinsey & Company in New York, and has put his own practical experience of banking consultancy together with the writings of academic theorists to recommend *Breaking up the Bank*. Analysis of McKinsey's voluminous studies of American banks shows that

> non-interest costs [of banks] ... have been only loosely linked to revenues. This is to be expected under oligopolistic pricing; in an oligopoly, pricing is determined not by price and cost competition, but rather by what the market will bear ... one of the essential features of an oligopoly is that most participants in the industry spend money not to make themselves stand out, but rather to prevent competitors from differentiating themselves.

Fortunately, according to other McKinsey research, the bottomless pit of one bank is the golden pond of the next, and a sensible swapping of activities could significantly increase the overall profitability of banking. Bryan believes that the complexities of large banks make them unmanageable but that, by using the techniques of securitisation – turning bank loan portfolios into tradable bonds – banks could transform their efficiency and profitability. Some banks will then concentrate on customer relationships and service – likely to be the majority – and subcontract all other services to specialists. Many of these already exist, as processors of credit cards or cheques, custodial and trustee functions, but Bryan argues persuasively that this disaggregation should go much further.

Bryan believes that securitisation has separated the function of banking into its constituent parts. This is how General Motors has become the largest supplier of mortgages in America, but GM not only finds and negotiates the mortgages, it also administers them. This is not necessary, and is done by GM only because it makes money from doing so. There are now businesses that specialise in banking loan documentation, others in the processing of mortgage repayments, while many savings and loans now just concentrate on finding and advising would-be home buyers, and do no lending of their own. Other specialists analyse the creditworthiness of GM's mortgage portfolio, insurance companies enhance its value by insuring investors against initial losses, while investment banks arrange to fund the portfolio of loans by converting the income flow of the loans into different types of bonds, each designed to give investors the investment return and maturity that they require. None of this would be possible without cheap computing, and most can now be done cheaper by specialists than by universal banks.

Bryan recommends that, now that banks don't have to do everything themselves, they should concentrate on what they ought to be able to do best; for most, that is advising companies and individuals on their financing problems. Banking size and mergers have always had more to do with banking egos and paranoia than with banking economics, with a justification that is no different from that of a century ago, though the banking world has changed completely since then. In the late-twentieth-century banking world of deposit insurance, money markets and telecommunication satellites, the original need for size and geographical coverage no longer exists, and postwar history suggests that rather than benefiting from economies of scale, banks suffer from the opposite.

Furthermore, technology is worsening the equation, for a personal computer today has four times the computing power of the IBM and PDP machines that I bought for the IIB in 1971, and costs a few hundred dollars compared to the hundreds of thousands that I paid then. Moreover the processing systems of the banks, quite apart from their cost, are strangling banking competitiveness with their rigidities. Banks are a portfolio of financial businesses, and another McKinsey study identified something like 150 quite distinct banking activities. Some of these are profit horror stories, supported by managerial ego, while others never fail to coin money, however badly managed they are. This came as no surprise to me, for I had used this as my justification to Jocelyn Hambro for employing Worden & Risberg some twenty years earlier. They were to advise on the structure of a bank that had grown from a balance sheet of £100 million to £1,000 million in just over ten years, and had substantially increased the range of its services. As microcomputer based banking systems are brought in to cut through the Gordian knot of the mainframe transaction system, the idea of distributed computing within banking, allied to Bryan's ideas on breaking up banking into its constituent parts, promises a renaissance of the local commercial bank – provided, that is, that the problems identified by Machiavelli can be overcome.

For while investment managers were getting more and more

information on the companies whose securities they bought, and using better analytical tools with which to reduce their risks and improve the rewards of their investing, lending bankers were going the other way. With more and more information, but less and less knowledge of the economics of their business, commercial bankers opted for size and the pursuit of the institutional imperative. Between 1955 and 1970, Citibank quadrupled the number of its international branches and trebled its staff to 37,000, while Midland doubled its staff to 32,000 and increased its branch numbers by 10 per cent to 2,200, but that was only the beginning. Fifteen years later, Midland was back to the same number of branches that it had had in 1955 but was employing 78,000 staff, nearly five times as many as thirty years previously.

'Product', the word that banks now prefer to 'service', came to dominate the structure of banking, for Citibank's downgrading of the geographical organisation of banking was successful in gaining business, and was followed by most banks. The pattern established in the late 1960s was to be the selling banker, but not the service banker, and based on the industry specialists pioneered by Wall Street banks; these would first be controlled, then assisted, and finally supported in their selling efforts by the credit department. The downgrading of the branch-based banker was justified by the growing complexity of the business of the banks' customers, the longer maturity needed if loans were to compete with bonds, and the difficulty of getting graduates to spend time in a branch, when all the real decisions were taken in head office.

This simultaneous change in the physical organisation of the banks, their increased numbers, and the disappearance of so much information into the information technology department, never to be seen again in comprehensible form, was bound to have some risks. In fact, the conversion of Citibank from a small-scale business, or of Midland from a series of personal, decentralised fiefdoms into a large and global institution, produced some quite unexpected dangers. When George Moore could gather the bank's key credit and lending officers in his room every week, or the responsibility of any Midland business could be laid at the door of some long-serving branch manager, then there was little room to confuse responsibility and accountability. The new structure became quite otherwise. Frequent change of jobs, rapid promotions and vast and confusing hierarchies created plentiful opportunities of 'delegating upwards'; in the end no one needed to be responsible for anything.

*

This new industry attitude comes out in Chernow's chiding of Morgans for their personal loan of $12 million to Charles Mitchell in the 1930s: 'Loyalty to clients was always the vice of the House of Morgan.' It is difficult to know what higher attribute is required of bankers, for, sooner or later on a tiger hunt, the beast is going to appear. When it does, the banker may well wish that he hadn't chosen tigers for his sport, or that he had chosen a better shot for his companion, but when the tiger charges, the only thing to do is fire, and fire again, and hope that your companion is standing firm. That is what Morgans and Mitchell both did; though disgraced, Mitchell remade his fortune by building up Blyth & Company, a Wall Street stockbroker, and repaid every penny of his debt. As Dennis Weatherstone of Morgans expresses it, banking is appreciating that there is a risk, that it must be taken, but it needs to be understood, and so contained and controlled, before it is taken. Morgans are still one of only two American banks with a prime credit rating from all three rating agencies, and that comes from thinking before acting.

Due diligence is a phrase that trips off bankers' lips with practised ease today, but discovering facts is merely the beginning of banking judgement. With Maxwell, Bond, Asdil Nadir, and many others of the same kind, few enough facts were unearthed until the money was lost, and excuses were needed but, since the earth was disturbed enough, many searchers must have been noted for their due indolence rather than diligence. But even with due diligence, bankers still need to consider the colour of Kreuger's socks. The attraction of a cause, religious, nationalist or environmental, is that it allows individuals to doff their personal morality, handing over judgement to a higher authority. This is equally true of institutions, and banks, because of their size and protected status, have now joined such better known counterparts as armies, churches, and political parties. But institutions, like nations, are neither moral nor immoral, merely amoral. The question of the 1990s is whether world prosperity can survive amoral bankers or whether it is not better served by those of whom it can be said that 'Loyalty was always the vice of the House of Morgan.' As independent responsibility slipped away from bankers, banks increasingly second-guessed their decisions. In turn, this encouraged 'transaction' rather than 'relationship' banking, though there is little evidence that any but a few of the very largest corporations ever wanted this, for explaining business problems to bankers is just too time consuming to be lightly undertaken. Transaction banking suited selling bankers, though, for it encouraged glory hunting, in an environment where self-publicised success produced real gains in the pay cheque.

The reason that Jocelyn Hambro had accepted my proposal for Worden & Risberg had nothing to do with my arguments, but with policy strains within the front room at Hambros. The Hambro family had twice risked all to capture the Italian market, but their 1945 support of Crown Prince, later King, Umberto did little to endear them to the masters of the new republic. So perhaps there should have been no surprise when the three main state-owned banks, who joined together to create Mediobanca as their investment-banking affiliate, chose Warburgs as its London agents. But there were some in Italy who regarded Mediobanca as the hidden agent of state capitalism, which would deliver Italy lock, stock and wine barrel to the communists, and in this was a chance for Hambros to restore its fortunes.

Among such critics were John McCaffery, the bank's representative in Italy. As an SOE commander based in Switzerland and Northern Italy, he had organised British support of the Italian resistance and, with these fighters, dreamed of the new Italy that would be born from the joint struggle against Mussolini and the Germans. He introduced Jocelyn to Michele Sindona, a brilliant Sicilian tax lawyer who made his name on the back of the Italian economic miracle of the 1950s, and built his influence by helping Archbishop Montini of Milan. Sindona had helped finance the Christian Democratic election campaigns and, as a CIA conduit in its financing of Italy's internal war against communism, had steered some CIA money to a children's orphanage that Montini had built while Archbishop. When Sindona bought control of the Milan based Banca Privata Finanziaria from the Istituto per le Opere di Religione (IOR, or the Vatican Bank) Hambros and Continental Illinois – then chaired by David Kennedy who would later become President Nixon's Secretary of the Treasury – each became 22 per cent shareholders.

Due diligence came up with all the right answers, for Italian society was still stuck in the world of the High Renaissance, where power was personal and alliances forever shifting, while the Vatican is one of the great financial powers of the world; it is also one of the key political structures of Italy, together with the Christian Democratic Party, the major business families and, though none of us knew it at the time, the Mafia. Sindona was a clever player of the American conglomerate game, and had won the American Libby company against a competing Nestlé bid, and this had brought the Italian financier onto the world stage. McCaffery was a good friend of Allen Dulles, head of the CIA, with whom he had worked closely when the latter headed the Office of Strategic Services from Switzerland during the war, so both British and American intelligence gave the okay to Sindona while the Vatican, visited personally, was enthusiastic. Their endorsement soon came in more practical form, for Hambros was given Vatican money to manage in the stock markets, as well as sizeable money market deposits. And corporate finance deals were attractive in Italy, for there the stockmarket was still nineteenth century in structure and practice, controlled by various family groups who manipulated the market between them so that, with the right alliances, $1 could always be bought for twenty cents.

In 1963 Montini became Pope Paul VI while, a year later, Prince Massimo Spada left the Vatican Bank to become a working director of Banca Privata and, not long after, the Vatican ceded control of Banca Unione to Sindona. As Chicago born Archbishop Marcinkus would say, once he became the Pope's financial mentor and responsible for the Vatican Bank, 'You can't run a Church on Hail Marys'. Together, but under the generalship of Sindona, Christian Italy and its foreign banking allies would wrest economic control away from the secular state and, of importance to Sindona and Hambros both, destroy the power of fellow Sicilian Enrico Cuccia of Mediobanca. To do this, Sindona planned to buy Bastogi, a large and moribund investment company, stuffed with cash and major stakes in key Italian companies.

Bastogi would give Sindona control of one of the largest pools of investment money in Europe, but was also a frontal attack on the Italian business establishment, one that it could not easily ignore. Sindona's ambitions were fuelled by McCaffery's son, who took over more and more of the responsibilities of his father, and was much more extreme in his views. There was, as well, growing Vatican concern about its revenues for, though the church was asset-rich, it was cash poor. Though the Papacy is a highly cost-effective tax-collecting institution, priests need the faithful if they are to collect, and increasingly affluent Western Europeans were giving up church going. The American church, richest of all and especially so in Chicago, argued that domestic needs constrained the amounts they could send the Papacy.

However, though income was falling, the call on Papal revenues was rising. The Italian state was becoming insistent that millions of dollars-worth of back taxes on the Church's investment profits be paid, while the East European Church, to which Marcinkus with his Lithuanian background was heavily committed, and the South American dioceses, all needed more and more financial support. Sindona had already made good money for the Church, for he had successfully sold its directly owned Italian industrial holdings, together with their politically embarrassing confrontations over workers' pay with communist or socialist trades unions. The funds had been turned instead into a portfolio of American properties and quoted shares; the Watergate office and residential complex, which included the Washington offices of the Democratic Party and the burglary of which would destroy the Nixon presidency, was one such investment.

But Jocelyn was cautious, fearing that Sindona was getting ahead of himself, and wanted to test Italian reactions first. So the initial, and successful, phase of the battle was the acquisition of La Centrale, a former electricity generator which, since the nationalisation of its business, had become a cash-rich investment company. La Centrale succumbed to the allies, and it appeared that so might Bastogi. Jocelyn remained hesitant, and felt that Sindona was going too fast, but McCaffery and his Vatican friends explained that Italy was different, and its unwritten rules gave more latitude than those of Britain or America. But other directors were worried about Hambro's increasingly large commitment to Italy, for to most Englishmen of this time both Italy, and the Italians, were a joke. It was a place of cheerful holidays, and a magnificent past, but not a serious industrial power, as more than enough people pointed out to me while I considered the IIB offer. Actually, this was no longer the case for Italian firms were regularly beating British firms to major civil engineering projects in what had once been the British empire, but perception had not yet caught up with reality.

The Bastogi deal required Hambros to take a much higher profile, if it was to drum up sufficient support for the next stage of the battle, and Dellborg brought in Westdeutsche Landesbank to front a public offer for Bastogi shares. The price was attractive, but no one tendered their shares, for the Bank of Italy let its charges know that selling to Sindona would be construed as an unfriendly act. Then disaster struck, for Hambro's German banking associate pulled out of the deal, and undermined Jocelyn's authority when, most embarrassedly, they telephoned Dellborg after the initial failure to say

I'm sorry Rolf, but we can't go along with you on Bastogi, for we don't like the murmuring about the Sindona connections. It seems he's more deeply involved with the Mafia, and laundering drug money, than any of us knew, and the word is that a lot of the long term investment funding for Bastogi is to come from those same sources.

That's impossible. We went to the Vatican for clearance on the fellow, and the only better recommendation would be God himself, and I'm a bit young to go and ask him. The Vatican wouldn't touch Sindona if what you say is true.

What makes you so sure of that? We aren't, and that's why we are pulling out.

Charlie, unlike his father Sir Charles, had never come to terms with the fact that the youngest branch of the family – Olaf and Jocelyn – had superseded his, the eldest. His grandfather Eric had been moody, and his uncertain judgement had left both his side of the family, and the bank, badly exposed after Britain went off gold in 1931. The result of the reorganisation of family shareholdings, necessary to maintain a united family front in face of the considerable Scandinavian block, gave Olaf's side of the family voting control. The partly called £10 'A' shares in the quoted Hambro Trust always received sufficient extra votes, regardless of how many extra £1 shares were issued, to maintain control, and Hambro Trust controlled Hambros Bank. Others shared Charlie's worries about Sindona but, though Jocelyn refused to continue with Bastogi, he equally refused Charlie's demands that Hambros dump Sindona, and sell its shareholding in Banca Privata; though Jocelyn accepted that Sindona's megalomania now made him dangerous, he found it hard to believe that he and the Vatican were partners with the Mafia. However, if his partners felt that he was wrong, then he was prepared to go, but only if Charles did not succeed him, for he was not willing to entrust his family's wealth to Charlie's judgement.

This was the function of the Worden & Risberg study, for Sporborg reckoned that he could use them to square this circle. The proposed operating committee, for which I had laboured, was the vehicle, though with changes that were not to my taste. Instead of being the chairman's inner cabinet, which I had advocated, it was a consensual body operating independently of the chairman of the bank, who would now be Charlie. This was unworkable in the long term for groups need leaders, especially so when painful decisions need to be made, such as allocation of capital. Under the new dispensation, for instance, the banking division insisted on charging interest on the money it borrowed, and then lent on as the capital of the investment banking division. The investment bankers, who had never paid interest before, claimed that this money should be free of charge, for it was their share of the group's capital. Since there was no one to bang heads together, and establish what was capital, what borrowing, and what was the appropriate cost for both, this became a festering sore between the two main activities of the bank, which needed to work in harmony to exploit all the opportunities before Hambros.

Nor did Charlie like it, quite understandably, and when the tanker crisis erupted some three years later, he was able to wrest back control of the bank from the Operating Committee. I did not like it either, for the strategic planning aspect of the committee was dropped, though I understood that well enough. Jocelyn had never disguised the reality that a close relationship with him meant difficulties with Charlie. I had disregarded those warnings, as I never thought he would step down so soon, so this was another reason for going to the IIB. I left Hambros at the end of 1971, when Jocelyn gave up as chairman of the bank, though he became the chairman of the new holding company proposed by Worden & Risberg. McCaffery resigned from the Hambros board, ceased to be their representative in Italy, and Charlie forced Sindona to buy back Hambro's stake in Banca Privata.

My experience at Hambros showed me that IIB's core business should be servicing Italian banks, and that to do this well and profitably the dealers needed regular and up-to-date information on their own, and the bank's positions. Since we were dealing in the forward markets, this meant 'ladders', or a print-out of all the deals done by the bank, listed by maturity date, by dealer, and showing both the net and gross exposure of the bank deal by deal. Dealers have an amazing ability, during a crisis, to deal for several hours at a stretch, maintaining positions in their mind and remembering each transaction in detail, until they have time to document them. New dealing-room technology has simplified much of this, but 'ladders' are still needed as the base with which to start the day. The trouble was that very few banks had what we wanted.

Most old-established banks, like Midland and Hambros, would take a few more years to realise that the development of the euro-markets had made dangerously obsolescent the traditional split of dealing activities between sterling money markets, foreign exchange, bonds, equities and foreign securities. Financial markets are driven by interest-rate considerations; the swap made major currencies equal, by eliminating exchange risk while Reuters was integrating market knowledge. Equally banks like Citibank, which had a treasury function, either had systems that were too big for us or regarded them as too much of a competitive advantage, and would not sell them. We found what we wanted at Anglo-Portuguese Bank, now part of Norwich Union Insurance but then a small trade bank, living on its own past but with an excellent dealing room.

Modified, this system gave the dealers the information base that they needed and it was this, together with the discipline established by the managers of the dealing room, that enabled the IIB, while I was managing director, never to lose money on its monthly forex-trading account – except once, when thanks were due to Sindona and the Vatican. But volume was the trouble, for forex markets were growing exponentially and my intention in developing IIB's forex reputation was also to attract deposits: dealers are like the rest of us, and would rather dial one telephone number than two. The IIB deliberately set out to attract overnight deposits from banks squaring their books and discovering they had too much money late in the afternoon. Our system produced the management information that enabled this money to be deployed however late in the day it came in, but contracts and confirmations still had to be drawn up manually, and delivered through banks of telex machines.

Many banks discouraged overnight deposits, because they were expensive and inconvenient to administer while, without an inte-grated dealing room, it was difficult to make profitable use of them. But I was conscious that we had to do everything in our power to get our name around the market. Whether overnight deposits came before forex deals or after did not much matter, provided other dealers telephoned our numbers and not those of other banks. As it happened, I knew that overnight money had a habit of sticking around for much longer than just a day, as well as building up in volume, and I also had a use for it: we lent to Scandinavian banks, on one to three months' maturity at LIBOR (cost of money) plus ¼–½ per cent, for the account of their customers, who then paid their banks rather more for this help than the banks paid us. We funded this Scandinavian bank lending out of the overnight and very short-term deposits that flooded in to us, but, with this and the growing forex relationships with Italy, the backlog of administration grew and grew. The more we tried to conquer it, the worse it got, though the situation was even more bizarre in New York.

There, our correspondent banks who cleared our dollar deals were hopelessly behindhand, with no idea of whether we owed them several tens of millions or they owed us. Most were so overwhelmed that, provided their counterparties came up with meaningful figures, they would sooner or later accept them, whatever it cost them in lost interest. We had a real interest in staying on top of these accounts, and argued our side of the story, including sending task forces to New York to agree the figures. The forex clerks strove manfully, staying until nine and ten in the evening to get the contracts out, agree the net position of the accounts, and clear their desks for the following morning. For much of this time they also had to struggle with building contractors – for I had monumentally boobed with the time needed to prepare the larger premises to which the bank was moving. Then the three-day week added paraffin lamps to bricklayers and marble cutters, when Prime Minister Heath took on the coal miners and lost. No doubt the position clerks needed their overtime pay, but what they really worked for was promotion.

Both Brett and Wiseman had been through this mill and insisted that recruitment into the dealing room come through this department. If banking in general could be a meritocracy, then the dealing room was the pinnacle for those with nothing to their name but their native wit. But it was obvious that we had to automate all the back office processes, which meant a complete banking system. There was no such thing available, at least not one that met the specifications I knew I wanted after my experience at Hambros. There should be only one source of information, and information would only be input once, when the deal was originally done. Figures easily become corrupted if they go through too many hands, or if there is no outside discipline to ensure that they are correct, so it seemed only logical that this common source of information should then become the only basis for running and reporting on the affairs of the bank. This way everyone had an incentive to see that the correct figures went into the system, from department managers to outside auditors, for the results reflected their managerial and professional competence. Arguing with department heads was hopeless when they all produced their own accounts, based on their departmental figures that came from God knows where. As at Hambros, so at Citibank, because once all the departmental results were added together, the figure was three to four times what the bank actually made.

Naturally, I thought that there had to be a way of making money out of this, for developing any banking system is expensive in time, not only that of the consultants needed, but all the staff and managers who must be intimately involved, if the final result is to work at all. Equally naturally for me, I talked too much and listened too little. The conversion of the Anglo-Portuguese system to the IIB's needs had been undertaken by a two-man information technology department, and the number two was quiet, competent and actually did the job. Nearly everyone in the bank realised this, except me, so the number two sensibly left for a better job.

Thus I was the only one to be surprised when the new system began to lag behind its various target dates. This was serious, not only because of the mounting pressure on the forex administration, but because we had invested in an IBM–360. This had cost a fortune to buy and, housed in a separate building because of its size and need for a controlled temperature, was costing another fortune to run. The investment justification had been that we could sell spare time on the machine, since its capacity was overlarge for the bank; alternatively, the new software would give us such a competitive advantage that our business would soon expand, or we could sell a package deal to smaller banks wishing to enter the forex market.

No time had been sold, no splendid new system was installed, and neither the manager nor the very expensive software consultants we were employing could tell me when one or the other might happen. This was a serious problem. IBIS, as the system came to be called, was designed to do everything; providing customers with smart and comprehensive contracts and accounts; establishing the internal market through which the treasury (a.k.a. Brett and Wiseman) would buy and sell money from the business-getting functions of the bank; giving departmental managers all the information needed to manage their specific functions; supplying the Bank of England's growing appetite for analytical breakdowns of the bank's balance sheet; and producing management and audited accounts for the shareholders. It could not be done manually, for we had reached a limit to the number of people that could be physically employed, and had only just completed our move to larger offices.

The system was also intended to support the bank's private banking business with a high-quality, personalised service, for the Guernsey office had got off to a stunning start, and I hoped to build up English business, as well, by attracting some of the newer firms of legal partnerships with this integrated banking service. All this was now at risk. Fortunately, I had a secret weapon. Patricia Drakes had joined the IIB from the accelerated promotion group of Shell and, as a clever accountant and excellent manager, I reckoned that she would be a fair match for computer babble. There were only two major software consultancies in Britain at the time, and we were employing one. The increasing capacity of computers suggested that IIB could get away with a bank-housed minicomputer, rather than the mainframe machine we had bought. Drakes reported that industry experience was that it was dangerous, but just acceptable, to change either machinery or consultant halfway through a project, but to do both was to court disaster. She was willing, though, to take over the job.

I disproved the slogan that 'you never get sacked for buying an IBM' by replacing manager and consultants, selling the IBM and its attendant building, though at some considerable loss, buying a DEC PDP–111, and handing over the IT function to Drakes. She was every bit as successful as I could have hoped. This international banking system has served IIB well over the years and a version was sold to the Midland Bank in 1984. By then, however, the second group of consultants had also been sacked, for they proved incapable of selling IBIS. Still owned by IIB and managed by Drakes, IBM minis have now replaced DEC machines and IBIS now has IBM as a minority shareholder, while over a third of London banks have now bought the IBIS system, and many of these have persuaded their parent banks to buy as well, for Drakes added another successful touch to the system.

IBIS is now modular, so banks buy only the elements they need for the business they do, and IBIS is run almost as a banking cooperative. Improvements or new modules are specified, and tested, by the bankers who have to use the system. The computer-systems designers act first as critics to the bankers' ideas, suggesting the ways that electronic blips can improve on procedures that were designed for quill pens, and then as executants of the agreed design. Schroders, for instance, installed IBIS over one weekend; the bank opened for business on the Monday morning with a computer system that had nothing in common with that on which its business had closed on the Friday night.

The pattern of computerisation has influenced the managerial structure of banking from the 1970s onwards, for this process was not preceded by any detailed analysis of what banks were doing and why, and how those procedures could be simplified by the computer. Instead, initial computer systems were a simple translation of quill-pen entries into computer keystrokes. The result is that, even today, banks have considerable difficulties with the first of their major errors with the technology that would destroy their exclusivity. Banks know how many accounts they've got; what few of them can work out is how many customers they have, or whether they make money out of them. Banking is driven by transaction systems, alien to the relationship nature of commercial banking in their handling of vast volumes of simple transactions, but so massive that no one knows how to change them. Over the years, bankers worldwide have thrown away billions on misconceived and inadequate computer systems or, perhaps less forgivably, by insisting on their need to reinvent the wheel.

Although investment bankers have recently accepted that it is cheaper and safer to buy standard systems and adopt their clerical procedures to the computer software, rather than the other way about, most commercial bankers still behave as if their bank is *sui generis*. John Ginarlis of PA Consulting, a competitor of McKinsey's, reckons that US spending on computers has now risen to 15 per cent of total costs or some $10 billion a year, while European banks have also begun to accelerate such investment. British commercial banks alone were spending just under £100 million a year in the mid–1980s, then shifted up to £150 million and, two years ago, moved up another gear, and are now spending in excess of £250-£300 million a year. Ginarlis puts it delicately, since bankers are the very people on whom PA depends for contracts: 'Spending programmes on this scale can develop a life of their own . . . A great deal of money can be and has been wasted in such circumstances . . . and this is all the more dangerous because . . . the major banks regard their levels of computer spending as a source of competitive advantage.'

Ginarlis might also have added that the information-technology departments of most banks have grown like Topsy, but starting from such a low intellectual base that these today are as terrified of the technology as are the senior bankers who purport to direct them. The trouble is that bankers, overburdened with innumerable problems, look for magical solutions. Sir John Quinton, as chairman of Barclays, summarised this credo when he stated: 'The impact of Information Technology is so radical that it will be a key determinant of success or failure in the industry; a key determinant of whether "banks", as a recognisable grouping, continue to exist; and a key determinant of the differentiation between competitors in financial services.'

True in the sense that computers are the key to cutting costs and returning decisions to the banker in the field, Quinton's remarks suggest that senior bankers still do not understand the working principle of the computer, which is that 'garbage in equals garbage out'. Nor, perhaps, did bankers misspend enough of their own youth listening to such anarchic individuals as Tom Lehrer, professor of mathematics at Harvard, and successful lyricist and recording singer. I still remember one appropriate line – 'plagiarise, plagiarise, don't plague your eyes' – for, if developing a software program is expensive, messy and fraught, copying it is altogether easier, while buying it from a satisfied user is safer and quicker still.

Computer-generated management information is, in the main, so opaque that bankers using it make medieval schoolmen, arguing over the number of angels that can dance on the head of a pin, seem brutally practical. Sensible remedial action is not easy, when corporate power is based on numbers of employees. Success in the bureaucratic jockeying for position goes to the best politician, not the best banker, for corrective measures become impossible without either profitability analysis or the expectation of imminent disaster. Without an agreed understanding of both the basic banking figures and the trends they show, it was all too easy to accept the new banking theory propagated by Citibank and other exponents of liability management, which was that money-market funding, diversification of the lending portfolio through syndication, and concentration on the biggest and the best of borrowers made banking risk-free.

Initially the IIB dealt with Moneyrex, which was the largest continental money broker. This was based in Milan, owned by Sindona, and managed by Carlo Bordoni, and McCaffery junior was much involved in this as well as in Sindona's two Italian banks. McCaffery was keen that the IIB should deal with them, and I was equally interested, for he promised to introduce me to Luigi Menini, who actually ran the Vatican Bank as well as serving on the Sindona boards. Apart from the Vatican, he promised other blue-chip business contacts, who I reckoned would not be coming via my shareholders, for, after the Bastogi failure, Sindona moved closer to the Vatican; more of Sindona's energies, and more of the Vatican's wealth, would be deployed in America where, Sindona felt, a self-made man was more appreciated than in class-ridden Europe. But business was always one-way, which was odd, for Sindona's banks had good reputations in Italy, an attractive business franchise, and their balance sheets showed them to be liquid. After a year of seeing money going out, but never coming in, I stopped renewing these deposits.

Possibly his Bastogi failure persuaded Sindona that pickings were easier in America; more likely, in my opinion, he was finding it more and more difficult to fund his wide-ranging corporate activities through the euromarkets. The pattern would be followed by all his imitators, with deposits from banks and funds from companies, posting through a hall of mirrors created by a complex and secretive web of interlocking companies and trusts. Good conjurors could fool nearly all the people all the time with this pattern, but they could never create cash flow out of illusions. The financial stringency that follows a crash exposed them all, whether Hatry and Kreuger in 1929, Sindona and Herstatt in 1974 or Maxwell and BCCI after 1987.

The La Centrale deal still required completing but, with Hambros out of the partnership, Sindona needed offshore companies and banks to shield his activities from the prying eyes of the Italian authorities. An international bank was necessary for his schemes, and the Pope's banker chose the priests' bank of Milan. Banco Ambrosiano was a solid Italian commercial bank, originally set up in opposition to the growing power of the 'secular' banks such as Banca Commerciale Italiana (BCI) and Credito Italiano. It had no international business worth the name, but it did have an ambitious young manager. Roberto Calvi came from a middle-class background, his father being a manager with BCI, but, rather than going to university, joined a good cavalry regiment instead. After meritorious war service in Russia, where he showed both moral and physical courage, he joined Ambrosiano and became a client of Carlo Canesi, a senior manager of the bank and, later, its chairman. No Italian gets anywhere without a powerful patron, a hangover so far from being Renaissance in style that it goes back to imperial Rome. More formal than the 'old-boy network' of the English establishment, it is equally effective and, when connected to the link between politicians and organised crime, enormously powerful.

Calvi had already proved himself by setting up Interitalia for Ambrosiano, in successful competition with IOS's Fonditalia mutual fund; after that, Canesi encouraged Calvi, who was an excellent linguist, to build up an international business for Ambrosiano. Calvi and Canesi were grateful when Sindona asked both to join with him and the Vatican, and Calvi gained another patron for, to complete the takeover of La Centrale, Banco Ambrosiano Holdings was established in Luxembourg, organised so as to shelter Ambrosiano's foreign dealings from the Bank of Italy.

Ownership of La Centrale violated Italy's 1936 banking law – patterned on the American 1933 laws – but official approval was given because La Centrale's holdings were predominantly financial and insurance businesses. In fact, it was fear of the Vatican and Sindona's friends in the Christian Democratic Party that won official approval despite the opposition of the technical levels of the Bank of Italy; these would have their revenge in 1982. Sindona introduced Calvi to Licio Gelli, head of the Propagande Due [P2] masonic lodge, at much the same time. As the senior commercial banker for Sindona, the Vatican and P2, Calvi formed the nexus of an influential though secretive linking of Italy's conservative forces, and his career went into overdrive. He became general manager of Ambrosiano in February 1971, managing director six months later, chairman in 1975 and, with Sindona in disgrace, from then to his suicide Calvi was God's banker.

I had also met the management of Franklin National in New York, and had not liked them. On that basis alone, I had refused them either a money market or a forex line – such are the pleasures of being an autocrat! – and I was right, though I did not know it at the time. Franklin was already bust by the early 1960s, having lost all its capital through bad debts. Franklin had been regularly warned by the regulators, and should have been closed down, but it was America's eighteenth largest bank and America's regulators had lost their experience of dealing with very large banking failures. Franklin also had friends in high places and, with Sindona's purchase, got more of them. When Sindona bought Franklin at a large premium to its market price in 1972, many of its bad debts were the result of loans to Long Island contractors, a business traditionally associated with the Mob, but whether Sindona was Mafia I never knew. No one in Italy liked to speculate, although I discovered soon that the Mafia – Camorra in Naples, and organised crime anywhere – was one of the powers of Italy.

The reason that IIB could get no Italian lending business was that no major contract was placed, no loan made, nor deal done, without substantial presents being distributed to those who had 'helped' the transaction. These sums were skimmed off the top as commissions, and distributed to the innumerable factions of the various political parties, this being the way they financed themselves. The banks were key to the payment process, which is why the parties kept such a tight hold of them. Equally, the political factions controlled the disbursement of state money, or contracts, which amounted to the same thing, and they remained conscious of their obligations to those who got out the vote. In Sicily and the south, this was the Mafia, who also ensured that everyone voted Christian Democrat, and building contracts were certainly their share of the spoils. This is the 'sotto governo' and, as Italy got richer, so did organised crime, for the embrace between banks, parties and contractors flourished, and the Mafia moved northwards. Drugs are no doubt profitable, but I doubt that these profits compare with regularly leeching a few percentage points out of the Italian economy; the current estimate is 12 per cent.

London bankers, as they found it increasingly easy to use the euromarkets, also found it easy to forget earlier lessons about banking liquidity. The dangers of this were brought sharply home to all of us late in 1973, as the reaction of the Arab oil states to the Yom Kippur war threw the whole of the developed world into turmoil. A large German bank had to be rescued that autumn; this was followed by the bankruptcy of an American bank, closely linked to President Nixon, and a large borrower on the euromarkets. Finally, interbank market funding for the whole of the British secondary banking sector just melted away. Bankers panicked; this was the first international crisis in forty years and, as no one had expected it, no one had much idea of how to deal with it.

Wall Street tottered as back offices collapsed, exposing the enormous bad debts that had built up during the boom, and private money left the Wall Street partnerships for good. In London property values collapsed, and the chairman of the National Westminster, Britain's second largest bank but the one whose aggressive hunt for business had exposed it most to the secondary banks, hurriedly put on a dressing gown one Sunday morning to deny that the bank was about to close its doors or had solvency problems. The key difference between then and the 1990s was that the banks were able to scramble out of their property and share-market loans; inflation reduced the real cost of their loans faster than unpaid interest increased them, whereas today the reverse is happening.

Nevertheless, Margaret Reid, the historian of the British crash, reckons that the necessary funding support marshalled by the Bank of England for the secondary – for which read property-lending – banks was as much as £3 billion; inflation since then means today's equivalent is a figure four times as high. Losses from the 1974 property crash have never been disclosed but Reid estimates that, adding those incurred by the Bank of England to those of its reluctant supporters, the figure was not less than £250 million. Quite modest really, even when quadrupled for inflation. It is possible that bankers lacked the time to read Reid's book, for they had a busy year of it in 1982, since publication coincided with the beginning of the Third

World debt crisis, but a couple of hours spared then might have saved many weeks, and several millions now.

By the summer of 1974, Italian banks could hardly borrow in the London market. The financial machinations of Sindona and political chaos in Italy, with its uncontrolled growth of state spending and borrowing, had meant that bankers were becoming wary of Italian loans, but the trigger for the crisis was the probability that the communists were about to become part of a Christian Democrat-led Italian coalition government. This 'opening to the left' was inherently implausible, and had more to do with the dishing of the Italian Socialists by the Christian Democrats than any serious attempt at reconciling a large and disenfranchised part of the Italian electorate. But it certainly turned London bankers paranoid about Italian 'country risk', and their feelings were not helped by two other horrors.

The first was the bankruptcy of Bankhaus Herstatt, a small German bank that had been gambling heavily in the forex markets. This failure came on top of announced multimillion-dollar forex losses by Lloyds Bank, Westdeutsche Landesbanke and Union Bank of Switzerland, as well as rumours of other major losses, many of which proved to be true. The Bundesbank (the German central bank) had no more recent experience than anyone else of banking crises, and closed Herstatt during trading hours. That was how postwar bankers first learned of counterparty risk. A bank's immediate trading partners may be safe, but the interrelationships of the trading and settlement system are enormous, worldwide and extremely complex. In the Herstatt case, this meant that banks who did not know they were dealing with Herstatt, suddenly found out that they were.

Bankers know that possession is nine tenths of the law, so Morgans, Chase and Citibank grabbed the clearing balances and other assets owned by Herstatt in its New York accounts, and just said 'Sue us' to other aggrieved parties. Those left without Herstatt security failed to complete their deals, sitting on whatever money they had. Hill Samuel found itself facing a potential loss of over $21 million as its counterparty contracts unravelled, though in the end, and after much expense, it lost not much more than a tenth of that. The position would have been clearer if Herstatt had been shut down after the day's settlements of forex and eurodollar trades. Herstatt hit London hard, for it was the world centre for forex and euromarket dealing, even though all these deals were cleared through New York. In the end the Bank of England set up a neutral account through which most of the Herstatt deals could be completed safely.

That was bad enough for the IIB, but we could excuse it as a unique mixture of German gambling and central-bank bungling. That excuse was no good for the failure of Sindona's overborrowed empire. An attempt to strengthen his home base, by merging his two Italian banks into Banca Privata Italiana, failed to stem growing rumours. His illiquidity was worsened as his political enemies lengthened the bureaucratic agreement to the merger, and Privata failed soon after the legal merger was completed, late in September. This was followed by the collapse of Franklin in October. At the time, this was America's largest bank failure, though the events of the 1980s would show that Sindona was a mere tyro, compared to those who would learn from him. This was the last straw for the IIB, and I well recall a conversation with a major London bank.

'We'll only lend three months' money if you pay the Italian premium of 1 per cent over LIBOR and even then my colleagues are not that keen on Italian risk, and we certainly won't go to six months.'

'That's bullshit, and you know it. You're happily dealing with us in forex, we're getting overnight money from you, and now you turn around and say we're not a London risk, but Italian. You know that's not the case, and what are you worried about anyway – that our shareholders are going to go belly-up after five hundred years?'

'If BCI and Credito are paying the premium, you've got to as well, whatever your exact legal status. Actually, since you're not a branch but a subsidiary bank, you ought to pay more than them because the risk is greater.'

'Like hell I will – not that another 1 per cent should make you willing to risk a deposit, if you really think things are that bad. Frankly, if I offered you the extra, you should take that as a sign that you ought not to lend, so we're in a catch–22 situation. It's a matter of principle – we'll either borrow at the market price, or not at all.'

'You won't be borrowing from us without it, so pay up or go without.'

This was when the IIB's forex strategy paid off for, by this time, we were the major marketmaker in the lire markets. Any bank that needed to exchange lire for dollars, for sterling, for Deutschmarks or whatever, had first to check the IIB price. Bcause the IIB was seen as efficient and knowledgeable in this most professional of banking activities, other banks' dealers continued to work with us whatever their managers or credit departments said. Bank dealers are a close-knit community, and also human. When forex deals were done with the IIB, deposit deals were done at the same time. Dealers were working with Ron, Alan or Jimmy, people they gossiped and drank with, and not some faceless institution of the credit department. I had interpreted my earlier conversations correctly, and the reason IIB survived the 1974 liquidity crisis was not its shareholders' support, even though, as I discovered afterwards, these were all liquid, with masses of unused lines with the New York banks.

The Bank of Sicily was the only one of the four that really pulled its weight during the crisis and, though the IIB funding book went from six months to three months, and then to less than one month, we lived through our dealing-room relationships and our private-bank deposits. The IIB was the only consortium bank to have more than 20 per cent of its deposits from outside the money markets; if these were aware that a crisis existed, they certainly did not ask to withdraw their money. The shareholders of Western American Bank were forced to buy out some £200 million of its loans and give it substantial deposit support in the money markets, and most other consortium banks were supported in a similar fashion. Other bank branches had to be supported by their parent banks, but the IIB survived on its own – not that the Italians ever appreciated how cheaply they got off.

There had been discussions of such a crisis happening in London, so the Bank of England turned the lessons of the domestic crisis to international use, and rallied other central bankers to the task of acting as lender of last resort. It was agreed that the lender of last resort for banks like the IIB should be the shareholders, supported by their own central bank, and shareholding banks were required to give letters of comfort to the Bank of England, stating that they would support their subsidiary. Actually Cobbold and I had both been worried about Italian political problems causing a funding crisis for the IIB, and we had already extracted such letters from the Italian board members, representing the parent banks. With Cobbold's encouragement I had called on them for help at the height of the crisis, and got no money for my pains, but plenty of ill will.

The reason became obvious two years later, when bad debts made it necessary to recapitalise the bank. The four chairmen, like good politicians, had put neither their undertakings to Cobbold, nor those to the Bank of England, to the boards of their parent banks, for they hoped that all would be well, and there would be no need to upset anyone.

14

Foggy Weather

'We are facing the upheaval that manufacturing has already gone through. Think of what happened to the engineering industry and the coal industry in the 1980s. We will go through the same thing because we have the same problems . . . The whole idea that we must save our people, and therefore we have to diversify, is wrong. We must cease to be the workers' cooperatives and become successful businesses.'

Brian Pitman, chief executive of Lloyds Bank,
to the Institute of Bankers

BANKERS HAVE LONG BEEN known as folk who lend an umbrella when the sun is shining, and demand it back as soon as rain threatens. English disquiet about the lack of banking support for the smaller company became public during 1991 when the *Sunday Times*, alerted by readers' complaints about banks doubling or trebling the cost of their services without warning to customers, though in concert among themselves, opened its columns to banking victims. The newspaper was inundated with thousands of stories detailing the high-handed and commercially crass behaviour of British banks, and the public uproar was sufficient to force the chancellor of the Exchequer to talk to bank chairmen, giving good photo opportunities to all. This apotheosis of the high-street bank into the *de haut en bas* style of Pierpoint Morgan was proclaimed by Sir John Quinton, then chairman of Barclays Bank; asked why it was that banks, unlike any other commercial business, changed the terms and costs of their contracts without discussion with their customers, Quinton simply replied: 'We hold the money.'

Banking customers, accustomed to thinking of the 'branch' as the 'bank', discovered in the crisis of the 1990s that computerised banking has no clear role for branches and – as their banks withdrew or reduced agreed credit limits, regardless of local circumstances – that their bank managers, whatever was asserted, had neither authority of their own, nor influence with their head office. Over the previous twenty years, these once powerful and influential figures of the local community had slowly ceased to be bankers and become instead junior salesmen for policies decided at head office. But, however blatant the banks' oligopolistic behaviour, initial threats of an official inquiry soon came to nothing.

This providential escape in 1992 may well have persuaded Brian Pitman, chief executive of Lloyds Bank, that he could succeed with a hostile banking bid, frowned upon by banking regulators on both sides of the Atlantic. His argument was that the country was over-banked, but Lloyds would accept its responsibility and dismember the Midland Bank for the good of the country, the banking industry, Lloyds' shareholders and, though not directly mentioned, him and his colleagues through their share options and bonus arrangements. Pitman's success in steamrollering his chairman and board into a bidding war with the Hongkong & Shanghai Banking Corporation, despite the obvious hostility of the Bank of England, was as surprising as it was politically insensitive. Hongkong already held 15 per cent of the Midland equity, generally regarded as sufficient to block any hostile bid, and talk of marriage between the two goes back as far as the late 1970s, when Bank of England opposition put paid to the romance. Matters had moved on since then. Proposals for a new marriage contract had been exchanged in 1985, cemented by the purchase of shares, and proved by some shuffling of European branches. This had been initiated by Sir Kit McMahon, formerly deputy governor of the Bank of England, Midland's chairman from 1986 onwards, and had the enthusiastic backing of Midland management and board alike.

Moreover, the Lloyds offer was embarrassing even to its supporters; it was conditional upon its bid, and that of its rival, being treated similarly by the relevant monopoly authorities, which was legally impossible under the provisions of the Treaty of Rome. The UK government could not take back the power of the European Commission to study the Hongkong bid, even had it wished to, and it was politically impossible as well. Any hopes entertained by Lloyds' directors that the public would roll over as easily as the chancellor had done the previous year were quickly dispelled, as the *Sunday Times* orchestrated public reaction, emphasising that while the country might be 'over-branched', it was far from 'over-banked'. Brave noises that Lloyds would continue to fight, despite the rejection of all its conditions, turned into an ignominious scuttle when Lloyds' board came to its senses and forced Pitman to abandon the battle. This hopeless – though expensive – bid might just reflect the usual megalomania of a successful banker, for Pitman has certainly been more adept than most in emphasising shareholder value and has profitably dismantled Lloyds' international activities.

More likely, it simply represents the intellectual poverty of senior bankers as they face a threat, not merely to banking profitability, but to the industry itself. Pitman, while claiming that earlier expansion was the consequence of the soft-heartedness of senior management, also mentioned the managerial toughness of Hanson, the Anglo-American industrial conglomerate, saying: 'That is management, not pussy-footing around.' The problem faced by senior bankers is that they are running financial conglomerates and ought to follow Hanson-like disciplines. However, they find this hard to accept, lack the tools to do the job, and cannot recognise that their lending and investment mistakes result from their abject failure to manage banking risk, or to manage within a changing world.

Commercial banking, as late as 1970, consisted of a few simple but economically vital services, offered through a complex geographical network. Banking is records and precedents, skills and resources, and these can be properly known only at the branch level, which is where most decisions were taken and all administration handled. The arcanum of banking was the handwritten, leatherbound ledger, together with the experience of lending – and therefore losing – money to many sorts of businesses, and from branches that differed in size and location, though all with their own economic and financial peculiarities. Head office could control branches passively, by ensuring through its banking inspectorate that managers kept within agreed procedures, but had no way of influencing them positively through budgets or volume targets. Commercial banking was a 'branch' culture for it was 'the bank in miniature'. For most commercial bankers, the promotion chain stopped when they found themselves in a branch and a town that they liked and that was big enough for their ambitions. Head office was only for the exceptionally ambitious, or those strange few that preferred central administration and control to running their own business.

The computer came as a godsend to banks, when social change stopped up the source of qualified clerks of the type portrayed by Jack Lemmon in the film *The Apartment* or Frank Dickens in the Bristow cartoon strip. Rather than reconsidering training procedures or pay scales, so as to attract back those who would have become bankers but had gone to university instead, senior bankers redefined banking. The banks' response owed much to their senior managers' wartime experience, for the first impact of the loss of cheap but clever labour was on branch clerical functions. Military lessons on how to turn unwilling civilians into competent soldiers were helpful, as branch functions were split into ever more discrete units and established on a production-line basis; young girls, not expected to stay beyond marriage, were the new cannon fodder.

The second stage of reorganisation was to develop staff and head-office functions, so as to make these jobs attractive to graduates, and to support or supplant the branch-management structure. This led to confusion among customers and bankers alike, for, though the branches looked the same, these steadily lost the knowledge and authority once incorporated in their professional staff. From the 1960s onwards, banking ledgers were replaced with computer files and, with banking split into barely understood functions, handled by ill-paid and under-trained functionaries, any decision of importance was referred up the line. Henry Ford would have been proud of the production-line techniques with which banking was deskilled. The arrogance of barely understood technologists then combined with the centralising tendencies of head offices, and bankers were persuaded that everything else, including judgement, could also be centralised. The banks proceeded to build themselves 'command and control' systems that Stalin himself would have envied.

Fortunately, as with communism, so with banking, and democracy crept back while the secret police were looking the other way. Two senior McKinsey specialists believe that systems spending by the US banks now

> represents a fundamental change in the way that banking services are being produced and delivered . . . Banking jobs are being displaced by automation in a manner similar to that of the automation of the US farm, a process which began in the last century. There, technology instigated a precipitous decline in farm employment that has now continued for almost a century.

Today, computer software has become clever enough, and hardware cheap enough, to enable computers to help banking judgement through decision support and 'expert' systems, though only at a decentralised, or branch, level; the problem is not computer power or memory, but convenience, confidence and information.

About 50 per cent of bank lending in America, both to companies and to individuals, is now made by 'non-banks', using industry standard software and the standard corporate controls for assessing profitability. For example, General Electric's financial operations outdo all but America's five largest banks. These new competitors are cheaper, quicker and often better than the banks. Despite Canute-like resistance by the regulators, the same tide is sweeping away European banking profits. The banks could compete, except that the same McKinsey study concludes that, though US banks' spending has definitely improved the quality, speed and convenience of many banking services, the cost has been increased capacity and more competition, so that 'banks are creating value and destroying profits'.

It is easier to copy than to invent, so establishing, let alone maintaining, a technological lead within banking is a near impossibility, yet banks continue to increase their spending with the proclaimed intention of doing just this. McKinsey calculate that 90 per cent of systems spending is concerned with 'essentially routine tasks, which provide few opportunities for distinctive performance and profits'. Computers can improve performance, but they still can't think, or replace the good adviser. Traditionally, the financial ganglia of local communities comprised the bank manager, the accountant and the lawyer; investment banking was the mirror image of commercial banking, for even in the late 1960s it consisted of complex and ever mutating services, but supplied from the simplicity of a single office. Like commercial banking, however, those who made the decisions emerged naturally from those who had initially either analysed or administered them.

The middle decades of the twentieth-century were always going to be hard for the Midland Bank. Britain was increasingly 'exporting weight and importing refinement' and Midland, with its gritty northern managers, was never popular within the City club, while its business franchise had always been in sharp contrast to that of its competitors. Much of British industrial success was originally based on family-controlled, vertically integrated, small-scale business – much like banking until the 1960s, in fact – and there seemed no pressing need to change this, despite the pre-First World War warnings of Midland Bank directors such as Dudley Docker. The creator of the Birmingham Small Arms engineering group, Docker was concerned at the increasing disparity between British, and American and German, manufacturing capabilities in the early decades of this century. The newly industrialising America and Germany were utilising the telegraph, graduate engineers and banking capital to create multinational business giants from the 1870s onwards.

The British were reluctant to borrow, to establish research departments or to allow their businesses to become any larger than could easily be controlled by the family. Between running US Steel or Siemens, and ruling India, there was no contest; Britain's best and brightest served the nation. Midland's chairman warned of the increasing vulnerability of British wealth throughout the interwar years; by the 1950s, it was becoming plain to all, and Jack Hambro remarked in 1960 (to Anthony Sampson for *Anatomy of Britain*): 'The traditional banks are like the British empire. There's nothing more to gain, and quite a lot to lose.' Docker's son in the 1950s was more concerned with using his position to pay for his gold-studded Rolls-Royce, and to allow his wife to display her fur coats and jewels on their frequent forays to the Côte d'Azur, than to reinvigorate a fading company.

The reckoning with reality for British business, and for the Midland, started with Warburg's takeover activities during the 1960s. These killed many of the Midland's biggest accounts, and the 1970s were even worse for the bank. When the Midland most needed bright recruits, banking conditions of employment failed to keep pace with social changes. European social programmes, and the GI bill in America, opened the universities to those who would once have become banking clerks. British banking, like the medieval Church, had long been an attractive and meritocratic career for those with talent but with neither higher education nor family connections, and banks had always attracted the brightest and the best of school-leavers; many of these were part of family traditions of employment, established over two or three generations. Though the 'branch' was still the 'bank' in 1970, the appeal of family succession, and banking as a career, was dying as Midland's war-depleted ranks faced the transatlantic assault of Citibank and its peers.

The best of the new university graduates had alternative careers to the commercial banks, including merchant banks, investment management and, increasingly, American or other foreign banks. The growing complexity of business, the proliferation of legislation, especially tax, prompted an increased professionalism within large and growing business corporations, as well as among legal and accountancy firms. The banks attempted to recruit graduates during the 1960s but failed, for they refused to change their methods of training. In consequence, the professional competence of branch managers began to decline just as that of their community counterparts – accountants, lawyers, corporate managers and investment bankers – was growing.

Citibank had similar staffing problems; it was stretched for talent and, when Walter Wriston took over from George Moore as president in 1967, the bank had only 250 platform officers, or bankers with the title of vice-president or above. Many of these, like Moore himself, were due to go, for retirement at sixty-five was the inflexible Citibank rule, even for chairmen. Though Citibank had started training courses during 1916, and recruited university graduates during the 1920s, after the Wall Street crash becoming a 'bankster' was most definitely not 'politically correct'. Moore had headed a 1948 committee that looked at what the bank was, where it was going and what needed to be done to get there, and these changes, together with others that he was able to push through once he became president in 1959, gave Citibank a five-year planning cycle. Moore made a big effort to attract graduates back to banking during the 1950s, when he took over responsibility for Citibank's domestic division, but this began to bear fruit only after some years of proselytising. This planning process became the motor that powered Citibank's growth, and enabled it to absorb the recruits that began to appear from the 1960s onwards.

Moore opened up another, unexpected source of future talent, once he took over the international division in 1956. 'Siberia', as he described his promotion, had an unusual benefit. Few Americans worked in this division, and all that did were old and tired. When Wriston was called in to set up a shadow organisation that would take the international division into the future, Moore realised that young Europeans, who once would have satisfied their taste for adventure and responsibility by joining their countries' colonial service, now lacked such an international challenge. Once these appreciated that foreign service with Citibank also meant American rates of pay, and citizenship, they lined up for jobs.

Moore and Wriston believed that planning for future management was a banking function, and not one to be delegated to the timid bureaucracy of a personnel department. The needs of Citibank forced them to establish a fast-track training system, for employees doubled while foreign branches quadrupled. Training was brief but intense, and based on Moore's experience of developing industry-specialist lending officers, then picking out high flyers from the more successful of these to be given a general training to equip them for future high office. The nature of the pickers, and the ambitions of the chosen, ensured that this would be a Darwinian process; once the guiding hand of the promoters left it, what was corporate competition became no-quarter civil war.

When Wriston was promoted to president in 1967, he called in McKinsey to analyse the bank's structure and prepare it for its return to its 'do anything, be everywhere' financial-services past. McKinsey worked openly with a widely selected task force and, by a joint and consensual decision, Citibank was reorganised into six profit-making businesses and a back-office. These were to be run by the new industry specialists, and guided by budgets drawn up in accordance with the five-year plan. The branches remained, and were increased, but they were no more than glorified post offices, handling the mail for customers and their graduate banker specialists. Wriston was in Moore and Mitchell's mould, an imaginative and driving salesman, and completed Moore's task of reducing Citibank's personal baronies into a well-crafted universal bank. But Moore was governed by his memories; Wriston honed this structure into a finely tuned selling machine, but one with no such governor sitting on top of its motor.

War and banking are both about taking risks on the basis of probabilities calculated from known precedents, existing skills and strengths, and the balance of certain risk against possible reward. So banking is fundamentally about doing, rather than managing. However brilliant the organisational structure, the planning, the marketing, the recruitment and the training, at the end of the day, as Olaf Hambro remarked, 'banking is about making more than you lose', whether by lending, issuing or dealing. Far from unquestioning obedience, banking required confident and intelligent business negotiators with minds of their own. The university option, as well as the bureaucratic impulse towards centralisation, increasingly produced the exact opposite. If bankers had to copy a service pattern of organisation, they should have looked to the navy and not the army. As the Falklands task force sailed through the South Atlantic, military and naval commanders were still at loggerheads. The army, fundamentally a nineteenth-century imperial institution, argued that the task was suicidal, for the task force had neither a secure base nor air cover, while the enemy were in superior numbers on a strongly defended shore.

The navy just drove southwards; too many beached captains, let alone the memory of Admiral Byng – shot on his own quarterdeck, as Voltaire quipped, 'to encourage the others' – reminded navy commanders that the final phrase in their commissions ('in this fail not at your peril') was not there for effect. The navy acted from a simpler and much older tradition than the army, and knew that chance, the confusion of battle and the unimaginable possibilities of the sea made too much cerebration dangerous. The task force sailed on towards battle, confident in Nelson's instructions that 'no captain can do very wrong who places his ship alongside that of an enemy'. The confusion of business is equal to that of battle, and the Midland's branch managers followed the navy style. They were always aware that even if banks only sacked staff who dipped their fingers in the till, their superiors still had the managerial equivalent of Siberia and the salt mines for those who failed.

Successful banking is single-ship action, for it is a personal response to specific financial needs. Though the advice and caution of superiors is necessary, banking judgement requires knowledge of the individual circumstances of the customer, and experience of the business nature of the locality. Banking success needs well-honed relationships which will provide economic intelligence, create business introductions and promote the banker within his chosen business community. It also needs time, since most of us learn more easily from burned fingers than fatherly prohibitions, and successful command of a battleship needs practice aplenty on smaller ships, as well as command at subordinate levels. Traditional bank training emphasised losing affordable sums of money when young, so as not to lose much larger amounts when older and in a position to break the bank. As the commercial banks junked this pattern, under the new pressures of graduate recruitment, the merchant banks were able to maintain their old ways.

The Midland might have equalled Citibank's growth, despite credit restrictions, since its thinking was considerably more imaginative than even Citibank's. Furthermore, the purchase of Samuel Montagu gave it an escape route from credit controls; although the Bank of England would not allow the English clearing banks to make currency loans until 1976, this restriction had been lifted from acceptance houses in 1957. The tenfold growth in Hambros' balance sheet over the decade showed the demand for such loans. There was considerable stock-market activity, too, for high taxation encouraged businessmen to convert income into tax-free capital through the flotation of their companies, and this enabled them to plan for tax-free inheritance at the same time. Furthermore, Midland had a winning scheme to attract support from Samuel Montagu and small-company owners for, eight years earlier, the bank had unveiled twenty-year farming loans and ten-year small-company loans. This commitment to business was what the English tradition had always lacked, compared to the American and German approach, and it quickly made Midland a leader in farming.

Moreover, quite apart from Citibank's perhaps flawed 1920s experience, the Midland could see the success that Hambros was making of hybrid banking, or look across the Channel at its correspondents. But since the death of Lord McKenna in 1943, the centuries-old leadership tradition of the Midland had ulcerated into turf struggles among the members of the general manager's committee. This was the most senior working position to which any Midland professional could aspire, below chief general manager, and the secrecy with which the bank conducted its affairs was demonstrated by its use of McKinsey. The bank needed an outside view of its structure, and chose McKinsey because of good reports from the newly merged National Westminster. But while Citibank, and Hambros with Worden & Risberg, brought commitment to restructuring proposals by allowing public discussion, in the Midland the conclusions were kept secret. More than ten years later the McKinsey proposals, which were never implemented, were kept in the bank's vault and neither Ian Morison, who became the bank's planning director, nor Tony Holmes, who wrote the bank's history, was allowed to look at these without the approval of the chief general manager.

Midland had rightly always given operating autonomy to its subsidiary companies, but increasing competition from both the American banks and the merchant banks required a clear vision of the group's future if cooperation among competing baronies was to be achieved. Growing confusion over lines of authority, made worse by the burking of the McKinsey proposals, worked against this, while secrecy and in-fighting destroyed any chance the bank might have had to rebuild a new business franchise.

The bank's many financial-service functions, including Samuel Montagu, were grouped into a new company. Midland Bank Finance Corporation was formed as a wholesale bank, with a capital of £10 million, and Midland complained for the next four years that MBFC had no lending power; this was because the 1967 sterling crisis was coincident with MBFC's creation, and the Bank of England blocked banks from increasing their balance-sheet totals, so that MBFC could only lend its capital. But Midland had bought Samuel Montagu for its renowned dealing skills, and Citibank and Hambros had both proved that currency lending could be profitable. The reason that MBFC did none of this was that Midland had taken a substantial foreign-exchange loss in the early 1950s, banking wrongly on a devaluation of sterling. Since then the forex markets had developed, so that currency borrowing could take place without an exchange risk, but obviously this news never seeped through to the Midland general manager's committee.

Midland decided to copy the American approach of calling officers, appointing four of its high fliers to represent both Midland and Samuel Montagu and supporting them with a small company-nursery unit to massage companies towards a flotation. But the recommendations of consultants were ignored; these appointees, well qualified though they were, had no authority, and no power to negotiate the difficult relationships between commercial and invest-ment bankers. Worse still, David Montagu was refused a seat on Midland's board by Sir Archibald Forbes, Midland's dour and highly numerate chairman, and, though not intended as a snub, it was taken as such, and Montagu left to compete as managing director of Orion Bank instead. This departure proved the investment bankers' suspicions of commercial bankers and, in the absence of a clear strategy for the merged group or good commercial leadership, the excellent dowry that Samuel Montagu had brought to the marriage was quite ignored. Montagu's successor was immediately appointed to the Midland board but, though a clever tax lawyer, he lacked the imaginative leadership that was needed if two such distinct banking cultures were to bed down together.

Usefully for individual bankers, banking deals take time to sour, so bureaucratisation of banking authority had advantages. It was encouraged by new banking procedures, as computerised adminis-tration and money-market funding transformed the relationship of branch and head office. The latter now identifies target customers, sets income and volume budgets by business type and industry, and has turned bankers from independent judges of customers' financial needs and ability to pay into proactive salesmen of financial products and seekers of lending mandates. Slowly between 1970 and 1990, the judgement of banking risk was divorced from the acceptance of the business. With a little luck, promotion ensured that both 'getters' and 'accepters' of bad business would be far removed from the scene if the business began to smell. But even if that did not occur, private ambition led bankers to do what was demanded of them, and not what they might think was right for the bank, since large bureau-cratic organisations do not reward those who question the quality of the Emperor's new clothes.

Edward Furash, formerly a senior vice president with Shawmut National Bank of New England, as well as a professor at Harvard categorised these changes thus:

Prior to 1970, bankers were overqualified and underpaid, and were thus able to offset the stupidities of the organisation. During the 1970s, as they were recruited by the treasury departments of the multinationals, they became fairly paid for their qualifications, and could still help the bank, even though it complained of being ruined by rising staff costs. By the 1980s, bankers were overpaid and under-qualified. What happened was inevitable, and was only a surprise to the large banking bureaucracies.

Computers and money markets encouraged banks to expand into more and more business areas, and to the geographical and physical complexity of the commercial banks was added the complexity of investment-banking services.

Many of these new services are far from simple, so the growing ingenuity of financial instruments with the complexity of relation-ships with customers who are as much competitors as clients, makes profitability-analysis essential. Yet most bankers, even today, do not recognise that 'profits' and 'profitability' are two separate words, with different meanings; and few banks have the financial controls that bankers insist are essential for their customers. The fundamental analysis of banking profits still assumes a monopoly of function, so there is no differentiation of risk or cost between the different types of liabilities and assets that all banks now have.

Banking analysis starts where it should end. It operates as a 'blind pool of risk' in which the market cost of all liabilities is deducted from the contracted income of all assets, to produce the interest spread. This is the gross profit of the bank, but the cost, stability and negotiability of current- and deposit-account balances differ, depending on the type, skills and ambitions of the banking customer, and these deposits have little in common with money-market deposits or longer-term funds raised from the security markets. Even more obviously, the nature of assets, in terms of the known incidence of bad debt, forced extension or even early repayment, differ enor-mously among borrowers, whether by industry, locality, size, type or the bank's known ability to handle certain types of difficult loan. Such a detailed knowledge of the source, use and risk of its funds was Midland's great strength, when it was buying other banks earlier in the century. Then such an analysis did not much matter, for commercial banking had a monopoly of skills and functions that others could not profitably replicate, so the customer had no choice but to pay for the banker's mistakes.

Today the comparative crudity of bank management systems,

compared to those of their manufacturing and service customers, is one of their most serious weaknesses. Lowell Bryan of McKinsey's shares the view of many senior bankers that the modern bank – global in its reach and universal in its capacity – is so complicated that it has become unmanageable. This explains the findings of an American study that four out of five banking mergers are unmitigated disasters. Only after the merger does the acquiring bank realise that much of the interest income, though booked as profit, has never been paid as cash, while the liabilities are mismatched to even the paying assets, leaving it vulnerable to any upward movement of interest rates. Banking chief executives respond in the traditional way to such a position of stress: they concentrate on the urgent tasks awaiting them, so as to avoid addressing the important ones.

Growth of income or reduction of costs are natural demands from business leaders faced with a crisis of profitability, but do not necessarily serve if the problem is systemic to the industry, and not a weakness of an individual company. This fundamental problem is untouched by growth in size. Brian Pitman of Lloyds has, more successfully than any of his other British competitors, shrunk the bank, simplified its managerial structure and improved shareholder returns. The need for the Midland merger was that the benefits of that process have ended, and only an acquisition could restart it, for Lloyds has failed to rethink the functions of a commercial bank, and how it needs to be organised and staffed in today's competitive marketplace. It is interesting that Lloyds' success with its international private-banking business, headquartered in Geneva, is in marked contrast to its indifferent results in the UK market; but in Switzerland, Lloyds had no precendents determining what it should do, how it should do it and what sort of people must be employed to do it.

A Midland takeover by Lloyds, had it been achieved, would only have produced an ersatz increase in operating income. Lloyds, and commercial banks generally, need to redefine commercial banking in an age where cheap computing power and instantaneous communications can create the authority of the local banker of the nineteenth century, together with the skills of the late twentieth-century global banker; only thus will banking increase its operating income, for then it will be the result of solving real business needs.

If banks follow policies that individual bankers know to be mad, one reason may well be the effect of what Warren Buffett, the outstanding investor of the postwar years, calls 'the institutional imperative' or the lesson that he was never taught at business school or as an analyst on Wall Street. Instead, while banking, investment management and business leadership were becoming institutionalised, Buffett and his partners retained personal responsibility and insisted on the necessary partnership of manager and owner. Buffett sold out his initial, and very profitable, postwar investment partnership and returned the proceeds to his shareholders in 1969, after consistently making them over 30 per cent a year, on the grounds that the stock market was overvalued. However, four years earlier Buffett had been tempted by its apparent undervaluation to buy a quoted New England textile business for $20 million. According to Buffett's own judgement, this 1965 investment was his worst ever, because: 'When a management with a reputation for brilliance tackles a business with a reputation for bad economics, it is the reputation of the business that remains intact. I just wish I hadn't been so energetic in creating examples.'

Despite this self-deprecation, Berkshire Hathaway is today worth over $9 billion, has sales of over $1.5 billion and employs more than 20,000 people. The shares have consistently performed five times better than those of the Standard & Poor's index of the US market, earning a compound rate of return of well over 20 per cent a year. The core of Berkshire Hathaway is four blue-chip American corporations, which have been held almost since the inception of the company and are never traded. The directly managed businesses are centred on a general insurance company, an important part of the financial-services industry as well as an activity whose history of boom and bust is at least as difficult as that of banking but, like banking, equally proficient in creating cash flow. When overcapacity during the boom threatens margins, Buffett and Charlie Munger, his insurance partner, just stop writing insurance, investing in the money or security markets instead, or paying off the company's bank borrowings.

Then, once the bust arrives, Munger is there, with unimpaired capacity, to write all the insurance that is needed, but only at a price which he considers profitable. His and Munger's job, says Buffett, is to allocate the capital to the various businesses, watch the numbers and cheer on the managers. An equally sensibly managed mortgage and savings bank (S&L), as well as several other low-tech businesses such as jewellery and candy stores, a local newspaper and a furniture supermarket, make up the rest of the unquoted investments. Buffett claims that he is highly 'risk-averse' as an investor, saying: 'Rule number 1; never lose money. Rule number 2; never forget rule number 1.' Buffett's portfolio proves his point that the surest way for an investment manager to make money is to invest in simple, essential and understandable businesses with proven, and even old, managers; many of them are in their sixties, some in their seventies and, until recently, one of the most successful was in her eighties.

However, there is a central-office complement of only a dozen people, including the cleaners, and a management structure unique within a business world dominated by institutional owners. No senior manager earns more than a $100,000 a year, though all are expected to earn more than this through their profit participations. However, these disappear when profits go down or fail to grow, and are not paid in cash but in shares. Most of all, business owners who become part of Berkshire Hathaway sell their businesses for shares, and are expected to keep the majority of them. Buffett is fond of saying, 'We believe in eating our own cooking.'

In recent years, and as the company has generated more and more cash, Buffett has been forced to expand the quoted portfolio by buying into large companies, with a well-established business franchise and competent management, but going through difficult times. This is why Berkshire Hathaway ended up with some 15 per cent of Salomon Brothers, and Buffett obviously believes that the banking franchise is worth money, however badly run the industry may be, for he has recently bought 10 per cent of Wells Fargo and a similar-sized stake in American Express. Banking shares, like Berkshire Hathaway, also represent complex financial-service businesses, but these have done much worse than the S&P index, let alone Buffett. The banks do, of course, have rather larger head offices, and their executives choose from the share-option menu rather than labouring in the kitchen.

They are also addicts of the 'institutional imperative' of Buffett, which he defines as

the wilting of rationality in the face of institutional dynamics; for instance:
* As if governed by Newton's first law of motion, an institution will resist any change in its current direction;
* Just as work expands to fill available time, corporate projects or acquisitions will materialise to soak up available funds;
* Any business craving of the leader, however foolish, will be quickly supported by detailed rates of return and strategic studies prepared by his troops;
* The behaviour of peer companies, whether they are expanding,

acquiring, setting executive compensation or whatever, will be mindlessly imitated.

And Buffett's investment in, and salvaging of, Salomon Brothers identifies the practicalities of these criticisms. By the time Henry Kaufman left Salomons in 1988, this trading machine had become unstoppable. Gutfreund was a superb trader but a hopeless manager, and the firm became a series of personal fiefdoms with unclear lines of command, ruled by Gutfreund's power to reward friends from the extraordinary profits made out of the US bond markets. Personal animosities came to a head in 1987, when market conditions choked off the profits flow for a while, and Gutfreund turned for help to Warren Buffett; Berkshire Hathaway invested $700 million in Salomon, saw off the corporate raider Ronald Perelman, and sat back to enjoy the 9 per cent interest on its convertible bonds, while waiting for Salomon's profits to improve, when it would convert the bonds into very favourably priced shares. That sensible game plan was blown out of the water by Salomon's greed.

As Salomon's success in the US bond auctions grew, and their position became so dominant and their squeeze on short sellers so painful, the Treasury limited the amount of any issue that could go to one bidder. By spring 1991, Salomon were getting around this by putting in bids on behalf of customers but unbeknown to them, lying about the volume of sales, and altering market contracts. As this became known, Gutfreund and four of his most senior managers were forced to resign. The Treasury only fined Salomon $290 million, as well as suspending them from acting for customers in the auctions for a year, so it must have satisfied itself that these were the actions of overkeen dealers, and not part of a criminal conspiracy to rig the market. Salomon was undoubtedly helped in its efforts to avoid the fate of Drexel Burham – fined $650 million and, in effect, forced into bankruptcy – by Buffett, who, arriving hotfoot to save his investment, immediately promised full and open cooperation with the authorities, and published a two-page Salomon *mea culpa* to shareholders. In this, he addressed Salomon's lacklustre performance for shareholders, remarking:

> There remain many jobs for which performance can be concretely measured, and ought to be . . . for employees who produce exceptional results for the firm, while operating honourably and without excessive risk, should expect to receive first class compensation . . . but employees producing mediocre returns . . . should expect their pay to

reflect this shortfall. In the past this has been neither the expectation at Salomon nor the practice . . . in the future top paid people will get much of their compensation in the form of stock . . . which motivates them to think like owners since [they must] hold the stock for at least five years, and [this] therefore exposes them to the risks of the business as well as the opportunities. Contrast this . . . with stock option plans, in which managers commit money only if the game has already been won, and then often move quickly to sell their shares.

After ten months as Chairman, Buffett brought in a successor, and returned to Omaha. The chief executive that he appointed in 1992 remains, and Deryck Maughan is the image of what went wrong with the English clearing banks. A generation earlier, this County Durham grammar-school boy would have ended up as a senior manager in one of them, having been recruited straight from school. Instead, the post-war state granted him a scholarship to university, and from there a Harkness fellowship took him to Stanford Business School; ten years in the UK Treasury were then followed by four years at Goldman Sachs. After being head-hunted by Salomon, Maughan quickly ensured that his new employers made money in Tokyo, to the envy of its US rivals and Japanese competitors. Buffett picked Maughan since he had shown in Tokyo the ability to plan and implement 'the tremendous amount of sewer and pipeline work' that Salomon needed if it was again to do 'first class business in a first class way'.

The manager of Midland's main branch in Norwich after the war was Henry Coe. He remained there to the annoyance of his head office for some twenty years since, like most managers of his day, he had no desire for further promotion. Coe was true to the unwritten Midland philosophy, which considered the branch manager to be the ultimate authority on local business and entitled to commit the bank for any amount. Tony Holmes succeeded Coe as the manager at Norwich before becoming one of the Midland's first regional managers as, late in the 1960s, the bank started to copy its competitors and dismantle the system that had powered its growth for most of the century. Holmes told me that, though Coe was a good banker for those customers that he liked, he was autocratic with his staff and reluctant to work with business people with whom he had no sympathy. Holmes himself, a clever and imaginative banker, ended up as a Midland general manager, but felt he had to rebuild Midland's Norwich image after Coe's long stay.

Yet it may be that this flattening-out of the idiosyncratic nature of local bankers resulted in more harm than good. Coe was certainly no saint, which perhaps helped him deal with difficult people. He never paid for a drink or a meal in any of my father's hotels but, equally, my father never expected him to; business in the community is about mutual help, particularly so in those days of high marginal taxation. Nor did Coe rely on his manager's salary. When I was sent to him, a completely green graduate with no idea of what a mortgage was, let alone whether I needed one, to discuss a loan for converting a tumbledown cottage, I reported back that Coe seemed willing enough, but very concerned about my health.

'You bloody fool!' said my father. 'Don't you know that's just Henry telling you you can have the loan, but you've got to take out a life-assurance policy through him!'

Coe, like most good managers of his day, earned nearly as much from life-assurance commissions as he did from the bank. From the bank's point of view, this was acceptable, though all banks had arcane rules about the level of pressure that could be exerted. Some banks allowed insurance brochures to be displayed openly on the manager's desk; others insisted that they be kept in the desk drawer – but this could be left open. It was good for the banks, since it improved the security behind their loans, and tied their managers into a network of mutual backscratching. The bank manager needed the expert support of the local insurance representative, who in turn need the banker's introductions, and both bank and insurance company reduced their salary costs.

The system had its disadvantages, which became more obvious as banks became more centralised. It encouraged independence among branch managers, and a concern for their customers' needs that would increasingly run counter to the bank's interests. And if the managers could do well, it seemed obvious that the bank could do even better, as well as supplying promising jobs for head-office apparatchiks. So it has proved, for the Midland bought out the insurance earnings of its managers in the late 1960s, setting up a centralised insurance-broking business in 1971. Insurance sales have been one of the success areas of the conglomerate bank, and bankers now happily believe that the future of their business lies in the foot-in-the-door approach of the Abbey Life salesman. Moreover, the personnel departments of the banks can move managers around every three years or so, ensuring that, unlike Coe, these have no chance of 'going native', developing too great a concern for their customers, or establishing any power base outside that of the head-office promotion ladder.

The disadvantages of this system are all on the customers' side. Most banking customers remain unaware of what it has meant to them, except for worsening service and loss of banking advice. The willingness of bankers to fall for the latest management theory never ceases to amaze me, and I had assumed this to be part of their naivety as businessmen, but I was assured by John Hunt that this was not so. Hunt, an Australian, is professor of organisational behaviour at the London Business School, and has frequently been frustrated in his consultancy assignments for banks – American, British and Australian.

Hunt has learned that senior bankers like to promote the newest management fad, to show that they are up to the minute in their thinking, but have no intention of changing anything. Successful bankers are those who have benefited from the very organisational weaknesses of which they complain. Though they may express concern over low managerial morale, and can even accept the reasons for the problem, Hunt's experience is that senior bankers are psychologically incapable of doing anything about it. In this the banks reflect the problem of military incompetence which, according to Norman Dixon, emeritus professor of Psychology of University College, London, is systemic. This former soldier argued in 'On the Psychology of Military Incompetence' that the very characteristics which are necessary to the smooth running of the military machine, and take peace-time soldiers to the top, are counterproductive to wartime success. The organisational virtues of orderliness, obedience, cleanliness and punctuality cannot compete, in warmaking or in banking, with opponents who are wily, innovative, flexible and resourceful in ambushing the enemy.

15

On The Ice

'A banker need not be popular; indeed, a good banker in a healthy capitalist society should probably be much disliked. People do not wish to trust their money to a hail-fellow-well-met but to a misanthrope who can say no. However a banker must not seem futile, ineffective or vaguely foolish. In contrast with the stern power of Morgan in 1907, that was precisely how his successors seemed, or were made to seem, in 1929.'

J K Galbraith in *The Great Crash*.

'**Y**OU'VE NOT ASKED ME about the most pertinent issue of all,' said Sir Archibald Forbes to Tony Holmes, as he finished interviewing him for the company history which was to celebrate Midland's 150th anniversary in 1986.

Of course, I can understand that you think you know the answer, or might be embarrassed by the question, but that doesn't excuse you. You should have questioned my reluctance to choose between Stuart Graham and Malcolm Wilcox as chief general manager in 1974, and asked why I split the bank between them as joint heads instead. I was frustrated, and wanted to be chief executive myself.

This 150-year company history was ready for publication when, early in 1986 Edwin Green, the bank's archivist and co-author, approached Ian Morison for help. Publication had been cancelled because Sir Donald Barron, the Midland's chairman, was adamant that it would do more harm than good, and he was not alone in wishing that this history had never been commissioned.

Midland's expensive, and ultimately disastrous, acquisition of California's blue-chip Crocker National Bank was so painful a memory that, as in any rightly written communist history, it needed to be edited out of existence. With consummate tact Morison, who was Midland's planning director, persuaded the powers-that-be that too many people knew of the history's commissioning for it to be dropped at such a late date. But the wound was so raw that history had to stop at 1976, and Midland's 150th anniversary was commemorated with only 140 years of its exploits. This was an extraordinary solution to the problem, even in as self-serving a publication as a company history. In fact, Holmes and Green's history of the Midland Bank is an exceptional model of its kind, though the ten years to 1986 could only be covered by brief notes. This was all the authors were allowed to do to memorialise the 10-year reign that effectively destroyed the Midland Bank. As Morison says 'Passions were too high, and the perspective too short, to enable anything sensible to be written at that time.'

Two years later the suppressed facts emerged over three issues of the Financial Times when in 1988, David Lascelles, the banking editor of the Financial Times, used these unpublished pages, and the memories of the participants in Midland's American madness, to record the story of Crocker and Midland. Lascelles' story was an awful warning against 'handing $500 million to someone [Midland] could neither understand nor control . . . after that, Crocker became like a Greek tragedy, working its way towards a fateful conclusion while the protagonists could only wring their hands and howl.' Civil servants can, perhaps, afford to delay, murmuring that 'the time is not ripe, the conjunction not yet opportune' but commanders who take that view, whether of regiments or of banks, deservedly end up dead or disgraced. The tragedy of modern banking management in general, and of Midland in particular, was that this was the fate, not of those that would not act, but of those that would, but who were then held back by the paralysis of superiors, their wills as frozen as those of a rabbit caught in the headlights of an approaching truck.

A Scottish chartered accountant with a background in manufacturing industry and war production, Forbes was chairman during the crucial decade of banking change 1964–1975, but was unable to reverse the postwar emasculation of the chairman's office. Forbes's solution turned out to be fatal for the Midland, however much it might have been based on his knowledge of the mutual dislike held by Graham and Wilcox for each other. It is more than possible that Forbes hoped that, with two relatively young managers each running half the bank, his successor would be able to achieve what he had failed to do – to grasp the executive leadership of the bank, and drive its management willy-nilly into looking critically at its performance and the bank's future. Graham was numerate but not literate, while Wilcox was his opposite, so Forbes must have calculated that his successor had an exceptional opportunity to do this.

If so, the choice of successor in 1976 doomed that hope. Sir William Armstrong had made his career within the civil service, ending up as secretary of the Cabinet Office and, as such, was better at smoothing away than grasping nettles. A sociable man, and not averse to an evening dram with the bank's managers as he travelled the country getting to know them, Armstrong queried one evening the wisdom of Midland's desire for Third World loans. Whatever Graham and Wilcox felt about the other, on this they were one and sharply told Armstrong that such decisions were for them to take, and that he was only there for flag-waving and image-building. Had Armstrong had Forbes's industrial background, he might have questioned this view of his role as chairman; as it was, he accepted the two as the business equivalent of his political bosses, and kept his mouth shut from then on. Moreover, Armstrong used his civil-service skills to create a committee structure to fill the role envisaged by McKinsey for a group chief executive, and to stop the animosity between Graham and Wilcox from tearing the bank apart.

A good example of the law of unintended consequences, the result of Forbes's initiative and Armstrong's committee thinking was that there was no one to take care of the Midland Bank itself. The problem faced by Graham and Wilcox was, and is, symptomatic of that of commercial bankers in all developed countries: how to increase corporate earnings when the bank already dominates its natural market. The problem was compounded for Midland in the 1970s since its corporate customer base was shrinking rather than growing. The Midland, as an institution, knew what was needed and what it had to do, for a planning team, established by McKenna in 1943, had trawled all levels of the bank for ideas on how the bank should respond. Among the business initiatives proposed, apart from greater discretion for managers and decentralisation of branch control, was the need for medium-term lending to industry. These views were expressed in the chairman's 1946 review, emphasising bankers' responsibility for 'looking beyond balance sheets, technical borrowing arrangements and the figures on a customer's account to the reality of the economic effort and achievement that lies behind them'.

This planning committee had identified Midland's major weakness, and one that Lord McKenna had already identified in the 1920s, when he had become the fiercest critic of the Bank of England's monetary policy with its overvalued currency that destroyed Britain's heavy industries and much of Midland's business franchise. But in the confusion of the postwar world, the bank's leadership fell into the hands of its general managers, and McKenna's plans to change Midland to meet the peacetime challenge died with him, as did the role of executive chairman. Nothing changed, not even a restructuring of the branch network to reflect the growing importance of the south-east and the southern Midlands, and certainly no looking to 'the reality of the economic effort and achievement' that lay behind customers' accounts. By 1960 Midland was no longer the biggest bank in Britain, let alone the world, and, as the bank declined, so Buggins's turn delivered ever more complacent and conventional senior managers to preside over its decline.

A second chance to rebuild the bank's business franchise came in 1956, when internal development ideas coincided with the hearings of the Radcliffe Committee, set up by the government for much the same reasons as the Macmillan Committee of 1931, a vague sense that British banking was failing industry and the country. Two chief general managers – one a rare interwar graduate recruit and the other a London-based banker – established the Hayward Committee to reconsider Midland's banking services. Their conclusions enabled the Midland to respond to the 1959 Radcliffe criticisms more promptly than any of its competitors, and with the right services. Twenty-year agricultural loans gave Midland leadership in farming, while the introduction of ten-year industrial loans was enthusiastically received by business spokesmen, in the light of widespread criticism of banks' industrial lending policies.

Such loans could have rebuilt Midland's declining portfolio of manufacturing companies, many of which were disappearing under Warburg's onslaught of forced industrial restructuring, for Midland at the same time was building Forward Trust. This developed from six branches into a nationwide business, with a branch structure parallel to that of the bank, and specialising in supporting small companies buying productive assets out of the earnings created by their purchase. Once again, internal feuding prevented any profitable implementation of good strategic thinking, and the unsatisfied demand of British companies for medium-term loans was met by Citibank's calling officers. Forbes approached Lloyds in 1967 to talk merger, as the only commercially sensible option for Midland in the general restructuring of the English banks, but was rebuffed.

Full disclosure of banking profits from 1970, the Bank of England's quid pro quo for permitting this new round of commercial banking mergers, disclosed the full damage of twenty years of complacent management. Midland had become one of the smallest of English deposit-taking banks, and the weakest in terms of capital adequacy. Not only had Barclays overtaken Midland as a deposit-gatherer late in the 1950s but Midland's profitability, by branch and employee, was significantly worse than any of its competitors'. These 1970 profit comparisons were facts that not even senior management could deny, and this news was combined with the almost simultaneous bankruptcy of Rolls-Royce, for which Midland was the main banker. The widespread sense of internal humiliation demanded a reconsideration of Midland's structure, which in 1970 remained much as it had been for the previous half-century. The problem was seen internally as the absence of clear leadership from a management which had degenerated into squabbling fiefdoms; the postwar bank was run by the general managers 'in committee', rather than in the Midland tradition of an executive chairman supported by a managing director or, like Citibank, with a strong president working with his predecessor as chairman.

McKinsey quickly spotted that Midland's system failed to allocate resources among competing baronies, to take thought for the morrow, or even ensure that agreed plans were implemented. Unfortunately, McKinsey's proposals for strengthening the leadership of the bank, and reconstructing institutionally the managerial vision of Holden and McKenna, fell foul of both Forbes and the general managers. The former felt strongly that a tougher and more numerate management was needed if Midland was to overcome the challenges facing it, and considered that the appointment of a group chief executive from within the bank would marginalise the chairman even more, while the latter regarded the proposals with horror. McKinsey was not only a threat to Buggins's turn, and therefore to the various protégés of the general managers, but might bring their managerial competence under scrutiny.

These proposals were rubbished as change for change's sake, and locked away within the bank's vaults. So Midland's new leadership in the mid–1970s faced a formidable challenge. Stuart Graham had already acted, before he became joint chief general manager, to set up a special sales department that would compete with Citibank in positively selling banking services to the largest corporate customers, and which could also act as an intensive-care unit for future casualties on the scale of Rolls-Royce. But the real banking need remained the gap in British banking between the weaknesses identified by the Macmillan and Radcliffe committees, what head offices thought they were doing to overcome these, and what was actually happening at branch and factory level.

One of the central problems of bank branches is their high cost, and this was made worse by the switch from corporate to personal business. As Midland's business loans declined, those to individuals and the professions grew from 17 per cent of the portfolio to over 40 per cent. Personal lending, now more popularly known to bankers as retail banking, can carry attractive lending spreads, particularly if the banks can set uncompetitive deposit rates. But retail banking does not generate the variety of banking services that are needed by any medium-sized manufacturer and exporter. These, and the fees they pay, are the justification of the commercial-banking branch network for, though large firms can afford treasury departments, medium-sized firms have little choice but to depend upon their bank; fees for services is how banks make their real money.

Midland could either support Wilcox and international banking, or modernise its branch network at the same time as it rebuilt its lending franchise. It could not do both, so far had its fortunes fallen as the result of the failures of the previous thirty years. The choice before Graham and Wilcox was stark; their answer equally so. Ian Morison, now professor of banking at Loughborough University but recruited to Midland in 1983 as its planning strategist, remembers it vividly:

> At the time, I was working with the Committee of London Clearing Banks, and putting together the agreed evidence of the banks for the Wilson Committee [yet another in the line of Macmillan and Radcliffe]. Nearly all the key conclusions in the international banking section ended 'except for the Midland bank', or some similar saving clause, but just before the final draft went off to the printers, I received a call from Graham, telling me to drop those final words. Midland had finally cracked, as the market saw it. In changing its international policy, Midland lost its distinctive edge, and became like all the other clearing banks.

Cooperation within a banking world increasingly influenced by Citibank's drive towards international pre-eminence had needed much more imagination and leadership than Midland's managers could find, and was destroyed by one of McKinsey's few acceptable recommendations.

Midland's new international division was Wilcox's baby, together with all the bank's other noncommercial banking activities. Once he assumed command in 1974, Wilcox commissioned a report from the Stanford Research Institute to consider alternative international-banking strategies to that of cooperation, and SRI found evidence of the decline of Midland in relation to other international banks, especially Citibank, which had become a key competitor for Midland's domestic business. The report recommended that Midland copy Citibank and do to others what was being done to it. By 1973, according to SRI, Citibank's non-American profits were 60 per cent of its total earnings, though the SRI report did not disclose that the bulk of this came from London forex-dealing profits, probably because they themselves did not know.

Actually, even banking auditors were finding these new markets hard to understand, and bankers were in no hurry to enlighten them, since they could be used to transfer profit to the most desirable of a bank's low-tax locations. Indeed, two of the most profitable and important business opportunities for Midland, as the premier correspondent bank that it was, were quite ignored in this study. Wilcox, like SRI, did not regard them as important, and it is doubtful whether anyone in Midland knew whether or not they were profitable. This was certainly not the case among the ranks of Morgan Guaranty, which in 1968 established EUROCLEAR to act as settlement agent for the ever rising volume of eurobond deals. This Luxembourg-based business quickly became the safest and most profitable way of participating in this vast new market, and none of the many market dealers even today has wrested any of its profitability away from Morgan, although jealous competitors established CEDEL a year later as an alternative service. Midland was involved in neither of these, yet most eurobond dealing was centred in London. By 1974, for private as opposed to state borrowers, this market had surpassed the issuing role of domestic bond markets.

In the early 1970s, too, the great majority of forex deals were initiated in London and the New York clearing – for most deals were in terms of the dollar – was a nightmare. IIB, like many major dealers, deserted the money-centre banks in favour of more efficient and responsive services, and chose Philadelphia National Bank instead. This set up in New York under US Edge Act banking legislation, which allows out-of-state specialised banking services, and developed an excellent 'bankers' bank'-style clearing house. Midland could have done the same, had it thought to enter this business. Though highly profitable to the US Edge Act banks, and in the mainstream of Midland's traditional business, correspondent banking was out of fashion. When the fashion cycle turned again in the late 1980s, it was too late for Midland, which had itself gone out of fashion.

Wilcox and Midland might have considered more closely the fashionable views of international diversification, particularly expansion into America. Citibank and other money-centre banks were beginning to lose ground to the domestically focused American regional banks, while Midland was already unsuccessfully competing with Citibank through the European-American Bank (EAB), an EBIC (European Bank Investment Company) joint venture which had entered the New York commercial and retail banking field through an acquisition in 1968. The American banking market, with its combination of national, regional and community banks, is the very opposite of oligopolistic English banking. Though a growth market for banking services, it is a highly competitive one, with considerable leapfrogging in banking salesmanship and services. Success requires management and marketing flexibility, for competition leads to the rapid development of specialist banking 'products'. The problems of EAB had indicated the complexity of this market, though Wilcox was quick to ascribe these to the difficulties of partnership control. Midland's disentanglement from EAB would be expensive.

Wilcox was an uncritical buyer of the SRI conclusions, for he was well known as a spit-and-polish warrior, renowned for rejecting complex reports because the stapling was not perfectly aligned with the paper's edge. In overturning Midland's traditional international policy, Wilcox, having already played his part in denying the Midland a captain, now removed the bank's rudder as well. From 1974 onwards Midland drifted to its destruction, driven only by the shifting winds of banking fashion and the short-term considerations of executive ambition. Though the bank's profits were running at less than £100 million a year, with shareholders' funds of some £450 million, Wilcox determined that Midland should establish an international 'presence'.

Wilcox first plunged into the syndicated loan market, converting the correspondent bankers that made up his division into Midland's international lending officers. The function of a correspondent banker is to ease business relationships between banks, so these cheerfully bought in loans by the gross, knowing that their job was to keep the correspondents happy, rather than bothering themselves with the quality of the loan or the value to the Midland of the connection. Midland's purchased loans of some £2 billion were mainly to South America and, as a participant in other banks' loans, it did not even benefit from Citibank-style fees. By the last years of the decade Wilcox was ready to buy, adding to the £2 billion of loans a further £2 billion of banking investments in France, Australia, Germany and America. With the exception of one rights issue of £100 million in 1978, all this was financed by interbank borrowing or loan capital.

If banks behave like Gadarene swine, it is that bankers are not only innumerate, but also illiterate: according to the Irish accountant Michael Lafferty, few bankers appreciate that 'same' and 'similar' are not synonyms. After editing the *Financial Times'* Lex column, Lafferty became the *FT*'s banking correspondent late in 1978. He persuaded the newspaper that banking should no longer be regarded as a purely domestic business, but be reported instead as an international and comparative business activity. What Lafferty saw from his journalistic perch was that the banking needs of the very largest multi-national companies are the same, whatever the apparent nationality given by its registered office. But these are few in number, certainly less than a thousand in total, while there are millions of companies whose banking needs and problems are similar, but far from being the same. Banking laws, national characteristics and industry structure ensure that this vast bulk of banking transactions make many distinct markets, not easily penetrated by international competitors, and very profitable to bankers not seduced by current fashions.

Lafferty brought a cold and uncomfortable outsider's eye to the hermetic world of banking, and within months had so enraged the British commercial banks that they asked the *FT* to sack him. Instead, Lafferty's *FT* campaign forced the bankers to accept that their accounts were meaningless and probably illegal in UK company law, and that their method of accounting for bad debts – the Leach-Lawson rules – had to be changed. As Lafferty says:

> Wilcox became very excited by what I was writing, and assured me that he would drum me out of the City. He was much like every other commercial banker of the time, however much Midland publicity promoted him as the banking genius of his generation. Wilcox simply didn't understand accountancy and, like all his colleagues, got into the most frightful muddles when he tried to theorise. As I told him, bankers are businessmen and, just because their business is money, that doesn't make them any more a financial expert than the corner shop grocer. Bankers don't like to be told this, of course, but you only have to look at banking results to see how true it is.

Once Midland decided that it would no longer be the 'bankers' bank', it had no clear international role. But there was one obvious acquisition for Midland, if it was to emulate Citibank as a global business. Standard Chartered Bank was a British overseas bank with good Asian connections, a large presence in South Africa and India, the owner of a decent-sized Californian bank, and a partner in MAIBL. Midland already owned over 20 per cent of Standard Chartered's equity, but Sir William Armstrong was terrified that its purchase would turn Midland's shareholders' meetings into a political battleground. Midland was not a significant lender to South Africa, but Armstrong had been suffering from 'rentacrowd' disturbances at shareholders' meetings, as one of the EBIC banks had made two high-profile loans to South African companies. So he vetoed any suggestion of a deal, once he knew that Graham would support his view, and without putting the idea to the board.

In the opinion of a later chairman, the Midland board would probably have agreed to the Standard Chartered purchase. Merger talks with Hongkong & Shanghai, already concerned about its long-term future, were looked at coolly by the Bank of England, as were Hongkong's later proposals for a takeover of the Royal Bank of Scotland. Wilcox felt the pressure of City criticism, with media comment implying not only that Midland was losing market share domestically, but also that it was unable to match the overseas diversification of its competitors. To increase the pressure, there was mounting American anxiety about the spate of US bank takeovers, and Wilcox knew that restrictive legislation was being considered by Congress. So when Tom Wilcox, chairman of Crocker National Bank, intimated early in 1980 that the two Wilcoxes could do business, the opportunity looked a godsend, for Crocker was a real blue-blood. Though it had lost ground in the market to Bank of America, Wells Fargo and Security Pacific, Crocker was one of the oldest and most respected of the Californian banks.

Tom Wilcox had spent most of his working life with Citibank, which he had joined from school at the age of fourteen, though Citibank later financed a university course for him; Malcolm Wilcox had a similar English and Midland background, but without the university. Both men had charm, when they wanted to use it; and both had considerable ambition. Apart from their common name, which both emphasised, each was likely to hear what he wanted. Cooperation seemed natural, for this had been Midland's way since the 1920s, and the banks needed each other. For Crocker, the Midland alliance promised money, prestige, the connections of Midland's correspondent banking network and the power to turn 'Atomic Tommy's' dream into reality. This was to make Crocker the J. P. Morgan of the West Coast, and so show his former Citibank superiors how wrong they had been in preferring Wriston to him as George Moore's successor.

For Midland, the Californian market was bigger than New York State, Citibank's domestic base, and growing faster. If California were a separate country, it would have the seventh largest economy in the world. So Crocker would allow Midland to finesse Citibank and leap ahead of its three English competitors. Resolving all Midland's growth and profit problems would also establish Wilcox as *primus inter pares* within Midland and the City of London. The rewards seemed enormous, the risks low, and the 1980 agreement with Midland left Crocker management with complete operational autonomy, though giving Midland 51 per cent ownership in return for an investment of $595 million. Of this, some $270 million was money subscribed for new shares, and Crocker had the right to call on Midland to invest a further $225 for another 6 per cent of Crocker, in shares priced at $90 each compared to the market price of $36.

The deal was greeted ecstatically by Wilcox's supporters in the City, yet, in his desperation to do a US deal, he handed over Midland's future to an Irish-American whose nature was scarcely comprehensible to the unimaginative and stolid Englishmen of the Midland Bank. Potential trouble was apparent in Atomic Tommy's insistence on calling the deal an alliance and not a merger. Potential became actual with his refusal to allow any Midland nominees on to his management team, his inability to find a representative office for Midland in Crocker's new thirty-eight-storey San Francisco office, to share offices in New York or Korea, or to give Midland any more information than any other shareholder.

More due diligence on Midland's part would have shown that all was not quite as it seemed. Tom Wilcox had joined Crocker in 1974 at the request of its board, who wanted a more dynamic banker to fine-tune Crocker's performance, so that it ceased to underperform its main rivals by 10 per cent a year. English tea in the afternoon, and porcelain tea sets, shocked the Citibank soul of Atomic Tommy, who had very different ambitions from those of his directors. Wilcox changed much of Crocker's solid and traditional lending culture irrevocably, for hired guns from the East Coast installed a typical Citibank package of specialist loan programmes: wine and farming, oil, gas and other energy sources, real estate and health were the industrial sectors in which Crocker would establish market leadership. No one could fault the courage of the new recruits, for one farmer alone was lent over $100 million, most of which was later written off; these loans had done much to increase overheads, without a commensurate improvement in earnings per share, and when Midland arrived on the scene, Crocker required support. It had run out of money, and morale had plummeted as sidelined Crocker managers watched their beloved bank being destroyed before their eyes. Wall Street wouldn't buy the Wilcox dream either and, without a trade investor, share prices and share-option values looked set to continue downwards.

Midland's promised new equity of $495 million enabled Crocker to increase its $19-billion balance sheet by 50 per cent, and Atomic Tommy proved his name by calling for Midland's cash far faster than planned, and whipping on his sales force. Though Crocker's nonperforming loans rose steadily throughout its 1982 quarterly reports, Poultry shut its ears to insistent whispers that further misunderstandings between Celts and Saxons were being added to the long historical record. Wall Street remained unimpressed by Atomic Tommy's idea of a satisfactory risk:return ratio; by January 1983 Midland's money had been fully committed, but Crocker's share price valued the bank at $675 million, compared to the $820 million Midland had paid for its 57 per cent. That was the year Midland and Crocker first became aware that most of their outstanding loans to Latin America would never be repaid.

Midland drifted steadily closer to debacle during the early 1980s, rather as a guard-mounting platoon at Dover Castle once marched stolidly towards the cliff edge. But Geoffrey Taylor, who was preparing to take over as Midland's chief executive during the summer of 1981, had no one to hiss at him, as did the sergeant to his tongue-tied guard commander: 'For God's sake, sir, say something, even if it's only Goodbye.' Taylor, a sound domestic banker from Midland's Yorkshire powerbase, was in a difficult position, for Sir William Armstrong died suddenly in 1980 and his designated successor was unable to take over until 1982. Sir David Barran presided as a temporary chairman, during which time both chief general managers handed over responsibility to Taylor; Malcolm Wilcox retired in June 1981, and Stuart Graham went six months later. This hiatus in leadership coincided with the recession of the early 1980s that devastated Britain's manufacturing heartlands, destroyed some

2 million industrial jobs, and finished off many of the core industries that made up Midland's business franchise.

Midland managers were fully occupied defending their home base, and extraterritorial problems had to be fitted in as time could be spared. This lack of attention was no problem for Tom Wilcox, since the only Midland connection that he recognised was the personal Tom-to-Malcolm one, and certainly not any formal one to the head of Midland's international division. This did not initially disturb John Harris, one of Midland's high flyers, Taylor's successor as head of international, and first of the postwar generation to be in line for the top job. Crocker was Taylor's problem, for he had been intimately involved in the negotiations with both Wilcoxes, which gave Crocker two seats on the Midland board, compared to only three seats for Midland on the board of its own subsidiary. Furthermore, Harris was busy enough sorting out the other $3 billion of the international division's spending. The first major task was to whip the international purchases into shape for many had been in varying degrees of trouble when bought.

Diplomatic care was needed to solve their immediate banking problems with Midland's help, while still maintaining the commitment of their managers to developing the banks with their own ideas. Especial care was needed with the German Trinkhaus & Burkhardt whose managers had been traumatised by their relations with Citibank, their previous owner, for Citibank had been quite unable to mollify Germans who were not only bankers, but touchy investment bankers. Harris succeeded in motivating these and the others, by giving them complete tactical freedom within mutually agreed long-term strategic objectives, the normal Midland way with its subsidiaries. Feathers in Poultry were ruffled by these changes, especially Harris's desired sale of some of Midland's international participations, but he ruffled them a lot more as 1982 produced dismal figures from Crocker. No one wanted to hear bad news, for Midland was committed to investing its final $113 million in Crocker during January 1983.

It was well disguised, so it could be ignored, but during 1982 Crocker's nonperforming loans – a euphemism for borrowers who are no longer paying interest – had nearly doubled to a figure not far short of Midland's total investment in Crocker. It looked as if Midland's money was being wasted. Yet, though the quality of the loan portfolio had worsened, Tom Wilcox reduced Crocker's 1982 provisions against bad debts by a third to $59 million, so enabling him to report another year of increased profits. The reality was that, even with this apparent sleight of hand, Crocker's earnings in 1982 were no better than those of 1977. Then it had been only half its present size, and now the trend of bad debts was upwards.

Theoretically, this was Wilcox's last hurrah, for in 1983 he handed over the chairmanship to his protégé John Place, who had joined him from Chase Manhattan. Place had come haring over to London in March that year, together with all his management team, and put on a 'dog and pony show' – in the way that only Americans know how – for 150 Midland bankers. From some of the audience, especially those whose trimmed-back budgets were financing this great new adventure, there were mutterings that 'bullshit baffles brains'. And Tom Wilcox still called the shots, for he remained chairman of the executive committee of the board, and that was where executive power lay in Crocker.

What Wilcox could no longer frustrate, though, was the annual inspections by the Office of the Comptroller of the Currency, one of the many federal agencies responsible for regulating the health of American banks. The regulators considered that Wilcox had treated them like low-level, impertinent clerks and, underpaid and under-regarded as his staff were, the Comptroller was inclined to agree. So the regulators often behaved with a sense of inferiority on their annual inspections, while the banks produced their 'rocket scientists'; these, intellectually secure in their Master of Business Administration higher degrees, used mathematics to prove that black was white. Unfortunately for Place, foreign ownership of Crocker gave the regulators an edge which they did not have with the domestic banks, whose generous approach to borrowers was becoming a matter of general concern. Michael Patriarca, a burly lawyer and one of the toughest of the OCC supervisors, took Wilcox's resignation as the opportunity to probe Crocker's loan book.

Wilcox had never allowed Midland to get close to Crocker's lending, though the bank had received due-diligence reports from everyone that mattered back in 1980, including sight of the OCC examiner's report; there was nothing to worry about. Now they learned differently, for the loan book was worse than anyone expected, and the news stunned Midland. Crocker had hundreds of millions of dollars in loans that could never be recovered. Where the borrowers had not gone bankrupt, they had just disappeared, and the value of the collateral – if it had any value at all – was in free fall. California's economy was heading southwards in the aftereffects of the energy boom of the 1970s, and the regulators identified an extra $300 million of nonperforming loans in their 1983 review.

This was before investigating the $2.8 billion of Latin American loans, even though Mexico, Brazil and Argentina had all defaulted. The required provisions of $107 million wiped out Crocker's profit for the year, producing a small loss of $10 million instead, and ruining everyone's Christmas.

American bankers live with Murphy's law, as the English do with Sod's law – what can go wrong, will go wrong – and no one could now pretend that Crocker was not trouble for Midland. Brian Goldthorpe, Harris's competitor for the top job in Midland, had become the head of risk management, after the tidal wave of business bankruptcies that had submerged Midland's branch managers. Geoffrey Taylor sent Goldthorpe to San Francisco in December 1983, deciding that if things were bad, it would be best to make a clean breast to shareholders. Goldthorpe discovered that Crocker had an excellent reporting system for bad debts, which Midland later adopted. This was called CATS, or Criticised Assets Tracking System, and had worked perfectly at identifying the growing crisis. But Crocker had split under the Wilcox chairmanship, between go-getting Citibank-type recruits with no loyalties except to their pay cheques and share options, and Crocker survivors. CATS was run by Crocker people, so Wilcox and his team appeared neither to listen to them nor to act on their information, which, of course, was kept well away from Midland.

Goldthorpe's analysis meant that both banks would have to settle down for a five-year haul to recovery. Crocker's autonomy was revoked, and Taylor had to choose between Harris and Goldthorpe as his Californian proconsul. Morison remembers Harris's joy when he heard that the board had approved his appointment; the decision was seen by Midland insiders as meaning that Harris had been picked to succeed Taylor. Harris quickly felt at home in San Francisco, for the Crocker style was much closer to the Midland that Harris had joined than the New York City banks from which Wilcox had recruited his management team. Many Crocker managers had been with the bank from school or university, and knew the bank's customers intimately from having served in the same branch or department for several years. It took time for Crocker managers to reciprocate Harris's feelings.

The Crocker people were highly suspicious of me, and of Midland generally, for Wilcox had made sure that there was no meeting of minds between the two banks. When Sir Donald Barron became chairman in 1982, he attempted to set up a coordination committee for the two banks, but it met only three times and achieved nothing, because Wilcox was determined that Midland would have no say at all in the way he ran Crocker. For heaven's sake, he wouldn't even show us Crocker's budget figures, even though we owned 51 per cent; and Taylor wasn't prepared to stand up for our rights. I knew that you could do nothing with Americans, unless you first get their commitment to what has to be done, when nothing is impossible. Our chief task was to save the bank, for it had no money left, and its losses were anyone's guess. There were some good managers fortunately, and after three months out there, and four weekend meetings going through the figures and refining the rescue plans, I had that commitment. This was to shrink the bank back to its core business of domestic banking in California.

So John Harris was surprised by Taylor's telephone call in April 1984, asking him to meet Frank Cahouet in Los Angeles and prepare a press release announcing that Cahouet had been appointed chairman of Crocker. Harris was vice-chairman to John Place, Wilcox's successor, and had only been in California for three months, but was left appalled by his meeting. He felt that the Midland had panicked and made a fatal error; the bank had lost heavily from Malcolm Wilcox's decision to stake reputation and money on Tom Wilcox and, to Harris, appointed Midland's supremo in California only in January, Taylor's decision seemed to be doubling the odds while still betting a similar combination. It was this decision that destroyed both Crocker and Midland, because:

Frank Cahouet was another Wilcox, a professional banker with little time or love for the English, but a towering ego, and an ambition that had nothing in common with what Midland needed from Crocker. In the event he turned out to be a better manager than Tom Wilcox, but this change of policy scuppered any chance that Midland might have had to retain its credibility or its money.

What Crocker needed was stability. I had been sent to work out, or clean out, the rotten parts of the loan book, and get Crocker back to what it had been and could be again – a good, high-quality Californian bank, with no nonsense about global banking, Citibank-style. For both strategy and work-out, I had the support of Brian, and so I knew I could rely on a team from the third floor at Poultry, if I needed them, but Cahouet would have none of it. These finally came out a year later, but then it was too late. For day-to-day business, I had the Crocker managers. These could not wait to rescue their bank from the East Coast mercenary that many considered Wilcox to be, complete with ludicrous growth-at-any-price instructions such as ordering the international department to write $500 million of loans within twelve weeks, just to meet budget.

We all knew – or thought we knew – what needed to be done, for we had discussed Crocker endlessly over the previous year and a half in Poultry. When we finally got everyone to agree that we had to revoke the autonomy of Crocker's management, it was to put the clock back. Crocker would be a domestic Californian bank, as Midland was a domestic English bank; international banking would develop jointly out of the needs of our domestic customers – two countries but one bank, rather like a banking version of Unilever or Royal Dutch Shell. Crocker was big, but not too big for Midland to handle, and Place was pliable although an optimist. That was all to the good, for Midland was running Crocker, with Place acting as front man.

Cahouet would have none of that; he brought in his own team of managers, just like Wilcox, and insisted that their motivation would be destroyed if Crocker was confined to California. He would only talk to the Midland board and just like Wilcox, frightened Taylor and his people with talk of class actions by minority shareholders, and similar nonsense. It's the story of the Californian banker, protesting to a farming customer about the savage blow with which he has just struck his mule. 'No, no,' says the farmer, readying himself for another tremendous blow between the mule's eyes, 'I'm not harming a bank asset, just getting its attention. Now I'll give it the message.' No Englishman that hasn't worked there can understand that Americans reach for their lawyers like other people take aspirin.

When Cahouet took over, the OCC insisted that all directors sign a letter agreeing to honour federal banking regulations and to meet the requirements identified by the OCC as necessary to get the bank back into shape. Wilcox was forced off the Crocker board soon after, and Cahouet sensibly covered his back, ordering another round of investigations, and making further bad-debt provisions of $148 million. But during 1984 the Comptroller's review procedures became a lot tougher. Patriarca, who was also struggling with Bank of America management at the same time, was quoted as saying: 'After Continental Illinois the whole relationship changed. We realised after all that examiners are not so stupid and bankers are not so smart.' So 1984 was another ruined Christmas for Midland, with Patriarca demanding a further $326 million of provisions, and coming hotfoot to see his opposite numbers in the Bank of England.

Midland was given a four-week deadline to come up with a recapitalisation that would save Crocker. Taylor and his colleagues felt that they were getting little support from their own regulators, when faced with such impossible deadlines. Cahouet was infuriated by Patriarca's demands, and leaped on a plane for London, missing the meeting through a diversion to Frankfurt caused by fog. But it was a pointless journey, even though Cahouet could have explained that American regulators start with impossible demands in order to obtain reasonable compliance, for Poultry had ceased to trust their own appointee. The Cahouet appointment destroyed Harris's career and stymied Goldthorpe's hopes, for Cahouet refused to accept Harris's authority, and Taylor for his part would not support his own man, believing that Cahouet – introduced through a head-hunting agency and on a salary three times that of Taylor – would do the Midland's bidding. But in summer 1984, with Crocker's shares at an all-time low of $17, and showing Midland a book loss of $600 million, Taylor learned at first hand what Harris had told him three months earlier.

Taylor was known for his dislike of confrontations, which was not surprising in someone who had been the protétgé and follower of the arrogant, unimaginative and tactless Malcolm Wilcox; diplomacy was essential then, but less desirable in a chief executive facing a crisis of unknown magnitude. Midland's management had already lost valuable time admitting to themselves that Wilcox's greatest coup, instead of putting the Midland Bank back into the world's top ten, was on course to destroy it instead because, as an international bank, Midland could not walk away from Crocker. Though only a 57 per cent shareholder, Midland was nevertheless at 100 per cent risk and, since it was likely that sooner or later Crocker would need more of Midland's money, the obvious thing to do was to buy the rest of Crocker's equity. Whatever illusions Poultry may have entertained about Cahouet disappeared, as he and the Crocker board rounded on the Midland's proposals, accusing them of acting like vultures in attempting to buy out the remaining shareholders on the cheap.

The Midland bid put the Crocker board in an invidious position. They had all signed the OCC agreement letter which required them to be prudent, but, if they were to get a higher bid from the Midland, they needed to put an optimistic gloss on the loan book. These concerns of the nonexecutive board members were not eased by the close-knit nature of the San Francisco business community, for this establishment was enraged when it realised that San Francisco's most blue-blooded bank was a can of worms, and the consequent rash of shareholder actions accused both Crocker and Midland management of negligence, incompetence and anything else that the lawyers reckoned actionable. Harris watched helplessly from California as the drama played itself out in Poultry. Harris was asked to return to London – ultimately he stayed for two years, parted from his wife and family, though not as Midland's hostage to Patriarca; rather, he felt:

> I had to stay on for Midland's sake, even though my position was anomalous, for I simply did not believe that Cahouet's interests were those of the Midland. I reported both to Taylor and to Cahouet. Cahouet was on the Midland board while Taylor was not on the Crocker board and loyalties and objectives became hopelessly confused. Though only in direct control of Crocker's credit and compliance departments, I felt I could limit further damage, and that I had to see it through.

Harris's problem was that strains were also developing in Poultry, as well as among the Crocker board members. Sir Donald Barron was far from happy to discover that Midland's board had been led by its executives into buying a bank which it could neither control nor manage. Early in 1983, at his insistence, Midland had become the first British commercial bank to employ a chartered accountant as finance director, and Taylor came to rely more and more on him. This did not always ease matters, for, as Goldthorpe was heard to say: 'If [Michael] Julien is chief executive of this bank, will someone please tell us so and, if he's not, will the real chief executive step forward?'

Ian Morison says:

> It's far from certain that Midland could have survived without Julien. He was a brilliant analyst, and a tremendous workaholic, and we needed both to get an understanding of what was happening in California, and to work out what to do about it – not only what, but how, for by this stage the risks were so frightening that the bank could no longer rely on finding whatever money it needed. Without him, the bank would never have agreed the purchase of the Crocker minority, nor Patriarca's required recapitalisation, within the time we were given. But it's true that he was power-hungry, though not, I think, out of any personal vainglory. It is just that Julien is very tidy-minded and can't bear mess. There's a lot of that in a large commercial bank, where things are done this way because that's the way they've always been done, so, if no one else would do it because no one else had appreciated the problem, Julien moved in to clean it up. The real weakness was that, like all good technicians, he fell in love with his solutions. Julien needed a backstop who would look at these and say: 'Yes, but does it make practical sense as well?' He didn't have that.

Michael Julien was another rocket scientist with figures, and had Barron's confidence, while Taylor needed his tables and charts. The Crocker problem was financial – where could Midland find the money to keep both banks afloat? – but it was also a managerial one. Julien accepted this, but had no confidence in commercial bankers as managers, at least not those wearing a Midland hat. As Goldthorpe remembers it:

> The question was who could best manage Crocker. Since we had all agreed that Crocker was to go back to its basic business, that should not have been a problem. Frankly, anyone who could manage Midland, with this country's industrial problems, would have had no difficulty with Crocker. But Julien wouldn't hear of it, so we ended up with Cahouet, and lost another year while both learned the same lesson, which is that you can't grow a bank out of trouble. You have to take the losses, cut the overheads and get back to the simple basics.

Right to the last minute the Crocker board refused to recommend Midland's bid, and it took a scathing attack on Cahouet, Crocker and the board as a whole by Thomas Jefferson Cunningham, Midland's American board representative and an associate of Henry Kissinger, to bring everyone to their senses. As he remarked, no one else would come up with the $375-million rescue package needed, and Midland were only doing it because they had no choice. Before Christmas 1984 Midland's treasury converted a £2-billion short position in the money markets to a £2-billion cash hoard; Crocker stocked its tills with cash, and manned them with extra staff, while both banks warned their main banking counterparties to be on guard. Both banks had reason for their fears, since the markets had not reacted at all calmly to the problems of Continental Illinois earlier that year.

In May 1984, the OCC had announced that it would guarantee the deposits of America's ten largest banks, but that had still not stopped a run on Continental Illinois, which had to borrow $4 billion from the Fed to cover the outflow of its deposits. Then the Comptroller asked Morgans to show banking solidarity by putting together a select group of fourteen of America's largest banks to provide a safety net for Continental's depositors of $4.5 billion. This was later increased to $5.5 billion from twenty-eight banks, but still the markets remained unimpressed, and in July the authorities finally had to seize the bank. But despite Crocker's announced loss of $324 million in January 1985, the markets took it calmly. Midland might have contrasted the markets' behaviour on that occasion with their response to Continental Illinois, and asked itself whether that meant it still retained some vestiges of its former reputation.

By this time, however, Midland was incapable of thinking straight. Cahouet, despite the strains of the previous six months, was still insisting on an international role for Crocker, quite independent of Midland. Relationships between Barron and Taylor were difficult. Barron had now moved even further from Sir Archibald Forbes's position, and felt that the bank must have a chairman with full executive power, whereas Taylor disliked the implicit criticism by Barron and the board of his executive performance. Ian Morison had been recruited by Goldthorpe early in 1983, who had produced a special report for Taylor on what systems Midland needed, to give management control over an increasingly risky business. The central risk-management team was one, a treasury function another, while Morison was to give Midland the chief of staff and planning function proposed by McKinsey ten years earlier. Goldthorpe and Taylor were both concerned about the navel-gazing habits into which Midland had fallen, and intended to open up the bank, but this promising start to Taylor's time at Midland was soon derailed by Crocker.

After the Committee of London Clearing Banks, Morison had worked with the Interbank Research Organisation, and Goldthorpe reckoned that Morison had the intellectual calibre and outside experience to envisage the changes needed in Midland. Goldthorpe was very concerned about the impact that the 1980/81 recession would have on Midland's future. Morison explains:

> Bankers spend so much time thinking about banking risk – credit risk, liquidity risk, counterparty risk and so on – that few of them ever think of the real risk they run. This became more obvious as deregulation proceeded, and technology and better information destroyed the intermediation function of banks. The real risk is that banks spend money which they can never get back, either by fees or by interest spreads. Midland just ran up against this risk faster than most other banks, because of what had happened to British industry.
>
> Midland's branches were in the wrong place, it was accustomed to dealing with large companies when the trend was towards the rebirth of small companies, and Crocker took away the money and energy that should have been spent on rethinking and rebuilding the domestic business. When the bank's PR people were asked to redesign the bank's griffin logo, to try and pull the group together, they asked people within the bank to ascribe visual images to each of the group companies. Crocker was a goat, standing isolated on a mountain, for Midland managers knew well enough that the bank's problems were

more deep-seated than an unfortunate investment in California. I remember the meeting at which a senior manager suggested that Crocker should be sold, and the atmosphere completely changed. The unmentionable had been mentioned, and without any real consideration, that suggestion became instead an assumption. The consequence was that, in the end, Midland suffered the pain and cost of reconstructing Crocker, but gained none of the benefits. It sold, just as it had bought, without sufficient consideration of the consequences.

Midland likes to pretend that it recovered the money it invested in Crocker, but the reality is far otherwise. It sold an absolutely clean business to Wells Fargo, for Midland took out some $3.7 billion of doubtful loans and those had a bad-debt cost further down the road. Moreover, this view ignores completely the opportunity cost of both the time of senior management over at least two years and the better use that could have been made of the $800 million tied up in Crocker. David Lascelles, as well as Midland insiders, put Midland's real loss at probably $1 billion. This was the largest loss ever incurred by a British bank, though National Westminster's American adventures would, by 1990, run it close. But when Crocker was sold in 1986, the bell was already tolling for Midland.

16

Abandon Ship

'The secret of life is honesty and fair dealing. If you can fake that, you've got it made.'

Groucho Marx

THE SEIZURE OF THE Bank of Credit and Commerce International in July 1991, led by the Bank of England and enforced by dozens of bank-regulatory authorities in sixty-nine countries around the world, was more akin to a drug bust than the usual sedate visit of a banking regulator. This was only appropriate for a bank which, it was claimed later, was actively known to America's Central Intelligence Agency and Britain's Secret Intelligence Service, and other users of its multifarious services, as the Bank of Crooks and Cocaine International. Initially, the numerous regulators were a little confused about why they had closed down BCCI. Some thought it was to reorganise the management, others to rebuild the capital, most because someone else had told them to do so, and a few because they considered themselves the helpless victims of a Western plot to humiliate and destroy Muslim bankers. The confusion was compounded by the cries of outrage from central banks of impoverished Third World countries, the public authorities of First World countries, and private depositors everywhere. It seemed that no one had warned them that BCCI was unsafe and their money at risk.

Some might have thought that the time for the regulators to act was when BCCI was convicted on charges of laundering drug money, after the 1988 arrests of senior BCCI officials in Florida. Banks everywhere were already helping an intergovernmental task force, which later reported that the drug money laundered each year amounts to some $85 billion, and recommended action to stop the conversion of this physically enormous mass of banknotes into legitimate business profits, via the banking system, as the easier way of cracking down on the drug barons. BCCI chose to specialise in the laundry business, but most Western banks benefit from these funds, however unknowingly, so central bankers may have thought 'least said, soonest mended'.

Robin Leigh-Pemberton, the governor of the Bank of England, remarked later to a committee of the House of Commons: 'There was an indication that certain things [in BCCI] were not well. Some transactions were false and deceitful . . . [but] if we closed down a bank every time we had a fraud, we would have rather fewer banks than we have.' As the BCCI smell became richer, the regulators set up a 'college' of those regulators most concerned with BCCI's activities. For BCCI had been clever in organising itself so that it could escape censure while regulators played pass-the-parcel with their surpervisory responsibilities. Closing down even a small bank is rather like choosing the nuclear option in war, and BCCI was not small: when it was closed, BCCI had total assets of some $20 billion. The suddenness of the regulatory action had less to do with depositors' safety, however, than with the realisation that, in civil-service speak, the time was overripe. Robert Morgenthau, Attorney General for Manhattan, had been pursuing the American end of BCCI on various racketeering, drug and bank offences. Over the several years he had been doing this, he had complained of receiving precious little support from the US Justice Department or the Bank of England. Now his case was almost ready, and Morgenthau was about to go public with his claim that BCCI was a criminal conspiracy, set up as such from the very outset to gather deposits which BCCI's guiding spirits would then despoil for their personal benefit.

The closure would unzip Morgenthau's mouth, but in the subsequent political squabble the regulators could always claim that they had acted first. The fallout was considerable; Agha Hasan Abedi, the bank's founder, Swaleh Naqvi, its chief executive, and Ghaith Pharon, a Saudi Arabian financier well known to Washington insiders, stand accused of bribing and corrupting central bankers, and defrauding the World Bank, the International Monetary Fund, the African Development Bank, and the Nigerian National Supply Company. Sheik Kamal Adham, another of the group pinpointed by Morgenthau and a former chief of the Saudi Arabian intelligence services, signed a plea-bargain agreement instead, promising to co-operate with the prosecutors and paying a $105-million fine – losing a few paperclips, was how one of his acquaintances described the effect of the fine on the Sheik's fortune. Much the same was true of the effect of BCCI's collapse on the fortunes of Sheik Zayed bin Sultan al-Nayan, the seventy-five-year-old ruler of Abu Dhabi and

77 per cent shareholder owner of BCCI. The *Financial Times* has calculated that the sheikdom's total exposure to BCCI is at least $9.4 billion, an expensive but hardly disastrous call an Abu Dhabi's daily oil royalties of $8 million or so.

What concerned Sheik Zayed rather more was the sullying of his image. All the Gulf rulers had been the target of con men, once their oil started flowing, and Sheik Zayed had been stung for $100 million in the late 1970s, on a commodity fraud. That was why BCCI appealed to him, as a Muslim bank that would protect the newly rich Arabs from the depredations of patronising Western bankers. The fact that depositors are getting back as much as 30 cents in the dollar is owed to the Sheik's willingness to put further money into BCCI, both before and after the regulators struck. The Sheik was more than a little aggrieved at what he considered to be the Bank of England's precipitate action, so much so that he took full-page advertisements in British newspapers to say so. After all, the Sheik's advisers had been working closely over the previous year with central-bank officials from London and Luxembourg and consultants from Price Waterhouse, BCCI's auditors, to simplify its legal structure and restore its capital. In April 1990 Sheik Zayed promised $2.2 billion of new capital and acquisition of BCCI's bad debts.

The Sheik had also agreed a new organisational structure for the bank, with at least a further $1 billion of invested capital, and he was expecting this plan to be accepted over the summer, thus putting BCCI firmly within the regulatory ambit of the Bank of England; he was just off on his holidays when his bank was closed down. Unfortunately for the Sheik, both the Bank of England and Price Waterhouse decided, somewhat late in the day, that the man who had the Sheik's ear was deeply involved in the scam himself. This has been denied by the man concerned and the events, so far as they have been told, suggest more cock-up than conspiracy. What is certain is that officials and banking regulators everywhere scuttled for the cover supplied by the Bank of England. This was the central bank most exposed to censure, and its position was exceptionally tricky since in fact, if not strictly legally, BCCI was run from London. Its largest branch structure was in the UK, and most of its head-office functions were in London.

Leigh-Pemberton claimed that only the report delivered to the Bank of England in July 1991 by Price Waterhouse finally gave 'evidence of massive and widespread fraud, going back over a number of years . . . The culture of the bank is criminal . . . [the report] provided both the first and the overwhelming evidence of the scale and the nature of the fraud . . . up to then no evidence of fraud on a scale to justify revocation [of BCCI's English banking license] existed.' Evidence of bank fraud is always easier to uncover after the event, and BCCI was an exceptionally dangerous beast for any civil servant to hunt. It was known to have close intelligence connections, being used by the spooks of the Arab world, as well as the CIA and SIS. Nor did it make any secret of its political and central-banking friends in politically sensitive countries, which it bought by the dozen. If those failed, it had serious associates to whom it could turn for advice and support, for, as a matter of deliberate policy, BCCI financed various good causes. These were chosen for being close to the hearts of influential people; among the latter were ex-president Jimmy Carter and the former UK prime minister James Callaghan, as well as Clark Clifford, a Washington lawyer, former US defence secretary and another of Morgenthau's targets.

These charitable donations may well have come out of depositors' pockets rather than profits, for Morgenthau is by no means sure that BCCI ever made a profit in its nineteen years of existence. No doubt the BCCI insiders took the view that with friends like theirs, who needed profits? A close intermingling of political power with financial clout has always been characteristic of banking, and only romantics would assume that, in a more democratic age, this might encourage prudence among politically weak and inadequately financed banking regulators. The use BCCI made of its connections is little different from the expectations of some American savings bankers. Charles Keating's main claim on history is the speed with which he turned the California-based, and profitable, Lincoln Savings Bank into a $3-billion loss to the banking regulators and, through them, to the American taxpayer. For a while, at least, Lincoln held the record as the greatest individual loss suffered by any one US bank, and part of that loss resulted from Lincoln's financial contributions. These included sums of over $1 million to five US senators, and dozens of other contributions to even better-placed local politicians.

Keating's naivety was exposed when he said to reporters: 'One question, among the many raised in recent weeks, has to do with whether my financial support in any way influenced several political figures to take up my cause. I want to say in the most forceful way I can: I certainly hope so.' History shows that, when luck deserts bankers, so also do their political friends. Keating is now in jail, while some of his erstwhile supporters are loud in their condemnation of the regulators of BCCI. BCCI was a 'Ponzi' swindle, but on a gigantic scale. (Ponzi was a 1920s banker, and perfected the use of early investors as the bait to bring in others; these early birds are paid out of the savings of late-coming customers, brought in by the apparent good fortune of the initial depositors, and the trick is to jump ship at the moment that the funds rise to their highest level, and before suspicions begin to affect confidence.)

According to the liquidators, BCCI ran its frauds to cover up four major banking errors, all of which stem from the late 1970s and early 1980s. One was the $633 million of treasury losses, which had been racked up by 1985; as a result of these the Bank of England had required BCCI to relocate its money dealing to Abu Dhabi, hardly a world financial centre; another was a bad debt of over $725 million from the Pakistan-owned Gulf shipping group; a third was the secret and illegal purchase of American banks for $346 million; and the fourth was a $500-million purchase by BCCI of its own shares. Ponzi left it just too late, before he jumped ship, but BCCI's perpetrators seem to have been much luckier with their accountants and regulators. The tragedy, of course, for BCCI's predominantly able and honest middle managers is that not only are their careers ruined, as well as the fortunes of their customers, but there was no need for dishonesty; banking is quite profitable enough without any need for scams.

BCCI was showered at birth with all manner of banking gifts, and I remember feeling most envious when this bank was set up at the same time as the IIB. The late 1960s saw a burgeoning confidence in the Arab world, for American oil reserves were running out, and Middle Eastern suppliers became central to the economies of the West. BCCI was superbly placed as Arab oil producers upped supplies, Western banks took their money and Western companies their orders. BCCI's business headquarters were in London, its legal domicile in Luxembourg and the Cayman Islands, and it had branches almost everywhere that a link was needed between the oil riches of the Gulf, and the banks and businesses of the developed and developing worlds. The IIB's business base of Italy seemed poor in comparison, and I was surprised that, in these years, BCCI did so little in the forex and money markets.

BCCI was staffed by the best of Pakistani commercial bankers, all trained in the British tradition and disgruntled by the wholesale nationalisation of Pakistan's private banks. The Bank of America, a founding investor, was in 1972 the largest bank in the world and celebrated for the profitability of its small-business and personal-banking activities. The Bank of America was much admired for its perspicacity in reserving for itself an important source of funds, particularly when, two years later, the Arab oil weapon was unveiled after the 1973 Yom Kippur war and every banker in the world was on pilgrimage to the Middle East. The management of BCCI and of the Bank of America looked cleverer still as the latter increased its stake from 25 per cent to nearly 50 per cent.

BCCI certainly made an impression on British high-street banking, opening over forty branches between 1972 and 1975, before the Bank of England called a halt to this headlong expansion. Even the Bank admitted that this branch network was profitable, when closing BCCI in 1991, though by this time the senior management of the bank itself stank from its corruption. Fish rot from the head, so some of the English branches must have been affected by head-office crookedness, but, even so, the success of this branch network is still remarkable, considering the historical difficulties of any bank quickly gaining profits from a new branch, and the overbranched nature of the English market. BCCI was helped in its penetration of the market by large and hard-working émigré communities, and the two prospered together. English business has always reacted well to the commercial stimulus of immigrants from the silk- and silver-working Huguenots of the seventeenth century onwards, but rarely did the indigenous banking industry fail them as it failed the Indian and Pakistani communities of the late twentieth century. BCCI bankers accepted that their customers hated paying tax, and were probably more than a little lax in watching over the interests of the revenue authorities, but British banks do no less through their Channel Islands and other overseas branches.

The Luxembourg monetary authorities asked the Bank to take responsibility for BCCI as early as 1985, knowing that they were incapable of doing the job, and conscious that the collapse of Luxembourg-based Banco Ambrosiano Holdings had done little for their reputation. The Bank refused, no doubt conscious that it itself had only just expelled BCCI's treasury function from London. Then in 1987 the Bank agreed to join Luxembourg's second best choice of a 'College of Regulators', and it was this that planned the final seizure. The Labour Party members of the Treasury and Civil Service Committee of the House of Commons tabled an amendment to the final report which, though voted down, puts in blunter terms the Committee's general conclusions, stating: 'We believe that the public, like us, will find it impossible to understand how . . . the Bank . . . could allow BCCI to continue to operate as a bank after

March 1990 by which time the Bank was aware of [1] dreadful weaknesses in BCCI's accounting controls [2] lousy management [3] the fact that one set of auditors, Ernst & Whinney, had had enough [4] drug money laundering by BCCI and [5] the existence of terrorist finance accounts at BCCI. If regulators at the Bank can tolerate this, we wonder if there is anything that they will not tolerate?'

It is easy for politicians to decry the regulators after the event, especially when few are noticeable for their support of the regulators when the suspect institution is opening branches, creating jobs and lending to supporters within their constituencies, while Michael Lafferty recalls:

No one was ever sure what was going on at BCCI. Bank of America were very coy about their shareholding, though they made it clear from the late 1970s onwards that they wanted to sell, were worried about BCCI, and had sold out by 1980. The Bank of England did its best to warn the market, but if no one listens what more can you do? I remember two articles I wrote in 1979 and 1980, helped by information from the Bank, and given considerable prominence by the FT.

One was on Abedi's ridiculous claim that BCCI had had no bad debts at all, despite just having opened some forty UK branches in less than three years, and that the Bank had forbidden BCCI to open any more. Then, when the 1979 Banking Act was published, another article made it very plain that BCCI had lobbied hard to be categorised as a bank, but that the Bank had only granted it the inferior status of Licensed Deposit Taker. BCCI, of course, was up to all the tricks, and made a virtue out of this. It kept 'bank' in its name; legally these were branches of an overseas bank, so the Bank could not deny it that. BCCI then claimed to its naive customers that it had a higher status than other high-street banks, because it was licensed by the Bank of England, and could put on its branch frontages LICENSED DEPOSIT TAKER, which was actually a message implying that such a firm was nowhere as safe as a bank. Warnings could not be plainer than that, and bankers seemed to have taken them on board, for few banks had much exposure to BCCI when it went down.

The Bank of England had another political problem, for BCCI was managed by Pakistani bankers, but financed from the Gulf. Pakistan was the base for Western resistance to the Russian occupation of Afghanistan, and important to Washington and London, while the sterling balances of the Gulf emirates were the largest remaining foreign holdings in the currency, and still important to the stability of the pound sterling. The last thing the Bank wanted to do was to upset the Gulf emirs and see sterling crucified as these changed their sterling funds into the more practical dollar. The importance of these sterling holdings had justified the dispatch of a British task force to Kuwait in 1961, when threatened by an Iraqi invasion. The Gulf was important, too, for Prime Minister Thatcher was forever going there, to get them to buy British military goods.

Upsetting the Gulf rulers would upset Mrs Thatcher, and that this was undesirable was well known. Sir Kit McMahon, with his rescue of Johnson Mathey Bankers in 1984 while deputy governor of the Bank, had maddened her. Though small, JMB was an important bank. It was one of the five controllers of the London gold market, and its failure would have seriously affected banking confidence. Unfortunately, JMB had got the growth bug, and made a series of disastrous loans to Pakistani shipping and trading companies, and was soon bankrupt. McMahon's judgement was right: the London market was comforted by the Bank's action, and the underlying gold business of Johnson Mathey Bankers was sound even if its commercial lending was erratic and ill-judged. The Bank of England retrieved all the money it had advanced for the rescue, together with interest.

But Mrs Thatcher was equally right to be annoyed. The Bank, though the 1979 Banking Act had given it the duty of monitoring and regulating banks' trading accounts, did not bother with all banks; those that it had traditionally supervised, and considered 'one of us', were still handled in the old way. So the Bank missed Johnson Mathey Bankers' change of management and style, and the fact that it had ceased to share the ethos of the London banking club as policed by the Bank. The result was that the 1979 Act became that of 1987, and the Bank lost further power to the Treasury.

BCCI was no Johnson Mathey, for it had the secret and complicated structure that seems the hallmark of international frauds. This served to confuse regulatory responsibility but never, according to Leigh-Pemberton, was there enough substantiated evidence to allow the regulators to act. But this, as the report of Lord Justice Bingham makes plain, is because the bank misunderstood its authority. As the FT commented on this report, it showed the bank to be 'a cowering midget, uncertain of its strength and anxious, at all costs, to avoid putting it to the test.'

Few central bankers desire, or even expect, to become martyrs. The fallout from the Sindona/Calvi affairs may initially have had more effect on central bank thinking than the formal expressions of the need for cooperation that resulted from the 1974 crisis. Allowing

Banco Ambrosiano to buy La Centrale in 1971 through a Luxembourg holding company had been against the wishes of the Bank of Italy. The real reason the authorities gave approval was fear of Sindona, the Vatican and their friends in the Christian Democratic Party. Calvi expanded Banco Ambrosiano Holdings on the back of La Centrale's money, buying other Italian banks and insurance companies and, despite its opaque structure, getting increasing support from the international banking community. Early in 1981 the Midland led a syndicate of sixteen banks which raised $40 million for BAH, and later that year, National Westminster and twenty-seven banks lent a further $75 million. Both groups made it just in time, for Ambrosiano was bust within the year. Nevertheless, its international lenders, including the two syndicates, were quite relaxed. Over $700 million was owed by BAH and its subsidiary companies to foreign depositors, and these had lent to BAH through the euromarkets, assuming that they were safe because of the concord reached among central bankers that each would support the overseas subsidiaries of its own banks.

The Bank of Italy refused to bail out lenders to BAH, arguing that the BIS agreements covered branches and subsidiaries of domestic banks, but not associated banks. This was the status of BAH, so that it could avoid the consolidation of its own figures into those of Ambrosiano, and thus keep the Bank of Italy's regulators at arm's length. It is also possible that the Bank of Italy felt that the foreign banks might have been more careful with their due-diligence inquiries, or wanted them to taste some of the medicine that they themselves had been forced to swallow. In 1978 the Bank of Italy undertook an American-style regulatory inquiry into Banco Ambrosiano. This investigation reported Calvi to be in absolute control of the bank, and that Ambrosiano had illegally exported some $20 millions' worth of lire through fake share-purchase deals.

In 1979, and in response to this 1978 report, the interested parties of the 'sotto governo' – intelligence departments, mafia, political figures, banking enemies, coup plotters or anyone else with an interest to protect – came together. The Bank of Italy, about the only honest non-politicised government institution in Italy, needed to be brought into line. It had to be punished for its foot-dragging over the 1974 reorganisation of Banca Privata Finanziaria and Banca Unione into Banca Privata Italiana, and the current bad-mouthing of Ambrosiano. The P2 connections quickly came up with a suitable, right-wing magistrate, who thereupon issued orders for the arrest of Paolo Baffi, governor of the Bank of Italy, and Mario Sarcinelli, head of banking supervision. Baffi was not imprisoned because of his age yet, though the charges were later shown to be false, the careers of both men were destroyed. The Bank of Italy was neutered and, from then on, investigations were done at arm's length; rather than detailed and lengthy on-the-spot examination of banking records, the intrusive regulatory approach of the American Office of the Comptroller of the Currency, the Bank of Italy asked for written reports from the bank itself, closer to the Bank of England's supervisory style.

This took the heat off Calvi, as did the murder of Giorgio Ambrosoli, the investigating magistrate reporting on the collapse of Sindona and Banca Privata Italiana. Some believe that this assassination was set up by Sindona, about to face an Italian trial and worried by Ambrosoli's findings that the commission of $6.5 million on the sale of Banca Cattolica del Veneto to Ambrosiano – another Vatican holding – was shared between a 'Milanese banker and an American archbishop'. Equally, others could have been worried about financial links between the CIA, the Christian Democratic party, and the Mafia, in all of which Sindona and Banca Privata were believed to be the central pivot. But the Magistrature was not as easily neutered and, by 1981, Calvi himself had been arrested, and charged with currency offences. After that, the position became hopeless as Calvi looked to his P2 and Vatican friends for help, and all turned away. Two thirds of Ambrosiano's euromarket deposits were lost between January and June 1982, and the run accelerated as the bank's management crisis continued, and domestic depositors panicked. Then Calvi disappeared from Milan, and his body was discovered hanging under Blackfriars Bridge in the City of London. A rather perfunctory Coroner's Court called it suicide; the Italians scoffed, pointing out sinister P2 masonic connections with 'black friars', mafia ritual with the bricks, stones and money discovered in Calvi's pockets, and the quite unexpected agility of the middle-aged Calvi, if indeed he had hanged himself there, and in the manner that it was claimed he did. The authorities found it impossible to staunch the continuing outflow and, as they had already discovered that Ambrosiano was insolvent by some $300 million or so, the bank was liquidated over one weekend, and 'Nuevo Ambrosiano' formed to take over the assets and to hold the remaining deposits.

The story of Ambrosiano's collapse, and Calvi's presumed suicide, was followed by Larry Gurin, a staff writer with the *Institutional Investor*, who later developed it as a book entitled *Death of a Banker*. A later Coroner's Court gave an open verdict on Calvi's death, though Gurin claims that jurors told him that they would have found for murder, had they known the financial background. Gurin reports that BAH was owed some $1.3 billion by a couple of dozen 'ghost companies', based in offshore, and incurious, tax havens such as Panama and Lichtenstein. Ambrosiano always claimed that these were beneficially owned by the Vatican and, though denied, this assertion is supported by Calvi's reported expectation that 'IOR [the Vatican Bank] would do its duty', as well as the support that Calvi received from Marcinkus after his arrest. More practical are the letters of patronage – though not a financial guarantee as such, bankers regard such letters as moral guarantees – that Marcinkus sent to Ambrosiano in August 1981 on behalf of the ghosts. The Vatican Bank was called upon to pay this debt, but denied liability, while Marcinckus was confined within the sovereign state of Vatican City, lest the Italian authorities get their hands on him. But over the months, and years, that followed, the Vatican were slowly forced to admit the ownership of at least ten of the ghost companies, with ownership of some going back to at least the early 1970s, and to agree that shares of Ambrosiano were pledged as collateral for these loans.

For Calvi and the Vatican were doing what Sindona had done, and what BCCI was doing, which was to use depositor's money to buy the shares of Ambosiano itself. The Vatican finally disgorged $250 million to BAH creditors 'in recognition of moral involvement'. Gurin reckons that $600 million of the $1.3 billion was for the purchase of Ambrosiano shares, and another $200 million from forex losses incurred by borrowing dollars to buy lire assets. What no one knows is what happened to the other $500 million, though suggestions abound, such as blackmail money to P2, financial support for right-wing Latin American *juntas* advised by P2, or simply pay-offs to various Christian Democratic politicians. Maybe the simplest answer is the right one, and this represents a continuation of the Vatican's stockmarket and forex dealing from the days of Sindona. The Vatican was worried about Church revenues in the early 1970s, for they were as badly affected by inflation as anyone, while Sindona prided himself on his stockmarket skills. Marcinkus was an ideal colleague for Sindona, since both at separate times were forced to pay fines to the SEC for securities market illegalities, and sign consent decrees not to violate US securities laws in future. Later in the decade, US officials were thwarted in their efforts to question Marcinkus about reports that the Vatican Bank was involved in an underworld racket to dispose of $1 billion of counterfeit bonds, as well as other money laundering. More importantly, Sindona had employed as his right-hand-man Carlo Bordoni, a forex dealer who had been sacked by Monte dei Pascei for indiscipline before joining Citibank, where he took enormous and unauthorised positions, which cost Citibank some tens of millions to unwind.

Bordoni was the ultimate rocket scientist, and I remember talking to him when he was managing director of Banca Unione. Everything he said made beautiful logic, for forex was a very profitable business at that time, except for his key assumption. Bordoni believed that all risk in the forex markets could be hedged away, and probably persuaded both Sindona and Marcinkus that this was so. As a matter of course, the IIB allowed Italian banking customers to warehouse deals over the month end, or whenever the Bank of Italy had an inspection. That allowed the banks to run positions well outside the limits set for them, make a small profit for the IIB – since the unwritten agreement was that these deals were taken back at cost, plus commission – and gain great good will. The Vatican certainly lost money with Bordoni, for IIB was caught out on a forex deal with Societa Generale Immobiliare in 1975. SGI was Italy's premier property company, as well as the developer and owners of Washington's Watergate complex, and controlled by the Vatican. It was claimed that the Vatican had sold to Sindona, though no one believed it for everyone thought it was the usual merry-go-round that both played with the markets and, in the event, IIB's loss was finally recompensed by the Bank of Italy. From 1974 to 1982 the lire lost half its value against the dollar – from L600 to L1400 – while dollar interest rates hit 20% at the end of the 1980s. It is difficult even for bankers to remember how rapidly compound interest turns small losses into big ones, and these years made compound interest work overtime, so churchmen would have found it difficult to know when to undo the deals, and accept their loss. This would have been particularly so for Marcinkus, since he had learned his dealing tricks from Sindona and Bordoni.

The tricks of Sindona, Calvi and BCCI were just state-of-the-art scams of the sort indulged in by American savings bankers during the 1980s. Americans are accustomed to fixed price mortgages, and savings-and-loans companies and savings banks – also called 'thrifts' – had the advantage that they could pay slightly higher interest rates than commercial banks. Bankers like Keating are familiar enough figures in the records of American banking, which has had rather more than its fair share of banking frauds. Thirty-year fixed-term mortgages financed by day-to-day or three-month deposit money always involved a tricky bank balancing act, and this was shown in the 1930s, when savings banks were in greater trouble than commercial banks. It worked again after the 1933 reforms, with stable money and bankers' ledgers, but by the 1970s inflation and competition from the money-market funds had upset this delicate equilibrium.

By 1980 many thrifts were bankrupt, and the politicians acted fast and foolishly to save them. The S&Ls were first allowed to convert the revenue losses, or negative-interest spreads that they had on their mortgage book, into a form of notional capital; this was an odd decision, since these revenue losses, or the difference between the income from the mortgage and the cost of the funding deposits, could never be recovered, whatever happened to house prices or inflation. This failed to solve the problem, so then the thrifts were permitted to do virtually any business that a commercial bank could do. The quid pro quo was that they lost their interest-rate advantage; this was an empty decision, for the money-market funds had been making a farce of interest-rate regulations for much of the previous decade.

Faced with a business-threatening crisis, the markets responded. Thrifts had always been supported by the government through federal agencies that would restore their liquidity by buying some of their mortgages from them. Salomon Brothers developed a way of converting these mortgages into bonds that could be traded on the securities markets. There was a growing demand for bonds, Salomons were the biggest players in the fixed-interest markets, and mortgage bonds yielded more than government bonds, while they were much more secure than junk bonds. There were considerable technical difficulties for, though mortgages may be for thirty years, on average people change houses or repay their loans every seven years. But once these uncertain income streams were converted into definite yields, via the derivative markets, the market took off. Those technical problems would have been insurmountable, except for the computer, which resolved all the many issues of administration as well as calculating the necessary income flows.

In the 1980s the rapidly cheapening computer was becoming an accustomed tool of administration, and 'disaggregation' was the name given to the administration of banking functions by specialised third-party suppliers. This can substantially reduce the costs of the banking system, and is now being intensively explored by the large American banks as a solution to an endemic problem of unprofitability. 'Securitisation' combines 'disintermediation' and 'disaggregation' to split banking into its many discrete activities. It has unbundled banking, while Lowell Bryan of McKinseys reckons it to be the first major advance in bank technology since modern deposit banking first evolved. Almost any business can participate in banking when 'banking' is seen as a series of subcontracted functions, such as finding borrowers, making loan judgements, documenting the loans, collecting interest and repayments due on these loans, funding them by the creation of traded bonds with maturities adjusted to meet investors' preferences, paying out the interest due on the bonds, and maintaining a trading, or secondary, market in these bonds. Securitisation helped square the circle of the thrifts' dilemma.

The problem was that Americans would not easily give up their fixed-rate mortgages, so securitisation enabled those thrifts that were good at business-getting to concentrate on originating business, while others specialised as administrators of mortgages. The answer for the thrifts, however, questions the basic nature of banking itself. Securitisation has enabled ATT (American Telephone & Telegraph) to establish a credit-card operation that, after two years of existence, was seriously challenging the long-established and highly profitable credit-card operations of the banks. With money-market funds for day-to-day savings, and credit cards and postal giro systems for transferring money, who needs banks? The banking structure, held in place for many years by the corset of a complacent bureaucracy, is now undergoing further trauma.

The Chicago derivative markets took the simple swaps developed in the London forex market into a whole new world. Interest-rate futures allow thrifts to hedge their interest-rate exposure, converting their pool of variable-rate deposits into fixed-interest obligations, and using the markets to deal against their fixed-income flows to equalise the two, while leaving a profit for the savings banker. The commercial banks make up the other side of these deals, convinced with Bordoni that all risk can be hedged away. Until the 1970s, the securities, money, foreign-exchange and commodity markets were separated by time and space, and also by knowledge and custom. From the 1970s onwards, electronics compressed time and space, and disseminated knowledge, and commodity-trading techniques found a new role within the financial markets. The development of commodity-style 'derivative' financial products substantially reduced the cost of dealing in the 'cash', or underlying markets of money, securities and foreign exchange.

This cost was reduced as much as tenfold in the share markets, though it also increased the price transparency of markets, and destroyed the barriers between them. By the middle 1980s, late-twentieth-century technology had allied with nineteenth-century commodity markets to link money markets to bond markets, share prices to foreign-exchange rates, in a way that has never existed before. This was the true global financial market, not the world-spanning offices of Citibank, Salomon or Nomura, and its parturition in October 1987 was as painful as any. This new market, like that of the previous century in its freedom but, in its speed and interlocking nature, more of the twenty-first century than of this, has made dealing cheaper, more widespread, but also more risky.

Henry Kaufman says:

> The use of derivative instruments has swept across the global financial landscape, multiplying in complexity, trading volume and amounts outstanding ... Only a decade ago, these products were in their infancy ... and confined to the United States. Five years ago, they had matured in this country, but were just beginning to develop elsewhere. Nowadays ... trading of derivative instruments often exceeds activity in the corresponding 'cash' markets of the US, Japan and the UK, and is growing rapidly almost everywhere else. Derivative instruments pose complex analytical problems ... private estimates put new interest-rate swaps arranged in 1991 at close to $1.5 trillion, up from $1.2 trillion in 1990 and barely $150 billion in 1985. Outstanding swaps now certainly exceed $2.5 trillion and may be approaching an astonishing $3 trillion. They contain significant submerged risk ... and the interdependencies among market participants in derivative instruments are intricate and potentially dangerous.

But not all savings bankers were up to such rapid changes in their business, nor the tricky intellectual conundrums posed by interest-rate futures. Many sold out, exhausted by the strains of the 1970s and fearful of the likely difficulties of the 1980s. Their successors were, all too often, Keating-type figures, who appreciated that desperate politicians, amenable regulators, an imaginative business mind and an easy conscience spelled profit from a business that never has a cash-flow problem until it finally goes bust. During the 1980s these bought S&Ls, and then spent their waking hours thinking up 'sweetheart deals' between managers, shareholders and customers. The object was to produce sham earnings for the shareholders and regulators, but legitimise the removal of real cash from the bank by managers and their friends.

Their efforts were made significantly more effective by some equally creative thinking on the part of Citibank and its Wall Street peers. By adroit financial engineering, the deposit-guarantee law could be stretched to cover a deposit of $1.2 million, as opposed to the $100,000 agreed by the legislators. Commissions on $1 million-plus deposits were juicy enough to justify real selling effort, particularly since a federally guaranteed deposit in a savings bank, brokered by Citibank, was something that even the most curmudgeonly skin-flint found difficult to fault. Interest rates were exceptionally attractive, for the more corrupt the S&L, the higher the rate it was prepared to pay; these were not interested in long-term business success, only the immediate property scam, and the higher the rate offered, the faster the money flooded in. Roosevelt's fears of 1933 were at last realised. With no capital left, there was nothing at risk, so gambling the customers' money made business sense and the 'brain-dead bank' was born. If it worked, the bank had something and, if it didn't, it was only other people's money that was lost. Why should they worry? The taxpayer would pay.

So successful was this alliance of imaginative banker with conservative bank – for what could be more respectable than a savings bank? – that in less than ten years the US savings-bank industry was gutted of some $200 billion. This bankrupted the federal fund that guaranteed these banks' depositors. Clearing up the mess, and compounding the interest on the money involved, will cost the American taxpayer some $500 million. Michael Lafferty puts it in perspective:

> The regulators were overtaken by events during the 1980s, for so many new financial instruments were developed, each with its own effect on banking risk, that it was a scramble to keep up with what was happening, even on McMahon's definition that the function of a regulator is to be one step behind – but only one step – those who are being regulated. It was hardly surprising if the Bank of England had little time to take notice of BCCI, for its powers only received legal backing with the 1979 Banking Act, by which time the unknown risks involved in off-balance-sheet use of the derivative markets were beginning to give central bankers nightmares.
>
> The idea of central bankers working together was undreamed of in the 1970s and early 1980s. The need for this only started during the late 1980s, as deregulation and computers made finance a worldwide matter. It was the Third World debt crisis and Banco Ambrosiano scandal, followed soon after by the 1984 collapse of Continental Illinois and Johnson Mathey Bankers, that brought home to regulators the increased risk. The possibility of a domestic default contaminating the global banking market, because of counterparty risk, had become

a reality when no one was looking. Banking risk has always been domino-like, one failure leading to a series, and involving the wider international community. But financial risk was localised, taking time to spread, and giving the authorities the chance to take preventive action. The derivative markets changed all that, and financial collapse is now an immediate threat to all main markets. This only became a risk during the last years of the 1980s, and regulators only slowly recognised this, though faster than the politicians and bankers themselves.

17

Every Man for Himself

'The City is becoming enveloped deeper and deeper in a baleful, mysterious crisis. Day by day thick clouds gather over the Stock Markets . . . This slow-killing agony has been going on now for about two months without coming to a head. The worst kind of fever would reach its climax in less time.'

The *Financial Times* reporting the Baring crisis of 1890

IN THE MID–1970s Lord Grade, the television mogul, decided to rescue the British film industry, a project which attracts rich romantics almost as regularly as Latin America entices bankers. Some £35 million was spent making *Raise the Titanic*, one of the cinema's all-time turkeys, and, once the pain had abated somewhat, Grade remarked that it would probably have been cheaper to lower the Atlantic. During the 1990s there will be calls to raise the banking *Titanic*, now accompanying many of its passengers to a watery grave; it will definitely be cheaper, and probably more effective, if legislators and taxpayers concentrate on the ocean level instead.

There are reasons why banking reform will dominate the 1990s, other than the prospect of a debt deflation that will hold world economic growth at well below sustainable levels and unemployment well above a politically acceptable rate, particularly among the middle-class middle managers. These are the people most at risk from the microcomputer and the credit crunch facing small companies. The demand could arise not from banking's usual errors, but from a sudden banking crisis caused by the new technology. Not much more than twenty years ago, a delighted banking world rediscovered the profitability of forex trading. Though interrupted by war and economic autarchy, this was something that banks had done for many centuries. Nevertheless, the banks lost scores of millions in their dealing rooms during the early 1970s, as they relearned the lessons of risk control. The Herstatt crisis, which was only the tip of that iceberg, put the financial system at considerable risk, for as banks stopped trusting one another, the international payments system became clogged.

Derivative trading has become the banker's favourite way of making money; the speed with which the market in interest-rate futures has grown makes the risks of the Herstatt years look like a game of tiddlywinks. The underlying reality is that the interest-rate risk, which bankers passed on to their borrowers during the 1960s with the variable-rate loan, has now been passed back to the bankers. Theoretically, the currency-swap market enables companies to raise money in those markets where they are best known and can find it cheapest; since this may entail borrowing fixed-rate Deutschmarks, when what the company wants is variable-rate dollars, the banks sometimes acted as introducers, finding a company whose position is strongest among dollar-based investors to swap with the Deutschmark borrowers. Since banks naturally act as intermediaries, no sooner had the introductions started than banks realised that they could make more money by standing in the middle, and warehousing a deal until such time as a suitable counterpart came along.

Encouraging the banks in this market-making approach ensures companies can pass the interest-rate risk back to their bankers, whenever it suits them to do so, by swapping variable-rate money for fixed-interest money, or vice versa. Since the banks have all significantly mismatched their loan books anyhow, because of the need for extra profits, the underlying interest-rate risks that they are running are not only considerable, but also unknown. Both the BIS and the New York Fed are frightened of these trends for Kaufman argues:

> A fundamental lesson from the developments of contemporary financial history [is that] stabilisation of the economy through monetary policy works through credit crunches. It does not work through the seamless, incremental fine-tuning that is possible in economic textbook models, but not in the real world . . . those involved in formulating monetary policy . . . are aware of this vulnerability . . . but can do little to smooth out the effects . . . financial innovation . . . has altered market conditions so thoroughly that each successive credit crunch has taken on unique features that defy standard analytical methods . . . the central bank is never going to know before the event exactly where credit restraint is going to hit, when it is going to hit, how hard it is going to be felt, and when the crunch will pass.

As a banker, I considered myself to be above the average in intelligence, though this does not say a lot; banking success requires shrewdness, rather than intelligence, and in that I was probably deficient. But even with good dealers, and a better than average management-information system, I found it difficult to comprehend all the risks that the IIB incurred in its forex positions. Today, those risks are much greater, and understanding them very much harder, and I doubt that most bankers have an inkling of what might go wrong in the $3,000-billion interest-rate swap market. This is why Kaufman's instinct that these derivative markets will be the source of the next round of financial stringency is worrying. The combination of a Herstatt counterparty problem and an LDC solvency crisis, but magnified many times, will certainly put central bankers on their mettle; it may even make gold popular again.

Even if this does not happen, or not just yet, the banks will still want to push reform to the fore. The underlying reason for the weakness of the US money-centre banks is that they have lost the profit subsidy that once was given them by their personal customers. Merrill Lynch introduced a money-market fund that could effectively compete against a bank current account in 1980, and American banks lost the advantage of paying their customers much less than money was worth, which had been the second leg of their fundamental profitability; loans to undoubted corporate borrowers had already been cut off by disintermediation and the commercial-paper market. McKinsey expect an equally dramatic profit turnaround in Europe, though when that happens is another question. The banks are lobbying hard against the introduction of Merrill Lynch-style money funds, having seen what happened to their American colleagues; since the German banks are most at risk, while the German Bundesbank dislikes anything that will weaken its control over monetary policy, reform may take some time. But French and Spanish banks have already lost much of their retail deposit subsidy and, as Canute proved a few centuries ago, attempting to deny the flowing of the tide only wets the feet.

As long ago as 1987, Gerald Corrigan, president of the Federal Reserve Bank of New York, argued:

> We have in my view excess capacity in large segments of banking and finance ... The historic value of the banking franchise is under great pressure. The institutionalisation of savings, the securitisation of financial assets and liabilities, the easy access to information ... are all symptomatic of a rapidly changing banking and financing environment, which has unquestionably undercut the once considerable value of the banking franchise.

Securitisation is now adding to banking capacity, though Lowell Bryan may be optimistic in his assessment of its importance; Citibank discovered the reason in the 1930s, for when people won't lend you money, they won't buy bonds from you either. As George Moore has remarked, bankers believe that bonds are good collateral until they try to sell them in a credit crunch. However attractive securitised mortgages, credit-card receivables and auto loans may look now as bonds, when another 1974 comes no one will buy them, for then only cash will be king.

Banking is the reflection of social as well as technological change, and none of this can be foreseen by legislators; yet as Machiavelli wrote, once a regime is in place, it is difficult to shift it. Investment banks are meant to live and die in the marketplace, without the benefit of government guarantees, yet counterparty risk means that these must be protected, since capital movements on behalf of investment managers and dealers now account for the vast bulk of forex transactions and international money transmissions. Once investment bankers realised they also had this safety net, they began to grow like Topsy. Drexel had drifted a long way from its days of glory as a Morgan bank, and a 1966 merger did nothing to improve its fortunes. But, though this pre-eminently WASP firm did not know it, from the 1970s onwards it had a secret weapon which would once again make it a star of the Wall Street universe. Unfortunately for Drexel, Michael Milken lacked the character of Pierpoint Morgan, although nothing of his drive and cleverness, and Drexel would burn itself out, taking many of the star financiers of the 1980s with it.

Milken, the son of an accountant and an extremely bright investment analyst, started working at Drexel during his summer vacations. He joined full-time in 1970 when he graduated from the Wharton School of Finance, probably America's most intellectually demanding business school. Kept in the boiler room at Drexel, Milken quickly realised that the majority of the sales staff were pushing tired ideas, neither better nor worse than anybody else's, but no help to a firm in terminal decline. He also quickly appreciated that investors are not unlike the firms that deal with them: because of their fear and greed, they and the markets consistently under- or overprice securities. Milken began to research junk bonds. These are either securities that have fallen from grace because the company that originally issued them has fallen on hard times or, more rarely, securities that have never been of investment quality. The middle

1970s were good years for Milken, and for Drexel Burnham as the bank became after a merger, for the 1974 crisis added new names to his investment universe. As his skills became more widely known, particularly in the bonds of the busted real-estate investment trusts, a group of investment managers coalesced around him.

Milken enabled these to give the American public what they wanted, and what their banks were not interested in supplying – a high running yield to keep up with rising prices, and the hope of some capital growth. Milken's judgement was justified, for many of his recommended bonds recovered their investment grade ratings, and the funds invested in them produced returns significantly better than funds invested in shares or investment-grade bonds. The junk bond funds were much more attractive than bank deposits – yielding more, promising capital growth, and often secured on the assets of large American companies.

Success breeds success within the investment world. As the managers did well, more money flowed into their funds; as more funds were floated on the back of this high-yielding growth-fund concept, more managers came to Milken for advice. Drexel partners found themselves making more money than the recent history of the firm gave them any right to expect, and Milken negotiated a deal with the partners that, effectively, made him a firm-within-the-firm. There was a problem, however; the demand for junk bonds was outrunning the supply.

Perhaps Milken and Drexel would still be in Philadelphia today, were it not for Fred Joseph, an out-of-luck investment banker looking to build a reputation. Joseph was an oddity, for he not only said he liked dealing with ambitious, medium-sized companies, but actually meant it. All investment bankers make such statements, since these are good for political and marketing image-building. Few do more, for big companies deliver big bucks; fees are generally a percentage of the face value of the deal, and big names give big clout within investment-banking parlours. Medium-sized companies are for commercial bankers, not investment bankers. The combination of Joseph and Milken made dreams come true for ambitious businessmen. Milken had built up one half of a traditional investment-banking franchise, which was the money, or investment, side. Joseph would build up the other: the issuers. These were businessmen with ambitions, needing money to make their companies grow. The combination of these two elements – investors and issuers – have been the foundation of investment success since the Dutch put together the money for the Dutch East India Company in 1602.

The issuers happily gave Milken the yield he wanted for his investors. Their companies were certainly not investment grade, their bankers were not interested, for they were chasing after Third World country loans, so it was either pay up to go without. But Joseph's customers reckoned that they could afford to meet Milken's needs. These businessmen either had their sights fixed on new business ideas, where margins were wide and competition low, or on larger companies within their own industry, which were fat, complacent and stuffed full of unused assets. These would make their acquirers very rich indeed, if only they could put the deal together, and no one minds paying high fees in such circumstances; the initial business deals of Drexel were extremely profitable for all concerned.

Then a new source of investor appeared in 1980, as the S&Ls were rescued from bankruptcy. Their regulator – the Federal Savings & Loan Insurance Corporation – could not afford to close them down and pay off their depositors. Instead, FSLIC helped them to stay in business by manipulation of their balance sheets, and encouraged them to find more profitable activities than making mortgage loans. These banks, with all their equity lost, had nothing further to lose; either Milken's bonds were good, which meant a profit on their funding costs and some recovery of shareholders' funds, or they failed, in which case FSLIC picked up the tab for lost deposits. But these brain dead banks had another attraction. Deposit insurance attracted depositors, and the higher the rate they offered, the more they got; financed by brokered deposits from the likes of Citibank, selling their mortgages to Salomon, and supplied with high-yielding junk bonds by Drexel, these honest but stupid S&Ls thought they were saving themselves. Their brighter, but crooked, colleagues had more direct ways of enjoying their brokered deposits.

Wall Street took off, as Uncle Sam underwrote all the funds that an investment banker could imagine needing: takeovers, reverse takeovers, poison-pill defences, management buyouts – all flourished in a world where money was, literally, no problem. Drexel had started lending to medium-sized, entrepreneurial companies that wanted to acquire the world, but they finished financing the management of America's largest companies as they bought their companies on the cheap from their own shareholders. By the 1980s Drexel had become the largest and most profitable Wall Street firm, and everyone else was sick with envy. Their rivals included Citibank, Drexel's commercial bankers, still doing for Drexel what they had done for Pierpoint Morgan in the great days of the business trusts.

What a recently restored investment bank could do, a proud and ambitious universal bank could do even better. But a 'proper' bank could do it in style, for it would have no need to sell paper when it could use its own money. So the bank-financed management buyout was born; instead of sharing the profit with investors, the banks would share it among themselves. Some 10 per cent by capitalised value of the New York equity market was bought back over these years, financed by borrowed money or junk bonds. Initially it was highly profitable, because of the enormous fees, and pretty soon the sum loaned by the US banks was as much as they had lent to developing countries. Milken at least was professional, laying off his risks on to his investors via the securities markets. Citibank, and other lenders of these Very Highly Leveraged Transactions, as the regulators finally classified them, were using depositors' money, and doubling and trebling their risk as bankers, investors and financiers. Hugh McCullock, the first comptroller, would not have been pleased: this was definitely not banking but 'splendid financiering' and, though the 'splendid financiers in banking' were neither McCullock's 'humbugs or rascals', they were worse; they were bureaucratic salesmen, chasing loan-volume budgets.

These were not solidly secured loans, nor did the borrowers have three ways to pay; instead, loan repayment was based on highly optimistic views of future cash flows. As competition mounted for the business, so also did the imagination of the bankers in identifying sources of cash flow for repayment. Furthermore, quite apart from the capitalist ethics of whether managers should be financed in order to cheat their shareholders, there was the banking principle involved in shafting your own customers. This had been the subject of anguished debate within Morgan Stanley when, ten years earlier, they first agreed to act in hostile takeovers. A decade later Citibank's lending officers were terrified that their colleagues in Citibank's VHLT division were hatching plots to take over their customers. It was only because of a newspaper story that in 1986 John Reed, the chairman, learned that this part of his bank had backed a corporate raid on Gillette, a valued and long-established Citibank customer.

By 1980 the social Darwinism of Citibank was beginning to mutate; by the mid–1980s it had become corporate cannibalism. The organisation of the bank was structured to create competition, for no one team was ever asked to look at something; it was always two or three, with the fastest and most aggressive getting the prize. One ex-Citibanker was quoted as saying: 'I had already been through a period when I felt I was under pressure to take more risk than appropriate. Either you have to obey your seniors or you have to leave. If you stay, you get painted as negative, and you become ineffective.' The result was confusion to banker and customer alike: Citibank spent $500 million buying two British stockbrokers, another $500 million on further stockbrokers to create a global securities capacity but, within a year of the final purchase, had changed policy, demotivated its new businesses, organised them and reorganised them, and finally closed them down, losing the bulk of its $1-billion people investment with the closures.

The position was even worse in Citibank's core business of lending. After the REIT bust, Walter Wriston had ordered a postmortem, very much on George Moore lines, into what had gone wrong. As a result, Wriston ordered his credit-risk supremo to circulate a memorandum to managers which said:

> If a lending officer thinks raises and promotions come from booking credit products, and if supervisors press for short-term bottom line performance – letting lending officers sell too hard or even violate credit tenets – the quality of the portfolio will suffer. Sometimes fed by performance motivated stock analysts, greed is the bugbear ... memories are short when a salesman is in hot pursuit.

Ten years after this, Citibank started paying bonuses for loan volumes. In a bank that ran on simple certainties – 'countries don't go broke', 'real estate values never fall' and 'overnight funding is always available' – that was to ask for trouble. The result, according to a damning and well-researched article in *Institutional Investor*, was that Citibank's whole credit culture fell apart. As another quote puts it: 'It went from "Let's get the right information so we can do it right" to "What's the shortest route to getting it done?" '

Success in retail banking during the 1980s helped plug the profit hole left by the desertion of the commercial banks' traditional customers, but it was not enough for either profitability or image. Arranging a mortgage for Mrs Jones, useful though it may be as a community service, did little to enhance the self-esteem of a financial master of the universe. A sinner's repentance is a glory to behold, and the world is now enjoying it, yet it might well have been cheaper for shareholders if the banks had never strayed in the first place. The British Trustee Savings Banks were beneficiaries of the Thatcher revolution, for they were privatised and then allowed to play all the best banking games. Since no one knew who owned them, and the

Treasury was unable to think of a convincing reason to keep the money for itself, the newly centralised management of these simple banks had a net dowry of £2.2 billion after its flotation in 1988. Like an earlier pools winner management adopted a policy of 'Spend, spend, spend', and lost every penny, just like the lucky lady of the lottery.

Though the TSB did their share of property lending, they preferred financiers, as did the Swiss. Even these stolid citizens got carried away, lending $1 billion to an unusual-for-a-Swiss charismatic take-over merchant. Unlike everyone else, though, the Swiss banking authorities thought this was not the way that bankers should behave. They produced a report criticising slack banking practices and ensured that those responsible were, if not sacked, certainly 'retired'. Everyone else preferred property, even though the losses of 1974 were less than a decade old. In 1987 Barclays appointed a new chairman, and Sir John Quinton was hailed as a meritocrat who could reverse Barclay's declining size and profits. Quinton was backed by a managing director from one of the founding families that still dominate Barclay's management. That same year Barclay's senior management had decided that the property market was over-heating, while Quinton himself encouraged the external warnings from the Bank of England about the dangers of too much property lending.

A year later Barclays raised £920 million from its shareholders, in order to reverse the loss of its first place within British banking to National Westminster. This gave the bank a massive unused lending capacity, for banking capital can translate into between ten and fifteen times as much of hard-core lending. Barclay's managers then had a problem, for they all had lending budgets to fulfil, and questions would be asked of anyone who allowed any slippage of Barclay's market leadership among high-profile borrowers. The inflation of the 1970s had helped to ameliorate the lending memories of the 1970s, and 'merchant property developers' sounded good. These promised their bankers that they would not get caught out like their predecessors. Instead of building for rent, they would build to sell, and their active trading would keep the banks' money turning over, earning fees as well as interest spreads.

Between 1987 and 1991 overall lending by English banks increased by a little over 60 per cent, but Barclay's property lending nearly trebled. All the banks made such property loans, as well as loans to finance the contractors who were making a reality out of the dreams of these new-style developers. The money certainly circulated until 1990, when bankers discovered again that property developers are just that, and all the 'merchant' means is that the bank has a charge on the individual unsaleable property, but not on a whole portfolio, nor on the borrowing company itself, and that when you need to sell, nobody wants to buy. British banks lent some £40 billion to property developers over the 1980s, of which some £17 billion came from the four English commercial banks. So 20 per cent vacancy rates and the problems of Canary Wharf explain bankers' present reluctance to lend on anything that is not both gilt-edged and guaranteed by God.

These banks had already written off some £8 billion for their adventures in Latin America and other places where British bankers' nannies warn their charges never to go, and no sooner was that over than the recession came. Scrooge would be embarrassed by the way the banks are recouping their fortunes by squeezing their individual and small-business customers. On the other hand, who else is there to pay? These banks now face further losses depending on the length and depth of the recession, estimated to be between some £17–20 billion. This should surprise no one who has heard senior bankers say: 'We can lend up to £100,000 for business on a credit-scoring basis, and we can lend over £5 million. What we can't do is make loans in the middle, because we don't have the people to make the judgements, and nor could we afford to do it, even if we had them.'

During the 1980s, property developers were romanced by bankers everywhere. There is now enough empty space around to keep US and British office users happy for the next ten to fifteen years, though not, of course, their developers or their bankers. 'Stay alive 'til '95' is the mantra chanted by American bankers and property developers as they go to bed each night, but their chances of so doing look bleak. Office vacancy rates of 20 per cent or more, rents unable to service the capital cost of the building, and computer systems scything through the ranks of office workers, all indicate that even low interest rates will be insufficient to hold back this grim reaper. With outstanding property debts of $160 billion, and values down by at least 25 per cent since their peak, American banks will have to swallow hard to digest the several hundred million dollar's worth of loans due to be refinanced over the next couple of years. It was a trend like this, as the Standard & Poor's rating agency gloomily reports, that wiped out the whole of the Texan banking industry during the mid- to late 1980s.

America is the place, of course, of wide open spaces, and the

Japanese banks own plenty of these. Of some $400 billion US-based lending by Japanese banks, $30–40 billion is secured on property, with most advanced in the dying months of the California property boom; vacancy rates are reported to be in the range of 30–50 per cent in the desirable downtown areas of Los Angeles and San Diego. Figures are bigger in Japan, of course. With only 10 per cent of the country's surface flat enough to be usable, the opportunities for developers' hype is much greater, which is why 100-year mortgages briefly became the norm for the family home. Fortunately, Japanese banks are not required to tell their shareholders how many of their debts are 'nonperforming', though their problems were described with typical central-bank understatement as 'serious but not lethal'. The *Financial Times* acquired a confidential estimate of Japanese bank property losses, which reckons that property bad and doubtful debts for the twenty-one major banks alone range between $177 and $224 billion, though the Bank of Japan was quoted by the *Financial Times* as saying: 'Nobody at this moment can possibly have an accurate estimate because the situation in real estate is so fluid.'

That's central-bank speak for the position is awful, prices are still falling, and for God's sake say nothing in case you frighten the children. Still, the Japanese banks can take comfort from one statistic; if they were stuffed by American banks with bad loans in California, they did the same to foreigners in Tokyo. Loans to property developers, and related businesses, amount to up to 9 per cent of Japanese bank-loan totals, but getting on for 20 per cent of the assets of foreign banks.

Britain's new investment bankers were caught out manipulating share prices on behalf of companies for which they were raising new money from existing shareholders, or advising on contested takeover battles. Attempts by the banks concerned to cover up these offences failed, and so did their next defence that 'what we were doing wasn't wrong and, if it was, then they were doing it first', because Mrs Thatcher's Conservative government in 1988 had a need for a blood sacrifice or two. The rise of the champagne-guzzling, Porsche-driving 'yuppie', particularly as displayed on TV news programmes, had given the government an image problem, for not all its supporters were as enthusiastic as were government ministers for capitalism, red in tooth and claw, particularly as demonstrated during the last hurrahs of a frenzied share market.

One of these was the bitter fight by Guinness for Distillers, a badly managed company with a stranglehold on Scotch whisky supply, and a real prize to any well-managed company who could overcome the nationalist supporters of virtually the last redoubt of the Scottish business establishment. Guinness won, then failed to keep its promises to the Scots, and an almighty row exploded. As lawyers were dragged in, questions were raised about the means used by Morgan Grenfell to support the price of Guinness shares, which were being tendered for Distillers shares.

The other row was over the acquisition by Blue Arrow, a fast-growing employment agency, of America's Manpower Incorporated. Manpower was much the older and more solidly established of the two companies, and its managers wanted cash, not shares, for their business. A rights issue of shares to existing shareholders was necessary to raise the cash to repay the temporary bank-borrowing arranged to make the purchase. This was for £837 million, the largest ever cash offer up to then organised on the London market and, it might seem, a trifle pricey for an employment agency. The issue was the responsibility of County Natwest, the investment-banking subsidiary of National Westminster, which, as one of England's 'Big Four' commercial banks, was trying to prove itself as a newly fashionable universal bank. The Blue Arrow rights issue failed to attract investors, who felt – rightly, as events were to prove – that the company was taking on more than it could handle.

National Westminster had two choices. It could admit failure and require the underwriters (guarantors of the issue, and large investment funds in their own right) to take up the shares. This would depress the share price, since investors would know that there was a 'tap' in the market, turned on whenever the market looked strong enough to allow the underwriters to get rid of their shares. It would also highlight the bank's inability to read the market, judge price levels and twist arms. Alternatively, the bank could stuff the shares into clients' portfolios, hold some themselves, get others to buy them with a guarantee against loss, and pretend the issue was much more successful than it had been. It chose to do the latter, and might well have succeeded but for the October 1987 price collapse, which gave the ousted American boss of Manpower the opportunity to return the compliment of his English successor when he regained control. As the share price fell, board squabbles intensified, market rumours grew, and the Bank of England called for an inquiry. The bank hid its embarrassment as best it could and, naturally, everyone in the National Westminster group proclaimed their absence, ignorance or innocence of these events or, best of all, all three.

Once overenthusiastic infractions of the City's code of practice would have been handled by the Take-Over Panel, much strengthened since Morgan Grenfell and Hambros had ignored it in their fight to keep Maxwell from gaining control of the *News of the World*. But this time the machinery of the law creaked into motion, to justify the recently passed Financial Services Act. This continued to enshrine the British principle of 'self-regulation' within financial markets, and in spite of the stinking corpse of the Gentleman Bankers' Code. Few City bankers believed that the actions of National Westminster, or of Morgan Grenfell, were much out of line with prevailing market practice. Once the event was in the open, though, the chairman of National Westminster, still protesting that the whole affair had nothing to do with him, was forced to resign together with three of his board colleagues. The bank fired many of the executives concerned, and hoped that memories were short.

The Bank of England, whipped on by the government, insisted that Morgan Grenfell sack its managing director and the team that had given Morgan Grenfell a reputation fearsome enough to equal that of Warburg in its 1960s heyday. The new law still needed a list of suitable suspects and the ideal list, in such circumstances, contains individuals who are neither too 'establishment', nor too senior. This allows any organisation foolish enough to be facing the wrong way when the political winds turn, to admit to a little overenthusiasm and possible bending of the letter of the law on the part of its regrettably undersupervised underlings, but still deny any intention to break the spirit of the law. Commissions of inquiry were appointed, lists drawn up, and tumbrils prepared. National Westminster supported its people; Morgan Grenfell, forgetting the Morgan principle of loyalty above all, threw theirs to the political lynch parties.

Five years after the events, and in a financial world that had changed completely from that which existed before October 1987, the various banking candidates loaded on to the tumbril have either been found not guilty, or had their trials suspended. In the case of four of the defendants in the Blue Arrow trial, this was not until after an appeal. After a trial lasting twelve months, costing the state some £40 million, and a three-day summing up, the jury were understandably bemused, and failed to understand the judge's direction. The trial of the bankers in the Guinness case was suspended; the two involved, abandoned by their employers, had destroyed both their fortunes and their health in attempting to defend themselves against the full might of the state. Morgan Grenfell, humiliated by its cowardice, soon ended up as a department of Deutsche Bank. Nearly all the banking victims have had their careers destroyed. The Serious Fraud Office was stigmatised for its incompetence. Even lawyers protested that including so many charges, and taking so long, was a perversion of justice.

But then justice was not the issue, so much as regulatory terrorism; if the law won't allow the regulators to get their way one way, then the state Exchequer will finance another way. Politics conquers money, and banks won't easily forget the experience. The state may have paid their court and legal costs, but five years' senior management time, sullied images, and worry have their price too.

American regulators are at least as frustrated as their British colleagues that financial life won't remain in the tidy boxes to which legislators have assigned it. They also have more cause to fret over the money lost by their earlier laxity. Charles Bowsher is Comptroller General of the General Accounting Office of Congress, and was warning early in the 1980s that the savings banks were on the road to perdition. Now that has been proved; the Resolution Trust Corporation, the agency set up to clean up the mess, has reported criminal behaviour in two out of every five of the savings banks that it has so far seized. Apart from their managers, the favourite responsible parties are their professional advisers. 'Misuse of accounting standards played an extremely large and, in some ways, pivotal role in the reckless growth of the Thrift industry, as well as in concealing the depth of its problems,' intones Richard Breedon, chairman of the US Securities and Exchange Commission. So also does everyone else, for the 1980s were a decade when no one wanted to know about the problems of the thrifts, a goodly percentage of which were already bankrupt as the decade opened.

Politicians did not wish to find the money to bail out the thrifts, and they were equally sure that their constituents should not bear the market price of their home loans. The Reagan administration wanted the 'market' to find the answer at the beginning of the decade and, at the end, did not want to upset the electorate and the presidential campaign of George Bush. The regulators learned from the sacking of a would-be reforming boss that there was no percentage in bravery, and that Congress did not want to be upset by talk of inadequate money and resources. And no one wanted to listen to Bowsher, least of all the administration, as he advised Congress that the bail-out was going to cost more, and take longer, than anyone was willing to contemplate. Now he is saying that the RTC is so incompetent that the ultimate cost cannot be calculated. Since his earlier estimate was $200 billion now, and $300 billion for the interest on the money over the next twenty to forty years of the clean-up, an 'uncalculable figure' will not be peanuts.

To add to the discomfiture of politicians and regulators alike, Bowsher reckons that the Federal Deposit Insurance Corporation is also bankrupt, and that the American taxpayer must finance a bail-out of the commercial banks as well. Though he does not reckon that this will be as expensive as that of the thrifts, he has advised Congress not to expect repayment of the $70-billion loan authorised for the FDIC. The administration denies both that the FDIC is bankrupt and that brain-dead banks are being left in business, as the FDIC does not have the funds to pay off their depositors and close them down. It is back to the old tunes, ten years further on, but with the commercial banks, rather than the thrifts, as piggy in the middle.

In the meantime, the regulators have discovered Racketeer Influenced and Corrupt Organisations (RICO) laws, which are loosely worded but have draconian impact. Originally designed to attack the business activities of hoodlums and drug barons, other federal laws now follow similar RICO procedures. This enables the Office of Thrift Supervision to attack anyone remotely concerned with the S&L scandals with punishment first, trial and judgement later. The Thrift Office extracted $41 million from one New York legal firm, which had advised Charles Keating and Lincoln Savings, by charging that the firm, and three specific partners, cooperated with Keating in violating the laws and deceiving regulators. The law firm was, in effect, put into receivership under the Thrift Office, for a cease and desist order was issued at the same time as notice of charges. As a result, the partnership had to pay 25–50 per cent of each partner's earnings into an escrow account; no partner was allowed to leave the partnership without millions of dollars as security against possible future fines; the use of partners' personal assets, and the level of their earnings, was restricted and subject to supervision by the Thrift Office; and the partnership lost its right to dissolve itself, take on new partners or otherwise modify itself, or to enter into unusual business transactions.

The practical result was that firm and partners either went out of business and into bankruptcy, or paid the blackmail. Naturally, the partnership cried 'uncle' and the Thrift Office has gone on to extract even more millions from other legal and accountancy firms. It is a great wheeze; using RICO enabled the authorities to threaten Milken with charges carrying fines of $18 billion and 520 years in jail. Since many of his closest collaborators had already turned state's evidence under similar pressure, Milken pleaded guilty to six technical offences and was sentenced to ten years in prison. It was made clear that this was to keep him talking and, if he did, cooperation would reduce the sentence by many years. Connie Bruck in *The Predators' Ball*, her riveting account of Milken and Drexel, comes to the conclusion that Milken had to be stopped; Milken feels the same. He has been reported as believing that, when Citibank and the others joined the party in the middle 1980s, prices of companies had gone too high, and corporate managers should have started raising equity and paying off debt. By that time, of course, the fees were too high, the game too exciting and the profits of success too enticing for anyone to leave the field, let alone the master tactician of the game.

The RICO laws were not designed for frustrated regulators, and these should remember the law of unintended consequences, which has been tripping up bankers these last two decades. If the technical tricks that caught Al Capone in the 1930s are suitable for bankers in the 1990s, there are only two conclusions. Either bankers are 'banksters', in which case Stalin had the right answer for them, though it did nothing for the Russian economy, or the regulators have been given an impossible task. If it is the latter, it is surely better to review the regulations, rather than subvert painfully acquired principles of law which have, on the whole, benefited the English-speaking peoples. Lynch law for bankers can easily lead to its use on others.

18

Clinging to the Wreckage

'If you see a Genevan banker jump out of the window, follow
him for there is sure to be money where he lands.'

> Voltaire commenting on his bankers

AFTER THE *TITANIC* SINKING, the US Coastguard instituted
an iceberg watch, which continues to this day. The problem is
not so much the icebergs themselves which, towering hundreds of
feet above the sea and weighing thousands of tons, are obvious to
the naked eye, but the growlers. These dark and ancient lumps of
ice are easily missed, even with the most up-to-date scanning devices,
yet their crystalline structure and titanium hardness enable them to
slit open modern hulls with the ease and speed of an electric tin-
opener. The sixteenth century accountant, Matthaus Schwartz,
would have recognised that the growlers of business cost, uncontrolled expansion and misused technology, have destroyed banking
profitability, rather than the icebergs of Third World, property and
VHLT debt. In his textbook on bookkeeping, Schwartz expressed
his contempt for those bankers who believe that they can keep
their accounts in their head, made up from variegated sources of
information, and he would have excoriated modern bankers as
'These little men [who] write down their dealings in poorly-kept
scrap-books, or on slips of paper, stick them on the wall, and make
their reckonings on the window-sill'.

Jacob Streider, the 1931 memorialist of Jacob Fugger the Rich, the
greatest of the Augsburg bankers, remarks that his hero obviously
understood Machiavelli's recommendation that politicians should
despise mere greed for power, for the true statesman keeps a cool
head and attempts only what is attainable. It was the secret noted
of the Rothschilds, two centuries ago, when it was commented that
they never sought an excessive profit, but always recognised the
appropriate limit for any transaction, for their true profit came from
spreading their energies over a great variety of constantly recurring

opportunities. Sir Archibald Forbes's frustration was partly that he was numerate, while most of Midland's general managers were not, though, in this, they are no different from the majority of bankers, all of whom can certainly calculate a percentage, add up a column of figures, or even deconstruct a balance sheet. Numeracy in the Rothschild style is best described by Matthaus Schwartz, the pupil and chief accountant of Fugger.

Schwartz had gone to Italy to learn the secrets of double-entry bookkeeping but claimed he learned there little more than nothing, compared to his experience with Fugger. For Schwartz, the importance of good and accurate accounts is that only thus can all the facets of the enterprise be truly reflected, as clearly as one's face in the shaving mirror. Even so, Schwartz argued that this is the less important function of good accounts; it is only by keeping proper accounts that bankers and businessmen are schooled to see things as they are, and not as they would have them be, to understand their business as a whole and not just in its detail. It was this dispassionate, rational scrutiny of risk versus reward that made Jacob Fugger the Rich.

While his colleagues were persuaded by the blandishments or threats of emperors, Fugger preferred smaller but more certain undertakings to these larger, riskier ones. A political and financial supporter of the house of Hapsburg, Fugger refused to lend to Charles V, the greatest emperor of his time, unless with proper security, and even then insisted that all contractual repayments be met, on time and in cash. So, rather than accepting the invitation of Herman Abs, one of the great German postwar bankers, to join the European Banks International Company, Midland would have done better to have asked how Abs and Deutsche Bank were rebuilding German industry.

British manufacturing was beginning to die, yet correspondent banking assumes a domestic base of exporting customers. Germany built up an awesome surplus on its manufacturing trade during the 1960s–70s, but Britain went the other way, and so did Midland's business. Between 1970 and 1980 loans to engineering companies halved as a percentage of Midland's total lending, and halved again over the following five years; over these same years loans to all manufacturing business, other than textiles, fell from 40 per cent of Midland's portfolio to less than 20 per cent. The Thatcher government believed in services rather than manufacturing, and a general lack of design quality had already resulted in British industry losing many of its export markets during 1960–70; domestic markets were attacked by imports from the middle 1970s onwards, and the 1980–81 recession speeded up this process.

A \$2: £1 rate of exchange at the start of the Thatcher decade acted like a giant enema on constipated management with clogged financial and labour controls; by the end of the 1980s British industry was efficient, but the cost of the clear-out meant that the traded-goods industry is now completely inadequate for the country's needs. During a decade when the banks were looking overseas for their borrowers, British demand for manufactured goods rose by some 30 per cent while domestic capacity increased by less then 2 per cent. Before 1981 the country had never run a deficit on its manufacturing trade with the rest of the world; since then it has never run a surplus. At the bottom of the worst depression since the 1930s, the country is running a deficit on its international trade of several billion pounds.

Once the Crocker crisis was over, Midland, the bank that most needed to encourage an industrial renaissance, found itself at last with a full-time chairman who was also its chief executive. Unfortunately, he was not a banker. Sir Kit McMahon became the would-be rescuer of the reputation of Britain's Midland Bank on the back of his considerable achievement as an economist, and the ability of this Australian academic to storm the English establishment. A very successful deputy governor of the Bank of England, McMahon went to the Midland to make money, for few central bankers are paid even a fraction of the rewards expected by commercial, let alone investment, bankers. It was not an easy task that McMahon had taken on, for Midland's staff were mortified by the speed and futility of the bank's decline, and McMahon appreciated the difficulties, saying to colleagues: 'Sometimes I feel keyed up with the challenge and excitement of it all, but at other times I want to jump into the nearest lake.'

McMahon moved fast to clean up Midland's balance sheet, sold off its Celtic bank subsidiaries to realise extra capital, raised new money through a rights issue, and brought in the Hongkong & Shanghai Bank as a 15 per cent shareholder for a trial marriage. Unfortunately, McMahon had all the prejudices of a former central banker, and one particularly enamoured of the American banking style. Nor was his judgement of people perfect and, in consequence, McMahon split Midland as Tom Wilcox had divided Crocker. John Harris was one of the casualties, and indeed nearly every Midland manager over forty was encouraged to take early retirement, while recruits poured in from the London branches of American banks. An executive minute of the board is rumoured to state that the Midland would, as a matter of policy, cease taking on any further Chase Manhattan recruits. McMahon was keen on the 'gee-whiz' business approach to banking problems; he was worried that he might seem too much of Hamlet figure, forever agonising over decisions. Ian Morison remembers:

> When I first joined Midland in 1983, there were perhaps four outsiders on the fourth [senior management] floor of Poultry, and what impressed me was the informal networks. Midland was hopelessly rigid, but worked, because everyone knew each other. These networks were made up of people at very different levels of authority, who had joined the bank together, gone on a particularly memorable or testing training course, or worked on a difficult hospital case, such as Rolls-Royce or those of 1980–81. When I left in 1988, there was only one Midland veteran left on the fourth floor, everyone else was an incomer, and the networks had largely gone. At the same time, of course, all the shared values had gone too, so there was no agreement on what Midland was, or should be.

Though McMahon recruited an able and powerful board, his underlying message to directors was to keep out. Geoffrey Taylor, who might have been a helpful board confidant, could never find an effective way to get through to his chairman. Not keen on testing questions anyway, McMahon became increasingly isolated within Midland, and a bank that had always got its strategy right, but failed in its tactical execution, now proceeded to get both wrong. The branch network was ignored, for all new recruits had been trained in the Hambro/Citibank style of head-office banking. This was a major error for – unfortunate though it may be for British businessmen – English commercial banking is based on branches handling provincial business, rather than the US style of independent main-street banks dealing with their customers' more complicated needs through correspondent relationships with money-centre banks.

Midland's costs were based on its branches, yet the cultural divorce between Poultry and the branches ensured that costs grew while income declined, and head-office rocket scientists produced ideas that not even branch managers could understand, let alone their customers. Forward Trust under Harris, and then Goldthorpe, had experimented successfully with 'lifestyle' loans, an approach to marketing bank loans developed initially by regional American banks. Translated by marketing gurus into strangely named banking accounts, in a vain attempt to give a brand name to a basic commodity through heavy TV advertising, these made the Midland look ludicrous. Only after several years of expensive marketing failure did Poultry accept what they had been consistently told by branch managers: these accounts were too expensive and not good enough. Once that was accepted, the accountants then discovered that they could not easily be handled by the bank's systems and were, anyway, unprofitable.

Whatever the faults of McMahon's strategic thinking, he had the intellectual ability to place Samuel Montagu correctly within the Midland. It became the international, wholesale and issuing bank of the group, as well as its central treasury. But even here the choice of people meant that these changes were cosmetic, rather than real, for Montagu's management remained alien to the core elements of Midland's business-getting function, and the bridges that were not built in the 1960s remained unbuilt in the 1980s. However, the treasury added another thorn to McMahon's crown by taking an enormous punt on interest-rate movements, getting it wrong, holding out obstinately, and finally losing millions when Midland could least afford either the publicity or the losses.

The circumstances of McMahon's arrival allowed him to eliminate the checks and balances that had developed within the bank; while these had held back the Midland, they had ensured diversity of viewpoint. The destruction of the Midland culture, and McMahon's recruitment of a clever group of managers alien to Midland thinking, created enormous volatility as well as exerting great pressure on McMahon himself. Sole leader and arbiter of the would-be 'new' Midland, a sociable and friendly man enjoying academic discussion with imaginative but practical subordinates became increasingly isolated. Managers learned caution within an environment where 'political correctness' became more important to the survival of a changed career than effectiveness. It is only fair to say that McMahon himself would not recognise this Midland insiders' picture but this, together with his failure to reverse the drift of Midland's fortunes, doomed him.

As the excesses of 1980s lending cut into banking profitability, both Midland and Hongkong & Shanghai were forced to reconsider their merger plans. As Midland slashed its dividend, the Bank of England acted to give Midland what it had lacked for half a century – a full-time executive chairman, working together with a chief executive, and neither of them Midland insiders. But whether

McMahon's successors will be able to reap where he sowed still seems doubtful. Morison remarked of his time at Midland:

> I always felt intuitively that it is the assymetric nature of information that gives bankers their opportunity as intermediaries, even though it does not always work in their favour. Borrowers always know more than the lender, whether they be companies borrowing from the bank, or banks taking money from depositors; similarly market makers ought to be in a better position than investors. A corporate raider once described the secret of his success to me as 'arbitraging between greed and ignorance'. Traditionally, banking has been rather like that.
>
> Here at Loughborough, I discovered an enormous academic literature on just this subject; if markets were perfect, there would be no need for banks. Everything financial intermediaries do could be done, instead, on the insurance, derivatives or securities markets. Markets are still far from perfect, though much better than they were, because modern technology makes information more widely available, more quickly, and from many more sources. Few senior bankers yet realise that these modern trends have gone a long way towards destroying 'the bankers' turn', or that traditional bankers no longer have a monopoly of functional skills which they can exercise within a compact business oligopoly. Midland in 1982 was in a very weak position, for its branches were predominantly outside the growing southeast area, it had not developed its skills in small company lending, and its costs were too high for its business volumes. I don't believe that much has changed for Midland over the last ten years, or that its management realises that this is a systemic weakness of banking, and one to which they are especially vulnerable.
>
> Bankers talk a lot about fee business, but most are unaware that there is an opportunity cost to this, and that it has significant capital costs of its own. Employing people, using premises, and obtaining knowledge in order to develop a new fee-earning business may show up as revenue, rather than capital, costs but it is all money which, otherwise, could be added back to the capital base. Moreover, few bankers ask themselves, in terms of their proposed fee-earning opportunities 'What is our valued added service, what do we do better than our competitors, why should customers come to us, rather than go to them?' When financial pressures arise, bankers tend to retreat to their traditional responses of cutting costs, or increasing charges and margins, rather than finding superior ways of adding value for their customers. That way, of course, lies decay, but it can take a long time to come in banking.

Colin Leach (the elder brother of the Rothschild banker Rodney Leach) was my other half in Robert Benson, Lonsdale's investment department, and developed his skills as an investment manager as I became more of a general banker. Later, while I was using electronics to help change the forex markets, he was doing the same within the securities markets. Colin was an investment director at Schroders when he was asked, in 1970, to set up a screen-based securities-dealing market. ARIEL (standing for Automated Realtime Investment Exchange Limited) was owned by the acceptance houses, and its function was to reduce the very high levels of regulated commissions that the investment managers were paying to stockbrokers. In 1971, after evaluating several American systems, ARIEL opened for business, having developed a new system earlier than planned and within cost budgets, an event rare enough in banking history to deserve remembrance.

ARIEL was so much of a technical success that the London Stock Exchange had to ensure that it was a commercial failure, to gain itself a final decade of uncompetitive existence. The Stock Exchange Council forbade any of its 'jobbers', or market makers, to join, so, though ARIEL was significantly cheaper than the stock market, it had insufficient liquidity to satisfy any but the most loyal investment manager. Worse still, and despite the efforts of Colin and his share-holders, the Stock Exchange Council persuaded the Bank of England to disallow the trading of British government bonds (gilts) on ARIEL. This it did, no doubt cognisant both of the importance of gilt commissions to the profitable health of the London markets, and the bloodbath then taking place on Wall Street. There, competitive pressures undermined the broking club with its regulated commissions much more quickly, and with it blew away most of the private capital that funded the Wall Street firms.

As the flow of investment funds grew to undreamed-of levels, inflation built up staff costs, while cutting away the value of capital required by the regulators to support business volumes. Like Salomon Brothers twenty years later, few firms bothered with management control, so that failure to invest in back-office functions, despite several years of a strong and active demand for equity investment, left Wall Street firms with a potential bad-debt time bomb ticking away within their capital. Though exceptional action was taken in the early 1970s, such as closing the market each week for at least a day to enable firms to catch up with the backlog, volume pressures did not ease, and the 1974 secondary banking crisis of London was mirrored by the near destruction of Wall Street. The 1973 oil-price rise detonated the bad-debt bomb in broking, as well as banking, back offices. Between 1968 and 1975, some 150

Wall Street firms closed or were absorbed, while nearly 300 regional firms disappeared.

Ownership and management of large companies had begun their divorce between the wars, but in the 1970s it was made absolute as investment banks and brokers joined the process, for electronics were beginning to destroy their historic monopoly of the securities markets. ARIEL tolled the death knell for the London private gentleman's club, if some fifteen years too early, as well as the very concept of central securities markets. INSTINET, the American software on which ARIEL was based, is now the core of Reuters securities-dealing system, and the American electronic market NASDAQ (National Association of Securities Dealers' Automated Quotations) is threatening the future of the New York Stock Exchange itself. It is the NASDAQ computer system that, with minor modifications, now runs the London Stock Exchange; this, or a similar electronic trading system, will, in time usurp it completely.

The growth and profitability of forex dealing during the 1970s, as well as the growth of Chicago's financial markets from 1980 onwards, hid this reality from banking strategists; instead, they assumed a false analogy between forex and securities markets. Forex transaction costs, like commodity-dealing costs, are of little importance to the traders who use the markets since these are insurance transactions, but the transaction costs of the securities markets are the key to investment performance; these represent a disproportionate amount of the expected annual return. The growing importance of capital movements to dealing in the forex markets, as well as the linking of all financial markets through the Chicago derivative markets, increased volumes at the same time as it reduced margins. Yet despite the destruction of so many Wall Street firms during the 1970s, and the commission-destroying objective of ARIEL, banks spent £1.5 billion on buying up London stockbrokers during the 1980s, just as soon as the ending of the club monopoly allowed them to do so.

The banks' timing was impeccable, buying at the very top of the market; no sooner had the deals been done than October 1987 happened. Then, the costs of repairing back-office systems, just as in Wall Street ten years earlier, cost further money, and this and bad debts has added at least another £4 billion to their initial purchase price. With all these extra, and expensively acquired, dealing skills, London-based banks needed to do something; they offered their services in the derivative markets to British local-government treasurers. With some £600 million of outstanding contracts owing to the banks, the courts decided that the government authorities in question had no power to do such business, and that the banks should have known. Long, expensive and time-consuming lawsuits are now in process to recover some of those losses. The lawyers are happy, even if their banking clients are not.

These investments are still not making money for their purchasers, though the former partners of these businesses are not complaining of their wealth. Indeed, the surprise was the banks' desire to buy, for the real dealing expertise in London did not reside in stockbrokers, who, under the British dispensation, were investment managers and purchase-and-sale agents. Dealing expertise was to be found either in the banks' own money market and forex-dealing rooms, or in the eurobond-dealing firms. These had never been allowed to join the London Stock Exchange club, even though they were – by size, turnover and profits – several times larger than even London's major stockjobbers and stockbrokers. The market for these eurobond dealers, however actively they dealt among themselves, were private European investors, with money managed out of the safe tax havens of Switzerland, Luxembourg and the Channel Islands.

Private customers were of no interest to banks chasing the lure of corporate and institutional business, even though the real value of the London stockbroking firms was that, like the banking Hoares, they had clients whose family fortunes they had managed for three or four generations. Long-standing family relationships were unceremoniously dumped, or driven away by outrageous pricing, but no sooner had the banks got rid of the only unique and valuable part of their acquisitions than policy changed. The new banking fashion is private banking, the business of these recently and expensively acquired firms, though, unfortunately, that business had been dismembered before anyone was told. Yet the basis of banking has always been the administration of customers' liquid wealth, the bridging of the liquidity gap between those who have money and those who need it, and the calculation and acceptance of the risks inherent in meeting savers' and borrowers' financial needs through the money and securities markets.

A century and a half ago, Emily Brontë was symptomatic of a moneyed class, however modest its wealth might be, enthusiastically embracing the railway age. Her investments, and those of hundreds of thousands of others, ensured that corporate debt replaced government debt as the largest constituent of the securities markets.

Institutions changed to satisfy these needs. US trust banks switched from their original business of managing land, and started to invest in the securities markets for the beneficiaries of the estates they managed; Scottish lawyers were transmuted into money managers and stockbrokers, while other Scots specialised as managers of investment trusts, as an efficient and safe way for investors to spread their savings across an exciting but risky world; these became more knowledgeable about the American market than New York bankers themselves. Half a century later these same investors began to dabble in shares rather than bonds. This switch became more marked after 1920, for the new electro-mechanical technologies required a larger equity base to support mass markets for cars, radios and the cinema, and to create water, electricity and telephone networks.

Commercial banks traditionally offered customers a money-management service, broking themselves or maintaining a list of approved stockbrokers, receiving and transmitting investment recommendations, and minding the account, and were thus the dis-tributors of the new investment trusts also. After 1945, however, the moneyed classes began to desert the securities markets as direct investors, and became indirect investors instead; rather than choose, and vote, their shares, tax made it more sensible to delegate both decisions to the managers of their company pension fund, their insurance company and their managed fund. Though tax incentives played a big part in this switch, an equally important reason was the desertion of this market by commercial and investment banks alike. Private investment business declined, for the banks chose not to distribute the new mutual funds, the modern successor of the investment trust. Inflation was one of the factors encouraging the change, though this worked against the interests of the banks; terri-fied of cannibalising their deposit base, the banks were unwilling to offer their customers a service to meet their needs.

The problem of banking is not its market, but its costs and its management, for there is a large market for personal banking services. This is primarily among the *Titanic*'s would-be steerage passengers of small and medium-sized businesses, but also the second-class passengers like Emily Brontë. There are even those first-class passengers who, appalled by the lack of interest shown in their affairs, took themselves off to the private bankers of Switzerland and Luxembourg or those few trust banks, like US Trust Company, that survived the banking cannibalism of the 1960s. Swiss banking is highly profitable, despite labour costs that make most foreign bankers blench; its base is the investment management of 'flight money' – or money held outside its country of residence – reckoned to be in excess of $2,000 billion.

These figures become insignificant, however, when compared to the 'Emily Brontë' market, for the Consumers' Federation of America reckon that Americans alone own investible assets worth more than $17,000 billion in total, while Citibank's estimates for the American 'rich' come to $4,000 billion – based on estimates that some 2 million Americans have net wealth (i.e. after debt) of over $800,000. Citibank reckons that the world asset base for private banking services to these 'High Net Worth individuals' comes to more than $7,000 billion, while American Express estimates are higher still. Yet the consequence of the banks' supplier-driven cost-recovery approach is that their new 'private banking' departments offer, on the whole, second-class accommodation, presented as first class and priced as a millionaire suite.

Most Americans prefer to be advised by almost anyone but a bank, and the numbers of America's registered financial planners trebled during the 1980s to over 16,000. The amount of money they managed rose tenfold over the same period, from $440 billion to some $4,600 billion, or 25 per cent of all assets owned by the American public. The level of regulation is minimal with, on average, one inspection every eleven years and, even then, the General Accounting Office of the US Congress reports that regulators find fault with six out of every seven inspections. Not surprisingly, everyone agrees that there is enormous fraud and incompetence, though no one knows how much this costs the American public. The GAO reckons some $200 million a year, the CFA reckons five times as much at $1 billion a year, while an American regulator in 1992 calculated that it was some 1 per cent of American wealth every year; as he put it: 'The financial planning industry is still in the days of the Wild West. The marshal hasn't ridden into town, and there's mayhem on the streets, with a lot of random shooting.'

Anyone but regulated and protected bankers, confronted with a market like this and the image that bankers still retain, would believe in Santa Claus. But all banks, wherever they are and whatever they do, have yet to come to terms with the technological revolution within the industry, what it has done to banking profits and the need to reduce costs and compete. They would prefer to lobby their local legislator for greater protection, improved defences against outsiders or, their long-term stand-by, permission to get bigger and do more. Banking costs are now so monstrous that bankers need to make money now, and not later. The very nature of banking, whose diversity of service once protected the customer, now exploits them.

'Competition and Credit Control' enabled the English commercial banks, after 1971, to enter the mortgage market in competition with the building societies or savings banks. This was in theory only, for the banks were not able to do much business until 1980, when the Bank of England finally freed them from all lending restrictions. Since then, the British mortgage market has been transformed, but not in a way that helps the banking customer. Until 1970 nearly all mortgages were repaid through regular instalments of interest and capital but, for the high taxpayer, it made sense to pay interest only, and repay the principal by saving through a tax-advantageous life-assurance policy. According to a report by the Office of Fair Trading, less than 7 per cent of mortgages in 1970 were repaid through endowment policies, but in 1991 the figure was 75 per cent, even though the tax benefits of life policies were removed in 1984. Now only 20 per cent of mortgages are straightforward repayment contracts, for the banks earn commission instead.

The average life policy used to secure a mortgage pays a commission which is equivalent to 80 per cent of all payments made during the first year. They can be higher still; one life company pays an upfront commission of £642 on a twenty-five-year endowment policy of £50 a month. Since 1989, after the coming into force of the Financial Services Act, tied agents like the banks have forced life companies to increase their commissions by 50 per cent; the banks need the money. The £162 million of life-company commissions received by Halifax Building Society in 1990 represented 16 per cent of the income of Britain's biggest savings bank, and 27 per cent of its profits. Not surprisingly, the life-company lobby fights hard to prevent any customers being told that it takes between five and ten years before buying a life policy will make as much for them as saving the same amount through a bank account, and that the 30–40 per cent of customers who are sold such policies and terminate them within the first three years, might as well throw their money on to the fire.

The banks now see their interest as supporting, rather than opposing, this obfuscation; much is said about the virtue of transparency in pricing, or letting customers know what financial services cost, but little is done because opacity, as it always has been, is in the interests of financial-market practitioners. Today, neither the Henry Coes, nor the awkward branch managers who gave me such a hard time with Westminster-Hambro, exist to protect customers from this institutionalised greed. The computer enables head office to target branch managers with monthly volumes of loan business, levels of fees to be extracted, and numbers of customers to be handed on to the insurance representatives. These have also changed since Coe's time. The OFT thinks there may well be implications for the competence of sales agents in the high staff turnover of insurance companies, with over 50 per cent of salesmen leaving before they have spent two years with their employer.

Bankers know the answer, but dare not say, for private estimates reckon that some 1.5 million Britons are now in a debt trap, with mortgages greater than the value of their home. The Bank of England estimates the figure as one million only – still one in ten of home owners – with an average shortfall of £6,000; this negative equity is reckoned to nearly double between 1992 and 1994, if prices continue to fall by 1 per cent a quarter, which is what analysts expect to happen. At least 300,000 of these are in danger of dispossession, as they are more than six months in arrears on their payments, while the Bank believes that all will have to maintain high levels of savings for several years in order to rebuild their personal balance sheets.

Those in danger of repossession are not allowed to sell their homes, for, if they do and there is a loss that they cannot meet, the banks must bear the bad-debt cost themselves. However, if the banks repossess the house and then sell it, the banks' insurers pay some, or all, of the difference, and chase the former home owner for the loss. Naturally, owners maintain their homes better than banks can look after empty properties, have a greater incentive to achieve as good a sale price as possible, and to do it as quickly as possible. None of this matters to the rigid bureaucracy of the banks, whether they be the quoted company version or the so-called 'mutual societies' of the Victorian era. Neither the current deflation of house prices, nor the general recession of business activity, is the specific fault of the banks. What is certainly true, though, is that the banks' mistaken business policies encouraged and fuelled the financial bubble, and it is the hangover from their enticement of customers to overborrow that now causes heartache.

German and regional American banks prove every day the value of the market for small-company lending and general banking services. Despite its cost and publicity, and the need for equity capital by businesses about to expand from medium to large, the Anglo-Saxon venture-capital industry has been a relative failure compared with the German banking approach to long-term support of business or the funds of private individuals. German bankers have been forced to keep their skills fresh because, since 1918, only the fleetest of foot among them have survived the series of catastrophes that finally culminated in the physical destruction of Germany and its institutions. Only banking judgement remained as collateral in the rubble of 1945's 'Stunde Zero', and even at the 1948 introduction of the Deutschmark, German bankers had little in the way of physical security, or legal title, to back their loans to entrepreneurs. Yet these, with their middle-sized companies, restored German engineering excellence over the next three decades, and those same banking skills are now doing the same for the ravished eastern Länder.

Of course, American and German banking tradition stresses the role of banks as business supporters, but it undoubtedly helps competitive attitudes that America has some 12,000 banks, Germany about 5,000, and that most of these are community-based, with local decisionmaking. With only three competitors, Midland's managers hardly had an incentive to change, however much their customers needed the skills of local, entrepreneurial bankers; a McKenna might see that Britain had become a 'less developed' industrial economy, but such vision was not vouchsafed by his general managers.

Lord Cobbold, as chairman of the IIB, had approved my refusal to make country loans but refusing to buy them was a serious mistake on my part; I had failed to apply to my own career the wisdom of John Maynard Keynes: a sound banker is one 'who when he is ruined, is ruined in a conventional and orthodox way along with his fellows, so that no one can really blame him'. By 1975, my longer-term plans had come to fruition. Alan Wiseman was regularly making some £100,000 a month from dealing, while the Guernsey bank, apart from supplying some £30 million of deposits to IIB's total funding requirements, was making profits of about £500,000 a year. And IBIS, though it was still in its money-eating development phase, was just coming into action. There was a small, Greek shipping department that justified itself by the loan spreads, the fees from the vessels' banking requirements, and the owners' deposits, but otherwise lending for the IIB cost far more than it brought in, and that was before bad debts.

The best way to cut overheads was to drop lending altogether, for the IIB was never going to get any Italian business, and the loan officers and their associated credit department were by far the most expensive part of the bank's overhead. Unfortunately, I needed to keep this to work out the bad debts, and with their overheads still there, I could not get costs sufficiently below revenue to rebuild the bank's capital. The question that I asked myself throughout 1976 was whether I could outrun the mistakes of my past. The answer was 'no', partly because the very success of Guernsey terrified Italian bankers envisaging a communist government, while the forex profits that IIB was making in London were coming from somewhere, and some of the ill will generated from Milan suggested that dealing rooms there were suffering. Relations between the shareholders were becoming strained, and all suggestions that the four should merge had died. The Bank of Naples was still going downhill, together with Naples and the south of Italy itself, while the San Paolo bank was beginning its rise to leadership of the Italian market; its use of the IIB as a training stage for forex dealing staff was irritating the others, even though all had had such an offer.

But these were minor problems, compared to the loan book. Once the auditors decided that recovery was far off, and insisted on looking at present values, rather than future hopes, the bank needed to be recapitalised. In my more optimistic moments over the previous eighteen months, I had recognised that the IIB was £5 million under water; when I was feeling pessimistic, and thinking of what I would do if I were to come in afresh, I reckoned that all the £10 million capital was at risk. I just hoped that with the dealing and fee-earning areas beginning to make real money, I would be able to ride out the storm. Unfortunately, the chairmen of the four shareholders had not prepared their own banks for such an unfortunate outcome to their brave venture, for their international departments had assured them they were getting a nice, simple, safe participating lender in country loans. Instead, they had ended up with something much more complicated and, at the time, messy and expensive.

Rather worse, the Italians then faced the embarrassment of explaining to their own boards − some of whom were political enemies − why they signed the Bank of England's letters, committing the shareholders to support IIB for capital and funding, without their approval. For this they needed a scapegoat and Rupert Raw, who was now chairman, was happy to supply me. I don't much blame him, for no doubt I would have done him the same service in his place, and he was tremendously conformist. His great desire was to run the IIB, do some simple country loans, and drive Wiseman mad with his questions. He wasn't sure about Guernsey, though he enjoyed his board-meeting trips there, for, as a lifelong civil-service administrator, he was suspicious of structures that thrive by virtue of being outside the institutional framework. All in all, he knew that the Italians were commercial bankers and that they, as well as he, found the business that I was developing complex and far from their experience.

I joined the Bank of England blacklist, for there is no excuse for someone who embarrasses a former governor, one of its ex-administrators and the current prime minister; one could be an error, but three has to be deliberate. I remembered the remark of a Texan engineering friend, when I asked him about his job move to one of the large bureaucratic firms that he had always condemned. 'I just got tired of picking shit with the chickens,' said he, and as that seemed to sum up my future in banking, I went back to my first love of investment instead.

In the long term, of course, there are advantages in unconventionality, and that is why the IIB has survived rather worse lending disasters than any I engineered, for there is banking life after lending, and IIB proves it. In a market dominated by banks very much bigger than itself, it has an entrenched market position and, with its excellent and specialised dealing room, makes a good return on its capital. IBIS now makes profits for IIB of nearly £1 million a year, simply by doing competently what had to be done anyway. And it would be making even better profits on its private-banking business, had Raw and the Italians been more decisive about what they did and did not want as a bank. 'Willing to wound, but afraid to strike' left the Guernsey bank in limbo, and Tony Hall, who had built up the business for me, left at the same time that I did and went to head Rea Brothers (Guernsey). Rea Brothers is a London acceptance house, but its Guernsey subsidiary turned out to have no free capital, offices but no staff, and only eight customers with total deposits of £30,000. Today, though no extra capital has ever been invested, the bank regularly shows profits of £2 million a year, and is one of the largest on the island.

My successor was found within the ranks of Samuel Montagu, a year or two after I had gone, and once Raw had expended the new capital on some simple country loans. If the shareholders hoped that such a background would make him sympathetic to commercial-banking susceptibilities, they were disappointed when he recommended selling off the bank's country loans. The early discounts were only 10 per cent or so, but when the board finally swallowed this painful suggestion, they had widened to 40 per cent. More lending profits were needed so a Samuel Montagu colleague, claiming to be a whiz on Australasia, was recruited. Once again, the shareholders had to take over the IIB portfolio of loans to confident, imaginative but very bust Australians. My successor followed me out of the door, sense finally prevailed, and Wiseman became IIB's managing director. Without that lending, IIB might have had Johnson Mathey Bankers instead, for the Bank of England has a high regard for IIB's dealing skills and the Italian jewellery trade is one of the main customers of the London gold market.

Yet in the years since I was dismissed, no one has asked again why IIB needs to lend, when it has a perfectly good banking business and its lending just wastes the money that would otherwise go to shareholders. But this is true of all banks, though the present crisis is forcing US money-centre banks to rethink their policy of being everywhere and doing everything. The principles of banking may be immutable, but the practice needs to change. Good bankers are opportunists, and in 1983 a senior banker at NMB (which in Dutch means the Netherlands Bank for Middle-sized Enterprises) bought a Uruguayan bank. This must have seemed double-Dutch logic to many of his fellow bankers, for only a few months before, at the Toronto jamboree of the 1982 International Monetary Fund, most bankers involved with the Third World had been bewailing their fate.

During the previous ten years, Western bankers had used these IMF meetings to pay court to the ministers of finance of Third World countries; now the begging bowl was reversed, and banks wanted their money back, but Mexico, Brazil and Argentina had all announced that, in a world of real, high and rising interest rates, they could no longer afford to repay them. Poland had said much the same thing six months earlier, but these new potential defaulters were supposed to be rich, capitalist and successful. The private banking debt of these three countries alone was $150 billion, far exceeding the capital of America's money-centre banks, and the outlook was bleak indeed. Default would mean that the capital of the Western banking system would be wiped out at a stroke; equally, it would cut off a substantial part of the world from international trade. The world economy had grown, and grown together, since 1930, and a similar financial catastrophe would have much worse economic results. Ever since that September meeting, country after country had refused to pay, and central bankers and government officials were searching desperately for palliatives that would keep the world afloat.

The Dutch banker could see the seeds of a new business, for he had spent much of his business life in Latin America, and the

Uruguayan bank was unique in having a licence to own a Brazilian branch. Though these countries were not paying their bankers, it wasn't because they had no money; most of them were rich in natural resources, and all of them had printing presses. What none of them had was sufficient foreign trade to earn the dollars necessary to service or repay their debt. The Dutch have always been entrepreneurial bankers, and had plenty of experience of East European barter trade, selling hard-currency goods to soft-currency countries in exchange for whatever goods they had, swapping these for yet other goods, until they had something that they could sell for hard currency, and so pay their own exporters.

NMB saw the LDC crisis as another barter business. (The euphemism 'less developed countries' has replaced the Politically Incorrect, if economically accurate, description 'underdeveloped countries'.) They calculated that there must be plenty of London or American bankers prepared to sell their Brazilian loans for what they could get. The Dutch would buy this dollar-denominated loan, go to the Brazilian authorities and swap dollar debt into cruzeiro debt, and use that as the initial asset for their bank. More importantly, thought NMB, what was good for them should be good for other European companies that wanted to invest in Latin America. It was good for these countries, too; they exchanged expensive foreign-currency debt for real investments in local manufacturing industry. The banks got hurt, and so did some of the local vested interests who disliked competition on their own private patch, but the process turned a dead weight of non-earning debt into something useful and productive. It took time for the idea to catch hold. Western bankers had to appreciate that their money was gone for ever, and they should take what they could get, while the governments needed time to appreciate that no one was going to bail them out of a mess of their own making.

Trading in this LDC debt was only $5 billion in 1983; in 1992 it was $250 billion. NMB is one of the big players in this market, a cross between a securities market and a forex market, in which some banks act as marketmakers, and others buy on behalf of their industrial clients, who are investing in the country concerned and need cheap, local investment funds. (Bankers learn fast; the likes of Maxwell, Trump and Olympia & York are generating a similar-sized market in busted corporate loans.) These funds are no longer that cheap: so successful has been the freeing of these once highly monopolistic and regulated markets that much of the aid money, and some of the bank loans, which was originally stolen and stashed in Swiss and New York banks, is now returning. The more this happens, the easier the balance of payments, the stronger the currency, and the more attractive the local securities markets.

After ten years, the debt crisis is over and the Western banking system has survived its toughest ever test, but it was touch and go at the time. As inflation went into reverse, and interest rates ceased to be negative and became positive in 1980, these new country-debtor customers ran down their clearing balances. Unbeknown to the country-loan department, most had begun to borrow heavily in the short-term money markets, using the treasury departments of the major New York banks. The first that anyone knew about a debt crisis was when these countries could no longer roll over their overnight deposits, and it looked as if the New York clearing system would melt down as the Herstatt crisis was replayed, but with the stakes raised a hundredfold.

That put the fear of God into the New York Fed and, ever since, it has argued that the world's payment system is too important to be left to the cavalier attentions of the commercial banks. Once that immediate crisis was over, the long-term problem needed to be addressed, and Citibank found the game had gone on too long, with too many banks dragged into it, for an easy answer to be found. That 1982 Toronto conference had forced central bankers, international financial organisations and commercial bankers into informal working partnerships. The meeting was criticised at the time as simply rearranging the *Titanic*'s deck chairs, but William Rhodes, a vice-chairman of Citibank who has spent the last ten years of his working life helping to resolve this problem, said of it: 'If greed often drives people apart, fear often brings them together.' The need was to pretend that all was well, and Mexico identified the answer.

The LDCs would continue to pay interest on their debt, subject to their bankers lending them the money they needed to do so. Provided the banks were getting their interest, never mind that they had lent it for just this purpose, their auditors would classify these loans as good, banking balance sheets would look sound, even if they weren't, and everyone would live to fight another day. And that's what happened, until the banks were profitable enough to write off some of the debts without harming their capital, or they got tired of waiting to be repaid, and took their loss by selling off their LDC debt to NMB and others. This time around, domestic banks in Thailand, and other such unlikely lenders, had replaced the American middle classes of the 1920s. They were just as mad as their predecessors, however, when they found out that things had gone wrong. The originators of these LDC loans have had to spend unbelievable amounts of time keeping fractious syndicates from declaring default on the loans, and so overturning the whole delicate process of managing the disaster; they also had to put up good money after bad, to enable their debtors to pay the interest due, and so prevent the loans being classified as bad, and often do it on behalf of recalcitrant syndicate members as well.

By the time the process was finished, Citibank and its peers had earned their origination fees ten times over; of course, these were booked as profits twenty years ago, whereas bankers' time more recently has been concerned with turning a 50 per cent write-off into one of 40 per cent, and syndicate members do not willingly pay fees for that. Citibank painfully discovered that Eli Wallich, a former governor of the Fed, was right, and Walter Wriston wrong; told that Wriston claimed countries don't go broke, Wallich remarked that the notion of sovereign immunity from debt default is as elusive as the smile on the vanishing face of the Cheshire cat.

Epilogue
Hollerin' For Help

'Men who don't take risks, won't drink champagne.'
Russian folk saying

THE MOST OBVIOUS DIFFERENCE between this century and the last can be seen in Hans Christian Andersen's tale of the Emperor's new clothes. In the fable, the child who remarks that the Emperor is not wearing an absolutely marvellous new suit, but is actually jaybird naked, is rewarded by a grateful Emperor, pleased to come across someone honest enough to tell him the truth. Any citizen of the twentieth century knows that the little horror would immediately be throttled by the secret police, and all those in earshot transferred to the gulag. Bankers keep quiet for the same reason, while economists only need to recall the fate of Nikolai Kondratiev to choose the consensus view. Kondratiev was foolish enough to assume that Stalin wanted facts, rather than illusions, about the progress of the 1928 Five-Year Plan and for his pains died, or was killed, in a Siberian labour camp, while his research institute and economic journal were both closed. Before misjudging his boss, however, and on the theory that success comes from knowing the enemy, he had studied the bones of capitalism back to the early eighteenth century. Using all available statistics, he identified what appeared to be a long cycle in economic affairs, lasting some fifty to sixty years.

Neither Marxist nor capitalist took a blind bit of notice of this statistical crank. In 1925, when Kondratiev published his studies, utopia had come, and it certainly wasn't in Moscow. Attitudes changed after 1930, by which time Kondratiev had disappeared, for his work on the long-run economic cycle had identified business troughs in 1745, 1790, 1844 and 1890 and extrapolated another one as due to arrive in 1930. It did.

Many theories have been propounded about business cycles, and as many disproved, while some economists deny their existence except in the perfervid imaginations of statisticians. But most agree that there is a stock cycle, lasting some three to four years; and a French physician identified what many economists reckon is a seven to eleven year investment cycle. Why it should be a doctor that used statistics so fruitfully, rather than an economist, suggests something about consensus views, though the good doctor had another explanation. As an early believer in time-and-motion studies, he wanted to know why marriages bunched, resulting in his pregnant patients not arriving smoothly at his clinic over the years, but coming in irregular batches.

In 1939 Joseph Schumpeter, teaching in America but a product of the great Austrian school of economics, published the comprehensive tome on business cycles, integrating all three into a theory of economic progress. The cycle begins in deepest gloom, with battered businessmen striving to survive and unemployment at persistently high levels. Bankers are exceptionally bloody-minded, politicians helpless, and no one is buying because all know that it will be cheaper still next year. This is the debt-deflation cycle of the 1930s, certainly Scandinavia and the UK in the 1990s, and possibly the rest of the world too. Then hope returns, and Keynes's 'animal spirits' have businessmen reinvesting. This second decade is very profitable, for nothing new has appeared for a long time, much equipment is worn out, everyone is tired of being depressed and making do until things get cheaper. People stop saving and start to spend again. The third decade is the time to be alive, for everyone is making good money, unemployment is a memory and a new world is at hand. Humanity has triumphed over its darker impulses and, according to Kondratiev, the upturn is always caused by a complete new business technique, and generally involves cheaper communications.

By the fourth decade, when bankers are becoming enthusiastic lenders once again and Dr Pangloss is much in demand at business conferences, subterranean forces are beginning to affect consumer demand and business confidence. The Kondratiev cycle peaks, and the relationship between raw-material prices and manufactured goods shifts in favour of the developed countries. Kondratiev believed that this was a sure sign of the turn, although he could adduce no reason for this shift of negotiating power. Commodity producers attempt to create cartels, to protect the price of their goods, and also borrow heavily to industrialise themselves. Protectionism begins to slow world trade, and the return on business investment begins to fall. Bankers ignore these warning signs, as well as the loss of bounce in both the stock and investment cycles, for they have discovered that a little more credit always supplies the answer. At some stage during this fifth decade, bankers completely lose their minds as banking becomes 'lend, lend, lend', as it was in the 1920s and 1980s. Then the bankers repent, and the cycle begins again, with bankers arguing that none of the mess is their fault, for they and their regulators are helpless victims of this, that or the other quite unexpected conjunction of fate.

Schumpeter's view is that these slumps are necessary, a period of 'creative destruction' as large bureaucratic business combines break up and free human ingenuity. Austrian economists started, not from philosophic theory as did the British, but from analysing the behaviour of businessmen – the microeconomics of what firms and their founders actually did, as opposed to what they ought to have done; Jacob Streider and his monograph on Fugger, was part of this school, destroyed by the Depression and the Nazis. Another was Friedrich von Hayek, who argued that capitalism is a discovery system. Hayek's market is not a financial reality, as most economists would have it, but an institution of society, rather like language or the law. People's wants and the resources and techniques of society are constantly changing, and the market discovers what works and what doesn't, for neither computer nor bureaucrat can predict the emergence of new knowledge, product innovations or original ideas, nor how people will react to them. This was Hayek's objection to any business regulation other than the law, since regulation assumed that society had been created by a designer, and so could easily be redesigned to a more modern and fashionable pattern, such as that of a Lenin or Hitler.

Banking securitisation has simply added another source of overcapacity to an industry that is in desperate need of Schumpeter's creative destruction. Throughout the twentieth century Midland and Citibank have vied for the title of the world's largest and most influential commercial bank. Each in its own time was the banking exemplar of the century, the industry's paradigm of what a bank should be, the physical embodiment of the world's leading financial power, the most imaginative and innovative of lenders, and the most aggressive of financial institutions. If banks such as these are on course for the breakers' yard, it simply reflects the terrible state of an industry that, in less than a generation, has been dragged from the nineteenth into the twenty-first century. One definition of a trillion is a one followed by twelve noughts – or a thousand billion. This is an incomprehensible number, though one that makes even the financial requirements of a disintegrated Soviet Union seem small change, but it is still not sufficient to contain the potential losses incurred by the world's banks during the 1980s, as they all attempted to replicate the driving aggression of Citibank.

It is the financial decisions taken in Frankfurt and Tokyo that now rock the world; and the errors of Midland and Citibank, and the example they gave to others, are both cause and consequence of this change. Yet no creative destruction will change the banks, for the present regulatory system is designed to preserve such monopoly profits as remain to banking. Regulation makes entry to the business difficult except to firms prepared to invest in an expensive distribution network, with considerable capital resources to meet the needs of the regulators, and sufficiently conventional in their business approach not to fall foul of the self-regulatory aspects of the existing banking club.

An industry, difficult for newcomers to enter because of regulatory barriers, yet impossible for established players to leave, leads to neither healthy banks nor efficient bankers. Only in the last decade have Americans had a convenient and nationwide domestic payments system, though this is no thanks to the banks, who enjoyed profits from the old slow methods that produced a useful float. It was created by the credit-card companies, at most semidetached from the commercial banks, and without any support from the Fed; until 1991 Citibank refused to allow its cardholders to benefit from the two national card networks, insisting that its machines were superior to others, but it finally had to face the reality of its customers' wants.

But is banking regulation necessary, particularly after its notorious 1980s failures? The academic answer is not clear cut, though it generally accepts that the supervisory system of the Bank of England which, until Lidderdale and Barings in 1890, supported the market rather than individual banks, worked adequately in protecting the financial system. For the first part of the nineteenth century, the Scottish financial system worked equally well, though without either a regulatory or supervisory function. Scots banking, unlike the English, allowed branching, and was also the first to introduce training; branch banking was known to improve the safety of bank depositors, though it worked against the commercial interests of the Bank of England.

The financial health of banking is of importance because banks have a dual role in creating and supporting prosperity. Lending is the key to the first, and the administration of the payments system is essential to the second. Gerald Corrigan of the New York Fed, Lowell Bryan of McKinsey and academic writers like Robert Litan of the Brookings Institute believe that deposit insurance works against the interests of the community, and that the international payments system needs to be isolated from commercial banking. The risks to the system of commercial-banking failure, whether of computer systems or of solvency, are now unacceptably high. Their suggested solutions have a basis in Dutch financial history. The Netherlands were the first bourgeois society, so banking was important to the Dutch in both their personal and business capacities.

They were also Calvinist and since, as a religion, this assumes that only a minority of the world is saved as the elect of God, the Dutch were persuaded that the world would enjoy more than its share of sinning. Good burghers that they were, the Dutch knew that this would be as much in the boardroom as in the bedroom. Bankruptcy came with degrees of sinfulness. Risk-taking in merchanting was essential for Dutch prosperity, and so bankruptcy as a result of shipwreck or some other commercial setback was more of a misdemeanour than a sin; going belly up while attempting a corner on the exchange was, however, quite definitely a spiritual felony. But not even the Dutch, with their nicely graded disapproval of money, would let commercial instincts threaten the trade on which the state's physical security rested.

The payments system was not run by the commercial banks, but by the state, and paid for by depositors. Like the Swiss banks three and a half centuries later, this Dutch payment bank charged interest to its depositors, but in return its guarantee of payment was as good as gold. Today, it is politically impossible to do away with deposit insurance; the limit in America was raised from $40,000 to $100,000 only in 1980, but was immediately subverted by the $1.2-million limit engineered on brokered deposits. The collapse of BCCI and some smaller specialised UK banks has released demands for an increase in the level agreed by the 1987 Banking Act. The suggestion of Bryan and others is that deposit insurance remains and, perhaps, becomes absolute. But only banks that specialise as depositary institutions would be granted this, and only such banks would have the right to access the international payments system.

Using the Basel agreements on capital adequacy, Litan and Bryan have shown that such an institution could be profitable, and make a fair return on shareholder equity, though investing depositors' funds only in short-term instruments, such as Treasury bills, prime short-term bank and commercial paper and other similar liquid investments. But theory isn't needed; this is the practical banking pattern of Hoare & Company, the principles on which Edmond Safra runs his Republic National Banks, and the business of the money-market funds. It was the way that the Trustee Savings Banks were run for many decades, even though the Treasury gave these banks rather less than a market rate of return on their depositors' money. Indeed, the Bryan proposals could be carried further, with the return to depositors guaranteed against inflation by the central bank.

This would certainly encourage the central bank to think hard about its money-supply policies, while losses incurred by the central bank through its guarantee would make politicians think carefully about the cost of their promises. The precedents all exist; the governor of the Bank of New Zealand is paid on an inverted scale to the rate of inflation; Germany's interwar hyperinflation now guarantees considerable independence for the Bundesbank; and the British government has been issuing index-linked bonds and saving certificates for the last decade. The deposit rate of such an institution would define the market rate; anything more than that, and 'buyer beware' would apply, for depositors and investors would clearly know that greater return comes with greater risk. Such risk-free depository institutions could be owned by banking groups or industrial companies, but these would be the only banks to be regulated.

All other banking or financial companies could do any banking business that they pleased, subject to their ability to attract depositors and so find the money to do it. This would almost certainly force banks back to their communities, to supplement their reliance on the money markets, but this is the management pattern that has enabled the American regional banks to thrive. The US money-centre banks are using the reverse pattern of this; disaggregation is the process of finding cheaper, third-party suppliers to take over the administration of big banks, for this now costs them more than they can afford if they are to improve their margins and generate the capital they need to survive. Banks would probably get smaller, and most would specialise in the many requirements of an industry influenced by securitisation techniques, but this would be an advantage. Even bankers admit that the modern bank is unmanageable. It would not prevent global Citibank-type structures from existing, provided that they showed the necessary holding-company skills of managing many different types of banks, and so could raise capital from investors. The supervisory central bank would then return to its pre-Lidderdale function; it would make money available to the financial system, in a crisis, but only to banks that could offer good security.

The commercial banks will argue that they need the subsidised profits of the retail depositor to pay for the payments system, domestic and international. The domestic economy does not require that banks control the payments system, though this is a valuable tool for controlling entry to banking. The Germans, Swiss and Dutch do very well with a post-office giro system, while the Americans made do with American Express cheques until plastic technology came along. As for the international payments system, the growth of capital movements made this the banking growth market of the 1980s. Interbank payments already go through a banking cooperative called SWIFT (Society for Worldwide Interbank Financial Transactions) and, using this, some banks developed a fee-earning service called 'global custody'. Its users were mainly the institutional money managers, and few complained of the cost, though the creation of this service put paid to a hidden source of earnings that all had enjoyed until then. But the service was good, and eased the money managers' job. The banks ganged up to prevent the institutional money managers accessing SWIFT, since it was feared that they intended to create a competitive service but have now relented.

Brian Pearse, the chief executive of the Midland Bank who replaced McMahon, has wondered aloud whether banks should be in money transmission at all, for department stores happily sell electrical goods without supplying the electricity. Money transmission was once the value-added service of banking, but technology has now made it just another commodity service, and one probably better done by computer specialists. Indeed, US General Electric is already in this business, a natural development of its electronic data interchange [EDI] services, which it sells to companies and to banks. EDI is one of the techniques destroying the layers of middle management that were once the hallmark of the large firm, but bankers find it hard to face the real implications of these changes. Pearse still argues that unprofitable business needs to be done in order to cover the fixed and heavy costs of banking, and he would wish to see the banks' UK money-transmission services merged, so as to make them viable through economies of scale.

What Bryan and his fellow consultants and academic writers are bringing about, whether the bankers will it or no, is a break-up of the enormous bureaucracies, currently called banks, built on functions that others can now do more efficiently. Securitisation and EDI are just elements of a technological revolution which is now forcing a redefinition of banking's value-added service. The comfortable world of assured banking profitability began to disappear when the computer destroyed first bankers' monopoly of skills in the 1970s, then their control of financial information during the 1980s, and it is now destroying the uniqueness of their administrative and money transmission functions. Well established banks can still make money; they just cannot make enough of it to continue to waste it in the style to which they have grown accustomed. Unfortunately, capitalism is not working as well as it might, for present banking regulation acts as the perfect mechanism to deny easy entrance to the banking industry, and so entrenches inefficiency.

As an investment director at Schroders, Colin Leach trained his juniors by making them analyse two anonymous companies. Both were family managed businesses but, while one had an excellent record of rising turnover, earnings per share, dividends and return on assets, the other had simply drifted. Naturally, the comparative price of the shares reflected these contrasting histories, and hence investors' expectations of future profits. Nearly all Colin's trainees picked the well managed company, whereupon he showed them that, over the next five years, the revitalised Imperial Tobacco Company made four or five times as much money for investors as did the excellently managed Marks & Spencer store chain. The purpose of the exercise was more than to impress on them the truth of the stock exchange adage: 'If conventional wisdom was right, we'd all be rich. It isn't, and we aren't.' It was to show that there is no such thing as absolute value in the stock market, and that all prices are relative, for the object of investment is to achieve the highest possible gain at the lowest possible risk. Banking, just as much as investment management, needs this same concentration on risk and reward because whether lending, dealing or advising, the banker's object also is to earn as much as possible at as low a cost as possible.

Though Keynes argued that slumps are caused by inadequate demand, and are not a business necessity to reduce over-indebtedness and inefficiencies, both he and the Austrians agreed on the central role of entrepreneurial endeavour. Indeed, Keynes reckoned that, in a slump, investment came before savings since, if no one is productively employed, no one can save whereas, once work commences, then savings rise to meet the demand. That is the reason for his semi-serious suggestion of the 1920s that the government seed disused coal mines with jamjars full of currency notes, fill them in, and offer the money to anyone prepared to recover it. The business activity generated would start the upswing. Today, there is no need to fill in the coalmines, for seventy years of communist rule has done it for us. The whole of the infrastructure of Russia and Eastern Europe needs to be rebuilt – and amongst the most important, *pace* Kondratiev, is transport – but it needs to be done by the entrepreneurial spirit, and not those of planners, whether of the Central Committee or of the banks.

Now the era of American financial supremacy is passing, but a similar concentration on domestic concerns by the German and Japanese monetary authorities may make the dollar's passing as painful as that of the pound sterling. It may be that we are condemned to follow Kondratiev's cycle by the hidden tides of our emotions; alternatively, by knowing our past history we might avoid repeating it and so help ourselves and our neighbours in the former Soviet bloc by allowing them to improve our own prosperity, while helping theirs. The West has the supply, but no demand, and the East has the demand, but neither supply nor money. This is what banks are for, but they need to be freed of their protection, for regulation has failed and Roosevelt's worst fears have been realised. 'It is Enterprise which builds and improves the world's possessions . . . if Enterprise is afoot, Wealth accumulates, whatever may be happening to Thrift,' said Keynes, desperate to get politicians to act during the misery of the Depression. And Enterprise needs enterprising bankers.

Today, as in 1890, we can choose the path of protectionism and slump, or that of trade and growth. Only governments can open trade barriers, but only banks and businesses should risk investment, for the analysis of reward is best pursued under the risk of loss. Given trade and the prospect of profit, investment appears without government aid, as do the necessary structures of commercial law; to assume that what was commonplace to our grandfathers is beyond our capacities is unnecessarily pessimistic. But banking reform this time around needs to take account of human nature. As Kaufman reports: 'Politicians prefer regulatory segmentation to regulatory effectiveness. They have a bias in favour of easy credit, minimal credit standards and forbearance.'

That's the way the bankers like it, too, for the stern and unbending image of a banker is an actor's make-believe, designed to deter their customers from a life of financial dissipation, when the money is their own. When it is other people's money, the banker can forget the acting. Banking reality is far different. Bankers have always needed romantic hearts since their merchanting background has always enticed them to travel further, and dare more, than other men. Many of today's bankers consider themselves risk-takers, for some remained in Beirut during the civil war, others opened banking offices in Moscow and Peking at the height of the Cold War, while many negotiated loans with the brutal and bloodthirsty dictators of Third World countries.

Francesco Datini (c. 1335–1410) was a colleague of theirs, and also of those Bardi and Perruzzi banking families whose trust was so much abused by the Plantagenets. Datini, whose life has been disinterred from his banking and household records by the Anglo-American Countess Iris Origo in *The Merchant of Prato*, took unimaginably greater risks. In addition to the ever present threat of brigands, pirates and shipwreck, let alone defaulting borrowers, was the undeclared hostage-taking war in the Mediterranean. Christian and Muslim bankers alike faced the real risk of ending as a hostage of the enemy or, rather worse, as merchandise themselves on the auction blocks of the Tunis, Algiers or Venice slave markets.

But bankers needed rebellious hearts, as well, for a proper observance of religious formalities was once considered to be as vital to the health of society as it was to the safety of the individual. Yet banking had to play fast and loose with such central religious precepts as that which condemned usury, or the lending of money at interest. The charitable foundation that honours Datini's name in Prato today bears witness to the doubts that early bankers had lest the business they did, and the mega-millions that they made, would press too heavily on their souls at the day of judgement. All the world's major monotheistic religions – Judaism, Christianity and Islam – once had absolute prohibitions against usury, or the lending of money at interest. These rules represented the prejudices of a landowning society, where the natural risks of farming were easily exacerbated by the moneylenders' desire for profit, as well as the fears of the weak faced with the strong. Yet even agricultural societies need bankers, for seed and fertiliser must be purchased before the harvest can be sown, let alone reaped, and the bridging of such gaps in business and personal income – or cash flows, in the jargon – is even more essential to a world of traders and manufacturers.

Considerable ingenuity was required of ecclesiastical lawyers to square the circle, for Medici Bank records show that even cardinals were keen to earn the market rate of interest on their fortunes, whatever Church law might decree. Italian lawyers provided the answers that society and bankers needed. Lending at interest might be against God's will, for, according to ecclesiastical lawyers if not practical banking experience, secured lending involves no risk to the lender. Exchanging money, however, was another matter entirely. The Italian merchant advancing Florentine soldii to the English supplier of wool ran the risk that, by the time he was repaid in English pounds, the comparative value of the two currencies had altered. The payment of a foreign-exchange risk premium was therefore legitimate; the unreasonably suspicious noted that those premiums bore an amazingly close resemblance to what the cost of interest would otherwise have been, but such considerations were overborne by the practical needs of trade. Modern churchmen accept bankers, just like the rest of us, but few find them lovable, for bankers have always allowed the letter, rather than the spirit, of the law to determine their morality.

The Protestant ethic quickly discovered practical reasons to allow bankers to pay and charge interest – so did Catholics, though it would take the French Revolution to sweep away the usury laws – but found it hard to accept that gains from trading in securities were equally legitimate. So society legislated against the securities markets in Holland (1611), and then England (1737), and these laws forced market participants to establish their own rules of conduct, since society's disapproval of their behaviour denied them the protection of the law. Marginalised first by Church law, then by social mores, bankers naturally looked to each other for their standards of morality.

Nor is it surprising that bankers have an affinity with horse racing. Since only the really successful can afford racehorses, bankers can publicise their success while also meeting potential customers, and a winning stable can advertise banking, as well as breeding, judgement. Banking decisions are little different, in principle, from those of bookmakers, for both have to measure risk, which is the very stuff of life. Bankers and bookies alike need to assess the runners and back the winners, while accepting that many of their choices will lose, often for reasons outside their control. The bookie calculates the odds, so as to reduce the costs of losing, and the banker does the same. Both use bloodlines, past performance, current conditions and the level of competition in picking whom to back, when, where and at what odds.

Banker and bookie need to cultivate self-control, for the skill of both is knowing how far to go, and with whom. The outside chance, with its possibility of an instant reversal of fortune, has always appealed to humanity – and humanity, surprising though it must seem to their customers, includes both bankers and bookies. The best way of ensuring judgement and self-control among bankers is for them once again to run the risk of bankruptcy.

Acknowledgements

A S HISTORY RECYCLED ITSELF in September 1992, it also brought a sharp pang of regret for my lost banking career. Italy's detractors yet again predicted its final demise in a financial and political armageddon while, just as in the 1970s, those Italian Houdinis continued to fool everyone. The IIB made another quick fortune in the forex markets for bank dealers came in early, and stayed late, while the Bank of England, ably abetted by the Treasury, stood ready to pay £1.20 for every £1.00 proferred it. There have been changes over the last twenty years, of course, for investment managers have now joined bankers in twisting the currency tails of macho politicians and George Soros, one such money manager, is said to have made profits of $1 billion from the crisis. Sam Brittan in the FT, quoting a new financial perodical called *Central Banking*, reckoned that the Bank of England, and its fellow central banks, deployed some £15–20 billion to defend sterling, and lost between £2.25 to £3 billion in the process. The magazine remarks of 'Black Wednesday' that 'it is just as if Norman Lamont had personally thrown entire hospitals and schools into the sea all afternoon'.

Such wilful refusal to heed, or even remember, the lessons of the 1970s, and the break-up of the Bretton Woods system, is a perfect example of Warren Buffett's 'institutional imperative' and my thanks go to all those politicians, anonymous bureaucrats and central bankers who helped set up this timely demonstration. Banking friends and contemporaries, such as Colin Leach and Jeremy Grafftey-Smith, were generous with their memories in recreating the heady excitements of those early years. Nat Butterfield of the Bermudan banking family, and Jim Pettit, formerly of the Philadelphia National Bank but now with the Willis Partnership, are ex-bankers turned head-hunters, and were equally generous with their time and contacts. However, banking egos are today so frail that to acknowledge the help of many other banking friends and acquaintances might terminally blight their careers; they know who they are, even if their superiors don't, and my thanks go to all of them.

No reader of this book can fail to note the enormous debt I owe to Jocelyn Hambro, and his family and colleagues such as Harry Sporborg, Rolf Dellborg, Otto Norland and Finn Arnessen. Equally, I owe much to my colleagues in the IIB, from those like Ron Brett, Alan Wiseman and Patricia Drakes, who stayed with the bank, to others such as Mario Perricone, Tony Hall, Hans Seeberg and Emmanuel Zurides who moved on; if I was slow to learn, it was not through any lack of effort on their part. Thanks are also due to Geoffrey Taylor, John Harris, Brian Goldthorpe, Tony Holmes and Ian Morison of Midland Bank; all these were in the eye of the Crocker storm, had their lives and careers permanently affected by it, but are now able to talk about it with some degree of detachment; how difficult this is, I found out for myself.

Ian Morison, now Professor of Banking at Loughborough University, and Philip Molyneux, reader in banking at the University College of North Wales, were especially helpful on the economic and industrial background of banking changes. Anyone who wants to understand this in greater, and more rigorous, detail, cannot do better than read *Changes in West European Banking*, written by Philip Molyneux in partnership with Professor Edward Gardner. If a story that is very complex in its timing and interaction is reasonably comprehensible, then much of the credit is due to Araminta Whitley, former investment manager and now literary agent, and to Brian Perman, my editor at Simon & Schuster. These persisted, even while I insisted on immersing them in the minutiae of banking, as the means of avoiding facing the pain of my own failure as a banker.

The views expressed, as well as any and all mistakes in the facts and interpretations of banking history, are all my own of course, and will not be universally accepted. Yet the survival of C. Hoare & Company over so many centuries, and the recent and successful establishment of J. O. Hambro & Company, persuade me that banking will, and can, change. The economics of book production are just as simple and brutal as those of lending, so much discussion with Rupert Hambro ended up on the cutting-room floor. But in less than ten years Rupert, with his father and two brothers, has created a more successful investment banking business than was achieved over three decades by the capable directors of Hambros Bank: the irresistible inertia created by the knowledge that one has money to lend steamrollers into the ground most bankers' imagination and flexibility.

And very much more than gratitude is due to my long-suffering wife; the writing of this book put her belief, that a resident writer is more fun as a husband than a travelling banker, under considerable stress.

Russell Taylor
London 1992

Index